COMPANY OF HEROES

OSPREY
PUBLISHING

ERIC POOLE

COMPANY
OF
HEROES

A Forgotten Medal of Honor and
Bravo Company's War in Vietnam

First published in Great Britain in 2015 by Osprey Publishing,
PO Box 883, Oxford, OX1 9PL, UK
PO Box 3985, New York, NY 10185-3985, USA
E-mail: info@ospreypublishing.com

Osprey Publishing is part of the Osprey Group

ISBN: 978 1 4728 0791 5
e-book ISBN: 978 1 4728 1339 8
PDF ISBN: 978 1 4728 1338 1

Index by Sandra Shotter
Typeset in Walbaum & Adobe Garamond Pro
Originated by PDQ Digital Media Solutions, Suffolk
Printed in China through Shanghai Offset Printing Products Ltd.

15 16 17 18 19 10 9 8 7 6 5 4 3 2 1

Front cover: A US Infantry patrol near Saigon, 1969. (The Granger Collection / Topfoto)
Front cover inset: Leslie Sabo Jr. in 1970, while on an M-60 machine-gun team. (Photo courtesy
of Rose Sabo Brown)

Osprey Publishing is supporting the Woodland Trust, the UK's leading woodland conservation
charity, by funding the dedication of trees.

www.ospreypublishing.com

CONTENTS

This book is dedicated to all veterans of the Vietnam War, but especially to the men of Bravo Company, 3rd Battalion, 506th Infantry Regiment, 101st Airborne Division (1969–70) and the following:

KIA January 28, 1970

Steven "Hungry" Dile, of Chambersburg, Pennsylvania
Peter Guzman, of Los Angeles
Frank Madrid, of Puerto de Luna, New Mexico
and John Shaffer, of Syracuse, New York

KIA February 17, 1970

Joe Honan, of Scranton, Pennsylvania

KIA February 25, 1970

Alan Johnson, of Medford, Massachusetts (died of wounds sustained on February 17, 1970)

KIA April 4, 1970

Gary Weekley, of Middlebourne, West Virginia

KIA April 8, 1970

Richard Calderon, of Silverbell, Arizona
Thomas Scarboro, of Asheville, North Carolina

KIA April 27, 1970

Bobby Koehler, of Philadelphia

KIA May 10, 1970

Larry DeBoer, of Grand Rapids, Michigan
James DeBrew, of Whitakers, North Carolina
Fred Harms, of Bartonville, Illinois
Thomas Merriman, of Paulding, Ohio
Ernie Moore, of Spring Lake, Michigan
Leslie Sabo Jr., of Ellwood City, Pennsylvania
Donald Smith, of Rantoul, Illinois
and Leslie Joe Wilbanks, of Gila Bend, Arizona

In the Jungles of Vietnam

(*To the tune of "Yellow Submarine"*)
Lyrics by G. Koziol, music by P. McCartney

In the land where I was born
Men were free to live their lives
To work all week and go to church
To raise their kids and kiss their wives
And then it came, right out of the blue,
We had to go to fight a war
So off we flew to a faraway land
And so we became this very tight band

(CHORUS)

We all lived in the jungles of Vietnam
The jungles of Vietnam, the jungles of Vietnam
We all lived in the jungles of Vietnam
The jungles of Vietnam, the jungles of Vietnam

And we fought, each day and night
It wasn't pretty; it was a horrible sight
We fought together for our fathers and mothers
We fought together, a band of brothers
We were young and tough and free
We were the men from Bravo Company

(CHORUS)

And then we came home from that faraway land
And we hoped to see a marching band
But what we got were protests and hate
No one knew the price that was paid,
Freedom's not free, you got to fight
And so we did, each day and night
And now we are back together again
Reunited, you and me

Because we are still the fighting men
Of Bravo Company

(CHORUS)

ACKNOWLEDGMENTS

In nearly 20 years as a newspaper reporter and columnist, I have received more than 30 regional, statewide and national journalism awards. I don't say that to brag – at least, not entirely – but to say that the greatest professional honor anyone has ever bestowed upon me has come from the Vietnam veterans who have called me "brother" in gratitude for my work covering their efforts to see their fallen comrade, Leslie H. Sabo Jr., receive the honor he earned so many years earlier.

Admittedly, that makes me a little uneasy. These were men who fought, bled, and watched their comrades die for one another and their country. Many of the veterans I wrote about in this book are alive today only because Sabo and others leapt, figuratively, into their graves. I, on the other hand, turned ten years old the month that helicopters rescued the last refugees from Saigon's rooftops, and my greatest worry in the world was that the Pittsburgh Penguins would blow a three-games-to-none lead against the New York Islanders in the 1975 Stanley Cup quarterfinals.

It still overwhelms me that the men who served during 1969–70 in Bravo Company, 3rd Battalion, 506th Infantry Regiment, 101st

Airborne Division – heirs and bearers to the much storied "Currahee" tradition – trusted me with the account that I told, starting with several reports in the *Ellwood City Ledger*, Sabo's hometown newspaper, and culminating with this book. I will be forever grateful to them for that trust. Without it I could never have told their story.

And I appreciate not only the trust of the men who sacrificed so much for our country and for one another but also their acceptance of me, a functionary of the dirty, rotten, stinking news media. Many Vietnam veterans feel hard done by the media, both in its news and entertainment forms, and not without reason. Vietnam was the first war in which the home front received wholly unfiltered reports from the battlefield. As a result, Americans – who had been sheltered from the brutality of war behind the natural obstacles of two oceans and sanitized written accounts by the likes of Ernie Pyle – had that horrific reality dumped into their living rooms every day by television and newspapers. The World War II image of American soldiers as Knights Templar was replaced by the "baby killer" Vietnam image.

Neither version was entirely accurate. Many US troops looted their way across Europe in 1944 and 1945, and one Currahee officer, as chronicled in Stephen Ambrose's book, *Band of Brothers*, was rumored to have gunned down more than a dozen captured German troops. Meanwhile, the majority of Vietnam veterans served with honor, just as their World War II forebears did. To an extent, the Bravo Company veterans had little choice but to trust me. Their hope was that Sabo would receive the US military's highest award for combat valor. And at the time, I was the only reporter looking to tell Sabo's story.

Ellwood City, Pennsylvania, where Leslie Sabo grew up, is one of those small towns where you might not know everybody else, but you're rarely more than one degree of separation from everyone else in town. Charlotte Price was my connection to the Sabos. Her son, Doug, is a Pennsylvania state trooper who raises bison on his farm just outside of town and was my son's youth baseball coach one year. Doug's wife, Karen, has had exercise classes with my wife. So, when Charlotte told me that she had a friend – who turned out to be Rose Sabo Brown – whose deceased husband was being considered for a military award I was determined to follow up on it. The result of that was "Act of Courage," which was published April 9, 2007, in the *Ellwood City Ledger*. That story received a first-place award in 2008 from the Pennsylvania Newspapers Association.

And it earned an even more significant prize from the men of Bravo Company. Because they decided I got their story right with my initial reports, many of them decided to reveal additional, and sometimes harrowing, parts of their stories, both while they were in Vietnam and after they returned home. I'm thankful to all of them for their service and for their openness in telling me about their experiences. I'm hopeful that this book does honor to them and to all Vietnam veterans who got no credit for their accomplishments and too much blame for the failures of others.

And if Leslie Sabo's surviving comrades suffered after he left them behind, so did his surviving family members. Rose Sabo Brown, Leslie's widow, was generous beyond what I had any right to expect with sharing her late husband's story. I was by her side when she received word that Leslie would be awarded the nation's most prestigious military award and she saw fit to include me in the list of people permitted to witness the eventual White House ceremony. I'm thankful for that as well.

When Leslie Sabo arrived in the United States at the age of two, he had an older brother, George, as his only friend. George Sabo, who traces his family lineage back hundreds of years to Hungarian nobility, talked with me about his brother until he could bear the pain of remembering no longer. But he was appreciative enough of my work to offer me thanks before some of the most prominent people in the United States. I thank you too, George.

No medal, no recognition – not even the Medal of Honor, one of the United States' most exclusive distinctions – will bring back Leslie Sabo. However, it honors his memory to note those men who survived a very bad day because of his heroism, and hopefully helps ease their pain.

Piecing this story together, as with any historical text written largely from primary sources – eyewitnesses – can be a matter of putting together a puzzle when all the pieces don't fit together cleanly. Sometimes, completing a work of military history requires reconciling conflicting reports. Even the central narrative of this book, Sabo's Medal of Honor citation, wasn't consistent with prior documentation. During World War II, Easy Company of the 101st Airborne's 506th Infantry Regiment was featured in Stephen Ambrose's book *Band of Brothers*. In the afterword to that book, Ambrose said, in reference to *Pegasus Bridge*, his previous D-Day book, "I felt it was my task to make my best judgment on what was true, what had been misremembered, what had been exaggerated by the old soldiers telling their war stories, what acts of heroism had been played down by a man too modest to brag on himself." But Ambrose went on to say that he changed his mind after *Pegasus Bridge*, and with *Band of Brothers* he sought out the guidance of the soldiers involved. Similarly input from Bravo Company veterans Richard Rios and Rick Brown was especially invaluable because they corrected mistakes I made in my prior coverage.

The work of other historians proved invaluable in both enriching the story of Bravo Company from November of 1969 to November of 1970. In particular, I owe a debt of gratitude to Major General Herbert Ross McMaster, a fellow rugby player and author of *Dereliction of Duty*, the comprehensive account of strategic failures in Washington, DC and Saigon during the war's early days. The book *Vietnam at War*, by Lieutenant General Phillip Davidson, was also crucial in providing context to Bravo Company's story.

The book *Twelve Days in May*, by Jerald Berry, former public information officer for 3rd Battalion, 506th Infantry Regiment, helped close some gaps in my narrative. Berry, motivated by respect and reverence for his comrades, assembled what is probably the most comprehensive account of the Cambodian campaign's northern thrust. This book represents the end of Leslie Sabo's story – the award of his Medal of Honor and the surrounding observation on May 16 and 17, 2012.

After attempting to obtain a publisher for various versions of this book for more than five years, Kate Moore of Osprey Publishing expressed an interest in my work. Any author worth his or her collection of rejection slips is painfully aware of the difficulty in winning a publisher's approval. Thanks, Kate, for your support and help in getting past the gatekeeper. And a big thank you to Commissioning Editor Emily Holmes, whose keen eye when reading this manuscript has saved me a great deal of embarrassment.

Finally, without the support of my wife, Dawna, and our children, Gareth and Calista, this book would not have been possible. At the age of 29, I was a full-time rugby bum when I met my then-future wife for the first time and caught, through her, a glimpse of my future. It was with the realization that no woman in her right mind would marry a man who paid the bills by delivering pizzas between scrums that I made my return to print journalism so many years ago. The three of you own a large piece of any success I might have.

Eric Poole
February 2014

PROLOGUE

Around 3:45pm on February 1, 2012, the telephone on Rose Sabo Brown's computer desk jangled to life. She had been expecting the call, and answered quickly. After a pause, she said "What?" then, "Yes, I'll hold." Finally, she put her hand over the speaker and mouthed three words, silent yet thunderous.

"*It's the President!*"

A few minutes later, President Barack Obama came on Sabo Brown's phone line and told her that Leslie H. Sabo Jr., the husband whose battlefield death had left her a widow more than four decades earlier, would receive the Medal of Honor, the US military's highest award for combat valor.

"I couldn't believe it," Sabo Brown said. "All the emotions just came rushing in."

With the President's telephone call, the United States, after nearly a half-century, completed one of its last remaining items of business from the Vietnam War. And while rewarding Sergeant Leslie Sabo for his sacrifice didn't change the war's outcome or the vicious manner in which it rent a nation in two, it fulfilled the most sacred pledge America's servicemen and women make to one another, and that the government makes to those who wear its uniform – to "never leave a fallen comrade behind."

Sabo's battle-shattered body made it home within a few days of his death, but his memory and the full story of his life's final hours was left behind, ultimately for decades. A menu of false stories – he stepped on a landmine, or was shot by a sniper, or died in the explosion of an ammunition store – arose to account for Sabo's fate, and his closed-casket funeral. Leslie Sabo's own father and namesake died without ever knowing that his son was entitled to a place in the pantheon of his adopted nation's greatest military heroes.

The Medal of Honor, paradoxically, is more often awarded in recognition of those who save the lives of their comrades than it is for the more conventional actions of combat, which would seem to repudiate the maxim of US history's most famous Army general, George Patton, who said, "You don't win wars by dying for your country. You win wars by making the other bastard die for his country." In fact, the Medal of Honor in general, and the award earned by Leslie Sabo in particular, argues forcefully against Patton.

You might not win wars by dying for your country, but you don't win them by making the other bastard die for his country. You win battles – and wars – by preventing your comrades from dying for their country.

When Sabo arrived in Vietnam, he was assigned to one of the 20th century's most storied military units, 506th Infantry Regiment, 101st Airborne Division, nicknamed the Currahees. The original Currahees were assembled in the summer of 1942 at Camp Toccoa, Georgia. More than 5,000 soldiers, in defiance of that old Army warning against volunteering for anything, signed up to be part of what was then a new experiment in American warfare – parachute infantry, a concept pioneered by Germany, the enemy they would eventually fight, in the Wehrmacht's successful invasions of Poland and the Netherlands. About one in three of those volunteers were chosen to be part of what was then known as the 506th Parachute Infantry Regiment. They trained the old-fashioned way, with innumerable sit-ups and pushups. And by running up Mount

Currahee, which loomed ominously over the Camp Toccoa parade ground, 3 miles up, 3 miles down.

After nearly two years of training, the original Currahees leapt from airplanes into the Normandy region, Cotentin Peninsula, on the early morning of June 6, 1944. The carnage they faced as a beyond-the-tip-of-the-spear unit forged thick bonds among the original Currahees, particularly within Easy Company, which would win fame years later through the book and Emmy-award-winning TV miniseries *Band of Brothers*.

When the original Currahees landed in Normandy, each one knew – from the newest buck private to Colonel Robert "Bourbon Bob" Sink, who commanded the 506th from its inception through to the war's end – exactly how doing his job would help his squad meet its objective, which would enable his company to succeed and allow the 506th Regiment and the 101st Airborne up through General Eisenhower and the rest of Allied Command to prevail in Operation *Overlord*, and eventually win the war in Europe. The line that connected the soldiers who wore the boots hitting the ground on D-Day to Germany's surrender was clear and easy to follow.[1]

The next generation of Currahees, particularly the ones who arrived in Vietnam late in 1969, didn't have that luxury. By the time Leslie Sabo and his comrades in Bravo Company, 3rd Battalion, 506th Infantry Regiment, 101st Airborne Division hit the line in January of 1970, no one seemed to have any idea, beyond killing the enemy, for winning the Vietnam War. Although the Tet Offensive nearly two years earlier failed to achieve any tactical objectives, the North Vietnamese scored a huge strategic victory by convincing Americans that the military was no closer to subduing the enemy than they had been upon arriving in the country half a decade earlier. The 1970 Vietnam Currahees had to have known that, in May of 1969, their fellow Screaming Eagles spilled gallons of blood and lost dozens of men in taking Hamburger Hill, only to give it back to the enemy a few weeks later. Nobody, it seemed, had any plan for winning the war, or any way to figure one out.

But they were the sons of men who had beaten back Hitler and Tojo. So the Vietnam Currahees went out into the field and fought like the original Currahees did. Bravo Company saw roughly the same amount of action in five months as Easy Company faced in 11. Deprived of a tactical cause or purpose, they fought for one another and forged a brotherhood, just as the original Currahees had. On their worst day, eight of them fell in a Cambodian jungle clearing so their comrades might live.

In its way, Bravo Company and the 506th Infantry Regiment might have distinguished itself during its 1969–70 stretch in Vietnam to an even greater degree than the World War II Currahees did. In *Band of Brothers*, author Stephen Ambrose dubbed Easy Company, "as good a rifle company as there was in the world." Like their World War II forebears, Bravo Company was composed largely of citizen soldiers drafted into the military. They were steelworkers, dropouts, new college and high school grads, dock workers, and laborers. They came from across the United States, although Pennsylvania was unusually well-represented, just as it was with Easy Company during World War II. Bravo Company boasted a Medal of Honor recipient, several Silver Stars, and more than a dozen Bronze Stars, the US military's fourth-highest award for combat valor. On its worst day, the company sustained nearly 50 percent casualties. And it more than honored the tradition begun a generation earlier.

In Vietnam, the use of combat parachute drops were all but abandoned in favor of more precise and effective helicopter assaults. But that didn't prevent two Bravo Company veterans – from a group of less than 200 soldiers – from moving on to places on the Army's elite Golden Knights parachuting team. The battalion's commander during that time is in the Army Aviation Hall of Fame.

By the final months of 1969, when Leslie Sabo and many of his comrades arrived in Vietnam, it was becoming increasingly clear that they weren't battling against communism, but rather on behalf of a brutal, corrupt string of South Vietnamese despots who enjoyed no credibility outside the immediate shadow of American guns.

Because their leaders failed to give them a worthwhile reason to fight and kill and die, they were forced to find their own just cause.

And that just cause was each other.

Unlike their original Currahee forebears, the Vietnam Currahees' war didn't end when they returned home. They were, in the words of one Vietnam War 101st Airborne Division intelligence officer, "made to feel ashamed of serving their country."[2] The brothers were separated for decades, not out of shame, but from the sorrow of having lost 18 of their own and the failure by their countrymen to acknowledge or even understand their pain. Lost through that estrangement would be the account of the one Currahee who had sacrificed more than any other for his comrades. That story would one day reunite a new band of brothers.

CHAPTER 1

Happy Birthday Olga and Stevie. I'm sorry I couldn't send you a card or write earlier but we had a very busy week also. I am low on funds. I hope you both enjoyed your birthdays, too bad I couldn't be there to enjoy it with you. George told me Roe went up so she represented both of us. When I called I was disappointed that you weren't home. I forgot that you worked on Sat. I wanted to call Fri, but there were too many people on the phones. At least I'll get to see everybody Sept. 13. I'm really looking forward to this. It was real nice to talk to George finally, it's been 4 months today since I left for the Army and that's been a long time to not even have talked to your only brother. You can see from the stationery where I'm writing from. It is real nice here, they have pool and ping pong tables, a game room, TV room, a lounge (where I'm at now), a place where you can play records and listen to them through ear phones, also a snack bar so [you] can see it really has a lot to offer. One more thing everything (even the stationery and envelope) is free. You pay for your food, but they also give you cake and punch during the day. At Fort Gordon, I never even knew they had this. I'm happy to hear that everything is fine at home with everyone. I hope you all enjoyed your summer, the kids will be going back to school. I know you're looking forward to that (but really, if I know Olga, she'll miss them). Well, that's all I have to write about, say hi to Tony, Stevie, and Michael for me and write back soon.

Letter from Leslie Sabo to George and Olga Sabo
Dated August 24, 1969 from Fort McClellan during advanced
individual training [1]

If Leslie Halasz Sabo Jr. took the Vietnam War personally, well, that was to have been expected, and his mother was a big part of the reason for that. Unlike many – perhaps even most – young men of the day, he was in favor of the war even before the Army sent him off to fight in it. Again, that probably shouldn't have surprised anyone. Even though he was a child of Hungarians born in Austria, America was the only country Sabo really knew, his family having emigrated shortly after his second birthday. But his family was acutely aware of its history and he grew up on stories of his parents' life prior to World War II in one of Hungary's wealthiest families. The Sabos left their homeland in 1944 as the Soviet Army was bearing down on them. When Hungary wound up on the Iron Curtain's communist side, they never returned.

Leslie's father, already in middle age when he brought his family across the Atlantic Ocean, succeeded in the United States. But considering his status in the homeland, it would be inaccurate to say he thrived there. Leslie adored his parents, especially his mother, the kind of woman who would have been decidedly less comfortable married (as she now was) to an industrial engineer at a western Pennsylvania steel mill than she would have been as wife of Hungary's prime minister – an outcome that would have been entirely possible in a different reality.

A reality that didn't include communism.

Sabo began his Vietnam combat tour on November 13, 1969, with Bravo Company, 3rd Battalion, 506th Infantry Regiment, 101st

Airborne Division, when it was being refitted for action – plenty of it, as it turned out – in 1970. Around 50 soldiers, which amounted to nearly half of the company's total manpower, joined the unit during the last three months of 1969 in Phan Thiet, a port city along Vietnam's coast northeast of Saigon. George Koziol, who would become one of Sabo's closest friends in Bravo Company, was part of that group. A 23-year-old native of Omaha, Nebraska, Koziol and 26-year-old Leslie Wilbanks were among the unit's oldest men. Their nicknames reflected that – Wilbanks was known as "Gramps" and Koziol was called simply "The Old Man," a nickname that would stick with him until he grew into it. With the influx of inexperienced soldiers, Currahees like platoon lieutenants John Shaffer, Alan Johnson, John Greene, and Teb Stocks, and non-commissioned officers like Steven Dile, Vernon Bruner, and "Little John" Roethlisberger – "As fine a man who ever put on a uniform," according to Bravo Company trooper Rick Brown – made up the steel of Bravo Company as 1970 dawned.[2]

Dile had turned 21 the previous September, which meant he was younger than some of the men he was taking into battle as a squad leader in Bravo's 3rd Platoon. But he was older than them in the one way that counted – combat experience. While Bravo Company's new arrivals were still in basic training, he was already slogging through the Vietnamese jungles. His personal maturity, well beyond his years, also helped him earn leadership bona fides, even among comrades much older than himself.

When Dile was only eight years old, his father was killed in a train accident. As the oldest of four children, he got the, "You're now the man of the house" speech at a very young age, and he took that responsibility seriously. He helped earn money for the family while working as a caddy at Scotland Golf Course near Chambersburg, Pennsylvania, and fostered a close relationship with his mother. Every year on Mother's Day, he took some of the money he earned carrying golf bags for men in families better off than his own, and bought her a cake.

"Steven became the father of the house," said his brother Keith. "He pulled my butt out of quite a few scrapes."[3]

In an army comprised largely of draftees, Dile had signed up in February of 1968, according to his younger brother Lee, out of empathy for Vietnamese children who suffered in war-ravaged villages. While attending Chambersburg Area Senior High School, Dile – like many other teens in the 1960s – was a massive Beatles fan, even to the point that he dressed like the band members. Hugely popular among the soldiers in Bravo Company, Dile would amuse his buddies by dancing around the barracks when they were back in base camp. Just as he helped out his siblings at every opportunity, he worked hard to help his "boonie brothers" – a fraternity restricted to Vietnam War combat soldiers who saw action in remote jungle areas – get acclimated to life in the combat zone, even while having fun.

"He helped me and he helped several others get their feet on the ground," said Michael DiLeo, who eventually would wear the mantle of non-commissioned leadership himself.

Dile won the nickname "Hungry," because he would cadge food from his comrades after finishing his own rations. Dile's appetite extended to drink as well as food. On one of Bravo Company's trips into the field, Dile had been assigned to remain at the firebase and have cases of soda waiting for his comrades' return, but Hungry got his hands on a case of beer and camouflaged it as soda. Hungry approached combat with the same enthusiasm as he showed for dancing and eating. He regularly volunteered for some of the most hazardous duty, like taking the lead on patrols into the jungle, known in military parlance as "walking point," and anticipated using his "bag of tricks" – a satchel of readily accessible hand grenades that hung from his belt – on the enemy.

"He was fearless," said Bravo Company trooper Jack Brickey, who had arrived in Vietnam at about the same time as Dile. "He was a good soldier. He just made you feel safe and comfortable."

Even before they arrived in Vietnam, the new arrivals had learned the general principles of soldiering – shooting, marching, and rudimentary battleground tactics – during basic and advanced individual training. But before the new guys could be trusted in the field, they got a week's worth of training specific to fighting in

Vietnam. Almost every combat unit had an in-country training regime. The 101st Airborne Division's was called "Screaming Eagle Replacement Training School," abbreviated as SERTS, which included lessons on how to spot a booby trap or a punji pit – a camouflaged hole designed to collapse beneath a man's weight and send him to be impaled on spikes in the hollow – to root through an enemy tunnel and how to walk point. They were taught to overcome the natural impulse to bunch together when under attack so a grenade couldn't take out more than one soldier. During those SERTS sessions, the "fresh meat" experienced live-fire simulated ambushes set by their fellow American soldiers in order to give the new arrivals a taste of the enemy's tactics from men who had already survived the experience.

But some lessons could be taught only by experienced soldiers like Dile or Frank Madrid of 3rd Platoon. "It was just kind of going through the jungle," Norm Friend said of the in-country training. Madrid could almost match Dile in combat familiarity and had even more life experience. The 25-year-old soldier, a native of Puerto De Luna, New Mexico, attended New Mexico Highlands University in Las Vegas, New Mexico, where he earned a degree in accounting, and was drafted in 1968 almost immediately following graduation.[4] Many Bravo Company soldiers like Madrid and Rios were college graduates and others like Sabo had been in college. Just in time for Christmas, Frederick Harms Jr. landed in Bravo Company on December 20. He had turned 21 the previous September while in advanced infantry training. A native of Bartonville in central Illinois, Harms attended Spoon River Junior College, Bradley University and Midstate College of Commerce before enlisting in the Army.[5] College-educated enlisted men were relatively common among Vietnam War combat units – about 25 percent of Vietnam troops had been in college, roughly twice the figure for their World War II counterparts.[6]

"They were the best," Brickey said of 3rd Platoon at the start of 1970. "Anytime there was shit, they sent us and that was because of Madrid and Hungry."

To a newly arrived private in Vietnam, packing a backpack properly could seem like a trivial matter, until he found himself in the field, getting resupplied every third day. In the meantime, he had to carry – up mountains, through streams, and into the jungle – every piece of equipment, ammunition, food, and water on his back. Suddenly, tactics for loading a backpack become almost as important as figuring out how to face the enemy. A C-ration can, packed poorly or in the wrong place, could poke into a soldier's back during a day-long march.

"You're carrying your house on your back," said "Kid Rick" Brown, who relied on Madrid and Dile for those lessons. "You're lost. You're going from a nice warm bed to the jungle."

And going from a goose-down pillow to a battle helmet. Sleeping in the field required some effort, especially during the monsoon season. While each man chased sleep in his own way, Norm Friend would rest his head atop his helmet and use his shoulder to bore a depression into the soft jungle floor.

"I didn't get much sleep that first night," Friend said. "But after that, I was so exhausted I could have slept anywhere."

After the first few days, the new arrivals could eat almost anywhere, too. Because of the physical exertion and an almost-constant diet of canned food, most soldiers lost weight during their combat tours. They also regarded any food from home as a delicacy. For Thanksgiving, one soldier's mother sent a packet of Hillsboro Farm pancake mix and a wide range of syrup, which was both thoughtful and useless because the typical soldier didn't have access to the milk and eggs necessary for turning pancake mix into pancakes. But by a fortuitous coincidence, the battalion cook was Hungarian, which presented an opportunity. Leslie Sabo, a child of Hungarian wealth, had learned a smattering of the language from hearing his parents speak it while growing up in Ellwood City, Pennsylvania. Sabo ingratiated himself with the cook through a common tongue, and got the Bravo Company soldiers some eggs and milk for a pancake feast.[7]

Christmas dawned wet, foggy, and miserable, especially for those soldiers who still had 11 months to go in their tour. For the occasion,

Bravo Company decorated a 2-foot tall Christmas tree, courtesy of a soldier's family. The holiday turned out to have been a mixed bag for one soldier about halfway through his combat tour. On that day, he learned that his wife had given birth. A few hours later, he fell down a mountain slope and broke his arm. He wouldn't return to the line for weeks.

The men of Bravo Company were a diverse lot, having arrived in Vietnam from all parts of the United States and beyond. As civilians, they might have read textbooks in college classrooms, run heavy equipment in farms, factories or construction sites, or driven a pencil in an office. Their Army training helped mold them into a unit. And they had one thing in common, from new arrivals – also called "cherries," for their status as combat virgins – to hardened veterans. All of them were preoccupied with their DEROS – Date Eligible for Return from Overseas. In plain language translated from Pentagon-acronym-speak, it was the day they were scheduled to leave Vietnam for "the world," as home was known to the troops. To the draftee combat soldier, the DEROS might have been even more important than rank and those nearing their DEROS were called "short timers."

At Christmas of 1969, Dick Freeling was one of the shortest of Bravo Company's short timers. A native of the Great Plains, Freeling saw a mountain for the first time in his life at basic training at Fort Lewis, Washington, where Mount Rainier was visible outside his barracks window. He had been a three-sport athlete in high school, the son of a Marine Corps World War II veteran. His mother died less than a year before he was drafted. After graduating from high school in 1966, he avoided the draft as a student at the University of Nebraska at Kearney. Once he flunked out, though, Uncle Sam came calling. For the new arrivals, being combat airlifted by helicopter hundreds of feet above double- and triple-canopy jungles was a bit of a shock, one which Freeling had already overcome.

"All of a sudden, you're 19 years old and this isn't watching the 6 o'clock news anymore," he said. "You are the guy in the helicopter. These people are not leaving that village because they want to. They are being driven out. And you are part of the force going in to make things hopefully better."[8]

On January 14, 48 hours after his DEROS, Freeling would make the trip from tropical Southeast Asia to his hometown of Kearney, Nebraska, where he was "the only one in town with a full suntan."

But as Freeling was preparing to vacate Vietnam, most of Bravo Company's soldiers had a countdown to DEROS that was in triple, rather than single, figures. Richard Calderon, nicknamed "Little Dickie," for his short stature, was among the new arrivals. Calderon, who played high school baseball and basketball while growing up in Silver Bell, Arizona, would become part of a small group of Hispanic soldiers who maintained communication security in the field by speaking Spanish. He had been drafted in 1969 and turned 20 during training.[9]

Calderon, who was assigned the job of radio telephone operator for squad leader Sergeant Vernon Bruner, swiftly became known as a man quick with a smile. Calderon's mischievous nature manifested itself when he noted Bruner's broad mustache and dark hair, and saddled his immediate superior with the nickname of "The Big Bandito" – a reference to "Frito Bandito," the cartoon mascot for Fritos corn chips. The Bandito, which was the Fritos mascot from 1967 to 1971, is now regarded as a politically incorrect perpetuation of negative Mexican stereotypes, which made it a little ironic for a Hispanic soldier to give that sobriquet to a white non-commissioned officer.

Leslie Wilbanks, of Gila Bend, Arizona, attended Arizona Western College and worked at the Bureau of Reclamation in Fresno, California. He was among the oldest soldiers in Bravo Company, including the officers. The Vietnam-era draft targeted men between the age of 18 and 26, and Wilbanks almost avoided it completely. He turned 27 in September of 1969, only months after being drafted. He joined Bravo Company on January 2.[10]

Sabo was assigned to 2nd Platoon, along with Koziol, Wilbanks, New York native Bruce Dancesia, and North Carolinian Ron Gooch. Bill Sorg, another 2nd Platoon soldier, was assigned to Bravo Company at about the same time, but he had begun his tour the previous August. Some of Sabo's comrades initially regarded him as an unlikely soldier. Sorg thought Sabo "looked like he should be someplace else."

In the not-too-distant future, though, Sabo would wind up exactly where Sorg needed him to be.

"He had a heart of gold and everything like that, but he was clumsy," Dancesia said.

Sabo's platoon was led by First Lieutenant Alan Johnson. A native of Medford, Massachusetts, Johnson had worked for the New England Telephone Company before enlisting. The 23-year-old officer had enlisted two years earlier and completed Officers' Candidate School at Fort Bragg, North Carolina, in January of 1969. He had also completed Special Forces training. He had a reputation as a lead-from-the-front officer that endeared him to the men in his platoon.[11]

Johnson was part of the company's officer staff with company commander Captain Larry Terbush and executive officer First Lieutenant David Palmer. The other platoon leaders were lieutenants Anthony Clough and John Shaffer. Within two months, all of them would be gone, either by way of transfer or death.

Most of Bravo Company's cherries had been part of 1969's draft class, the last one picked entirely by local draft boards based on federally mandated quotas, oldest to youngest. The first Vietnam War draft lottery would be held in December, just as soldiers like Sabo and Rick Brown were beginning their combat tours. But Brown was an exception. A native of Columbia Station, Ohio, he joined up because it looked as if he would be drafted at some point in a decision that was influenced both by circumstance and family history – his father had served in the Marines during World War II and earned a Purple Heart during fighting in the Pacific. After graduating from Columbia Station High School with the Class of 1969, Brown – a three-sport letterwinner who was a basketball standout – planned to attend Oberlin College not far from his home.[12]

"I decided to get my two years out of the way and [then] go to college," said Brown.

Ruben Rueda, who was less than a year older than "Kid Rick," landed in Vietnam as a reluctant warrior. Already none too large, he tried to lose weight in an effort to fail his pre-induction physical. When the physical deemed him stout enough for service, Rueda's father offered him $5,000 to dodge the draft and run for Canada. It was a difficult decision. Both Rueda and his father, a successful store owner in Los Angeles, opposed the war. Before being drafted, Rueda was among the regulars at Vietnam War protests in Hollywood. But even though he was opposed to the war, Rueda didn't want to run away.

"I told my father I was going. It was the right thing to do. I was proud and I wanted to make my dad proud."

Robert Koehler's combat tour began Thanksgiving week, one month after his 20th birthday. A graduate of North Catholic High School in Philadelphia, he had been drafted the previous June. Before leaving for Vietnam, Koehler extracted a promise from his father to care for the sports car he left behind. In return, the soldier vowed to attend St Joseph's College when his hitch was up. Koehler set aside a portion of his Army pay for those classes.[13]

When the draft notice came for Norm Friend in early 1969, he was too busy to protest the war. His wife, Ardie, was well into her third trimester, and the couple was preparing to move into their own place when Uncle Sam invited Norm to the party in Southeast Asia. He quit his job at a loading dock and Ardie made plans to spend the next two years – the length of her newlywed husband's military hitch – living with her parents.

"Instead of taking the rest of the stuff out of the car, we packed up and went back home," Ardie said.

In May, heading into a weekend with Norm's induction scheduled for the following Monday and Ardie well past her due date, her doctor put her on drugs to induce labor. And even that didn't work. On Sunday, after going without food or sleep for two full days, she gorged at a relative's graduation party and fell into a deep sleep, which ended when she went into labor. She went to the hospital. Norm went to his draft physical.

Norm learned about the birth of his son while waiting for the bus that would take him to basic training.

"They said, 'You have a baby boy,'" Ardie Friend said about the conflicted feelings over her son's birth. "Five minutes later, they said, 'Get on the bus.' You have the joy of a child and your husband isn't there."

Before leaving for training Norm Friend got more than a child. He accepted advice from his older half-brother, who earned a Silver Star with the 82nd Airborne Division and would go on to make a career out of the Army.

"He said, 'Whatever you do, don't ever volunteer for anything.'"

So, of course, once Friend got to basic training – which he described as "Really, a pain in the ass" – the drill instructor immediately asked for volunteers. Volunteer firefighters. With a training platoon filled with young men from small towns across America, the sergeant had no trouble finding a few, and he put them to work keeping the barracks furnace lit and clean. Friend's drill instructor was a tall, thin sergeant named Rutledge who dabbled in classical piano on the side. But if that hobby seemed too effete for a man in such a rugged job, Friend later recalled that Rutledge didn't skimp on the physical demands of basic training. Friend said the other two platoons in his training company were carted between venues, while Rutledge made his charges run. They also had to carry one another, piggy-back style, to and from their barracks at mealtime and negotiate a set of monkey bars before they ate. Skipping the monkey bars was an offense punishable by forfeiture of meals.

"I kind of figured it would be like that," Friend said of the physical demands. "I guess it was good because it got us into shape."

By the time they arrived in Vietnam in the last three months of 1969, the newest Currahees had gone through more than a half-year of training designed to turn steelworkers like Sabo, working men like Friend, college students like Koziol, and newly minted high school graduates like Brown into soldiers. During the process of boot camp and advanced individual training, they learned how to march and shoot and polish their shoes the Army way, and possibly even some elementary tips on the jungle warfare they were destined to wage. They were trained in the use of an Army infantry company's entire arsenal, including automatic rifles, the .60 caliber machine gun, 81mm mortars and M-79 grenade launchers.

When the 101st Airborne Division was instituted during World War II, it was an all-volunteer paratrooper outfit and every Screaming Eagle was required to earn jump classification. By 1969, that was no longer a requirement. In Vietnam, Army leadership had adopted helicopter-based air assault as a substitute for airborne drops. Even though jump certification was no longer a requirement, some soldiers still opted to earn jump wings. Richard "Dick" Freeling took his paratrooper certification, because it got him another $50 a month, effectively doubling his pay as a buck private.

"I never deluded myself into thinking I was going anyplace but to Vietnam," Freeling said. "I knew the only way to survive in that situation was to be as physically fit as you can be."[14]

Peter Guzman, Sabo, Brown, and Friend were distinctive in another way – all were married men. Guzman, 20, was drafted in early 1969 and arrived in Vietnam the following September after completing his training. A Los Angeles native, Guzman played football in high school and left behind a wife, Rose Marie.

Sabo received his initial entry training after being drafted in April of 1969 at Fort Jackson, South Carolina, and went through basic training at Fort Gordon, Georgia. He took his advanced individual infantry training at Fort McClellan, Alabama, which was eventually closed in 1995 under a recommendation by the Defense Department's Base Realignment and Closure Commission. During his training he earned sharpshooter's badges for the .60 caliber machine gun and automatic rifle – most likely the M-16, the most commonly used automatic rifle in the Army at that time.

Sabo's proficiency with a rifle shouldn't have been surprising. Once he learned the mechanics of actually firing the weapon, shooting would have been all sighting and angles, just like pool, a game he understood and played well.

Among the recruits camaraderie was fostered, often in the cruelest of ways. Army policy proved woefully inadequate for some ethnic names. Because it didn't recognize apostrophes, Ray D'Angelo became, on his fatigues and footlockers and anything else that bore his name, Dangelo, to be pronounced "dangle-o." That is, when they weren't calling him "dago" or "wop." Insults and ethnic slurs are typically part of the bonding process within any large group of men and that type of name-calling wasn't extraordinary. In any event, it's certain that Leslie Sabo didn't participate in the anti-Italian language. His hometown of Ellwood City, Pennsylvania, was populated largely by Italian Catholics, and both he and his brother had married women from Italian families. Sabo himself came in for some ribbing on account of his gangly appearance and a pair of Army-issued BCGs – "birth control glasses" – so called because their appearance alone was enough to dissuade any attention from the opposite sex.

The good-natured insults and jibes notwithstanding, Sabo and the remaining cherries were welcomed into the Screaming Eagles fraternity by the time they completed their in-country jungle training. SERTS also gave the experienced soldiers an opportunity to play a trick on the new arrivals. Koziol and several other soldiers in Bravo Company remembered being told that they would be out of danger, driving trucks in the rear echelon.

"They told everyone that. The next day, we were on the battlefield."[15]

And they learned the most important lesson of all, that the men of Bravo Company were their brothers. And that each one of them was his brother's keeper. Even more than Sabo's ability to wield a weapon, his fundamental unselfishness might have been his greatest asset as a soldier. And he possessed that gift long before he took his oath as a soldier. The Army merely honed it.

As 1969 came to a close, Bravo Company was up to nearly its full complement and engaging in combat operations in Binh Dinh province looking for enemy soldiers in the thick and mountainous jungles in South Vietnam's Central Highlands region. For most of the recent draftees, military service was an interruption, not a part, of their life's plan. But after nearly a year honing their combat skills, they had all become soldiers. Even after all their training, though, a significant portion of Bravo Company was green, with no combat experience as 1970 dawned. That would change quickly.

CHAPTER 2

How's everything at home with you and Tony, Stevie and Michael? I guess you're wondering about me, I'm fine. Really things aren't too bad at all, when I arrived in Nam, I was at a replacement center for two days, then they gave me my orders to go to the 101st Airborne, I'm a grounded eagle. What's funny about that is the reason I didn't go airborne was so I wouldn't end up where I am now, but I really don't mind coming here. It is a good unit and the guys stick together, I'm in the base camp now waiting to go out into the field when I go nobody knows, probably not for a few days, maybe longer. They haven't seen any action for two months, the ARVN [Army of the Republic of Vietnam] are supposed to do all the fighting and we're here to give them a hand. They say we'll be back in base camp for Christmas. So everything looks good. Tomorrow, we eat a big Thanksgiving dinner but it could never compare with what I'd eat at home. The worst thing is not getting mail but I think it helps me from getting real homesick, things being new and different helped some too. They say time goes real fast once you're out in the field. By the way tell Roe not to send me any big packages with a lot of cookies and stuff because ... I'll have to carry that much more if I'm in the field, see we carry over a hundred pounds to begin with. Tell everybody Happy Thanksgiving for me, especially Roe because I forgot to in my last letter.

Leslie Sabo letter to his brother, George, and George's wife, Olga
Sent November 26, 1969 from Ban Me Thuot

The 1969 class of draftees landed in Vietnam during the year's last few months, as America's war effort was deteriorating, both on the battlefront and back home. At about the same time, the nation was shaken – and the combat soldiers' reputation shattered – by news that hundreds of civilians, including infants, were massacred by US soldiers the previous year in the village of My Lai.[1] In a war that by all accounts hinged on the ability by both sides to win hearts and minds, the My Lai incident was an enormous setback in a conflict that originated more than 20 years previously. In 1946, as a war-weary world began to heal from the misery of World War II – which had effectively begun in eastern Asia 14 years earlier with Japan's successful invasion of Manchuria – Vietnam was just beginning its 30-year war for independence.

Under political leader Ho Chi Minh and General Vo Nguyen Giap – the term "General" being a misnomer at the time, because Giap commanded literally only a few dozen troops – the Vietnamese liberation forces known as the Viet Minh formed. During World War II, they had fought alongside the Americans and Chinese Nationalists against the Japanese. After the war, the Viet Minh turned against the French colonial rulers in an effort that had inconsistent support until 1949, when the Chinese Communists, under Mao Tse-Tung, defeated the Nationalists, led by Chiang Kai-Shek. This had multiple profound impacts on fighting in what was then called French Indo-China – which included the present-day nations of Vietnam, Laos, and Cambodia.

With China on Vietnam's northern border, the Communist Viet Minh had a large well-appointed ally to provide economic and materiel support, and training. Within a few years, the once ragtag Viet Minh was able to crush the French at Dien Bien Phu and drive them from Vietnam.[2] The French had been guilty of underestimating their Vietnamese adversaries and Giap, whose training was in history, not military tactics. But Giap proved a quick study. He learned from his tactical mistakes and didn't repeat them. Additionally, he commanded a force of men highly motivated by the prospect of overthrowing the French.

The Viet Minh developed a three-tiered system for their ground forces during the First Indo-China War against the French (1946–54) – the Second Indo-China War (1955–75) would pit the North Vietnamese against American forces. The Main Force, which was the most prestigious, was what most would regard as a conventional army. Within a few years of beginning its war for independence against France, the Main Force rebels were well-organized, with a traditional division-regiment-battalion-company arrangement, along with artillery and antiaircraft sections. They operated throughout North and South Vietnam, and in Laos and Cambodia, under direct orders from the military commander-in-chief.

The second group was the Regional Forces, recruited from a province or district within each of Vietnam's provinces. Regional units were usually the equivalent of a battalion, fewer than 1,000 soldiers, and rather less well-organized and armed than the Regular Forces. Their primary assignment was to carry out defensive military operations within their area and reconnaissance for Main Force units in preparation for offensives in their region. They were commanded indirectly by the military commander-in-chief through territorial commanders who were in charge of military operations and a wide range of political and economic strategies, including taxation.

The third group was the Popular Forces, mostly guerrillas. They had no uniforms, little training, and were poorly armed. From a military function, they set up ambushes and set booby traps. Eventually, the last two would be referred to collectively as the Viet Cong.

Throughout the war, the North Vietnamese military had a promotion system similar to that which existed in American professional baseball. Just as a ballplayer could work his way up from the low minor leagues in Class A to Class AA or Class AAA in the high minors and eventually to the major leagues, the best Popular Force soldiers could earn promotions to the Regional Forces and the Main Force. This ensured that even the Main Force's lowest-ranking soldiers were experienced, battle-tested veterans.[3]

In 1954, French General Henri Navarre inexplicably expected to use Dien Bien Phu – effectively at the bottom of a bowl surrounded by mountains – as an outpost from which to launch attacks against the enemy. In fact Giap lined the surrounding mountains with artillery guns that pounded down on the French paratrooper garrison from above. In a matter of weeks from March into early May, 1954, the Viet Minh overran Dien Bien Phu and killed, wounded, or captured virtually the entire 14,000-man garrison. The defeat effectively ended France's colonial influence in Southeast Asia.[4]

The United States assumed oversight of Vietnamese politics, at least in the country's southern half after the Geneva accords that divided Vietnam at the 17th parallel. Under the agreement, a national vote scheduled for 1956 was to have decided who would rule the nation, which was led by Ho Chi Minh in the north and Ngo Dinh Diem in the south. That election, however, never took place, and North Vietnamese leaders began to support revolution in the South.[5]

By early 1963, President John F. Kennedy had poured more than 16,000 US advisors into South Vietnam to train the nation's military and help deal with what was then a war of insurgency. But Kennedy had lost faith in the corrupt and inept Diem and, after the well-publicized self-immolation of a Buddhist monk in response to religious persecution by the Catholic Diem, the President approved a military coup against the South Vietnamese leader. That coup led to Diem's death, only a few weeks before Kennedy himself was assassinated.[6] Since Kennedy's death, historians have vigorously debated whether the 35th President would have disengaged from Vietnam had he lived. The question is a central plot point in the movie *JFK*, whose director, Oliver Stone, was a twice-wounded Vietnam veteran who believed that Kennedy would have avoided escalating the war.

That contention is debatable at best, considering the realities that would have constrained Kennedy just as they did his successor, Lyndon Johnson. After the fall of China in 1949 during Harry Truman's presidency and the ensuing Republican-led Red Scare Congressional hearings, Democrats had been particularly vulnerable to charges of being "soft on communism." Kennedy and Johnson, both Democrats, most likely simply did not have the luxury of abandoning Vietnam to the Communists. In the words of Lieutenant General Phillip Davidson, who served as chief intelligence officer for General William Westmoreland and General Creighton Abrams in Vietnam:

> Of course Truman had *not* "lost China." The United States could not lose what it never possessed, and there was no practical action that Truman could have taken in 1949 to prevent China from falling to the Communists. These facts, however, did not reduce the political mileage the Republicans made out of China's "loss" and would make again out of another Asiatic defeat. A Democratic president could not see Vietnam fall to communism without inviting a devastating political attack at home.[7]

Balanced against that principle were two other caveats for Johnson. First was the warning, issued initially by General Douglas MacArthur, to avoid a land war in Southeast Asia. Secondly, and perhaps most importantly, the United States had to be mindful when beginning combat operations in Vietnam that an overwhelming strike could provoke the Soviet Union or China, both communist nations armed with nuclear weapons.[8]

Johnson undertook that muddled mission in 1964 when he sent combat troops into Vietnam. Execution of that effort fell to Defense Secretary Robert McNamara and his "Whiz Kids" – a nickname that would, as Vietnam turned into a quagmire, become ruefully ironic – who attempted to micromanage the conflict to the point of selecting targets for bombing raids, under the principle of "graduated military pressure."[9]

Much of the military leadership, including Westmoreland and Abrams, had been junior officers during World War II, a conflict radically unlike Vietnam. Westmoreland, in charge of the entire US effort through Military Assistance Command, Vietnam (MACV), realized that the combined American–Republic of Vietnam forces could prevail only by eliminating the North Vietnamese resistance.

With that, Westmoreland adopted a strategy of "Find, Fix, and Finish," which referred to the practice of "Finding" the enemy, trapping, or "Fixing," him in place, and then using superior firepower to "Finish" him. In theory, at least, that was how Westmoreland planned to win the war. In reality, it spawned the "body count" strategy, where progress was measured by the number of enemy troops killed. McNamara, more a statistician than a military theorist – indeed, he and the "Whiz Kids" were contemptuous of the military top brass – set an objective of killing enemy soldiers faster than the North Vietnamese could replace them, which he called the "crossover point." But even finding the enemy turned out to be problematic. Concealed beneath thick jungles and often in tunnels, the North Vietnamese were virtually invisible from the air, which neutralized the Americans' greatest advantage. Even attempts to employ technology in the exercise of finding the enemy failed. For a time, US forces used an automated "people sniffer," which located large concentrations of urine. But the North Vietnamese got wind – no pun intended – of that trick and thwarted the Americans by leaving buckets of urine hanging from trees and moving down the trail.[10]

The "body count" mandate filtered from McNamara's Pentagon to military leaders such as Westmoreland and eventually to commanders in the field. Combat officers, particularly company commanders who typically held the rank of captain, were under extreme pressure to produce large body counts. With so much hinging on the body count statistics, widespread killings of civilians were all but inevitable.[11] Davidson, Westmoreland's chief intelligence officer, said the Americans had reached the "crossover point" in 1967, although those figures might have been swelled by civilians who were reclassified as enemy troops.

Body count proved not only to be counterproductive – killing civilians, either deliberately or as collateral losses, was an evident obstacle in winning the hearts and minds of their surviving friends and relatives – but also a faulty method of measuring progress.

That deficiency was brutally exposed at the beginning of 1968. On January 30, the North Vietnamese launched coordinated attacks on multiple cities, including the capital, Saigon, in South Vietnam and laid siege to the Marine Corps base at Khe Sanh, near the demilitarized zone separating North from South Vietnam. The attack began during Vietnam's Tet holiday, which had been a truce period in previous years, so it caught the South Vietnamese by surprise. Westmoreland and his staff knew an offensive was imminent, but didn't realize how great the enemy's commitment would be. In total 40,000 troops would take part in the operation.

Initially, the attack, called the General Offensive and Uprising by the North Vietnamese leadership and known as the Tet Offensive by the Americans, registered some successes for the enemy, which took the city of Hue and reached the US Embassy grounds in Saigon. The Communists' stated objectives were to overthrow the government of President Nguyen Van Thieu and trigger an uprising of communist sympathizers in South Vietnam. The purpose of North Vietnam's siege of Khe Sanh is a thornier one. Most observers treat it as a diversionary feint, although Davidson, who had been on Westmoreland's staff at the time, said it defied logic to use more than 20,000 North Vietnamese troops in the exercise of diverting about 6,000 Marines. One counterargument to Davidson's claim is that Giap, who masterminded the Tet Offensive, had counted on Westmoreland to reinforce Khe Sanh, but the US general refused to do what his enemy wanted him to do. Davidson believed Giap had attempted to replicate his triumph of 14 years earlier at Dien Bien Phu.[12] One plausible argument was that Giap might have wanted to pin down the garrison at Khe Sanh out of fear that the Americans might try to cut the Ho Chi Minh Trail at its most vulnerable point in Laos near the border between North and South Vietnam. The trail, which ran along the Vietnamese borders with Laos and

Cambodia, was the main thoroughfare for supplies and troops moving from North to South Vietnam. Because the United States had refused to enter either Laos or Cambodia out of respect for both nations' nominal neutrality, the North Vietnamese could operate without fear of reprisals along the trail network.[13]

Regardless of whether Khe Sanh was a diversion or an additional prong of the Tet Offensive, it quickly became clear that the North Vietnamese would achieve precisely none of their tactical objectives. Their gains in South Vietnam were dislodged by late March, the South Vietnamese people declined to join the uprising – Davidson asserted that the South Vietnamese Army fought with more courage and aptitude than they had before or ever would again – and enemy forces never came close to overrunning the Marines at Khe Sanh before the siege broke in early April.[14] Further, the North Vietnamese losses, more than 100,000 killed, wounded, or captured in Tet's three phases running through September, were so crippling that the Viet Cong guerrilla forces would never again be a significant factor in the war.

Tet was a tactical victory for the US and South Vietnamese but a strategic victory for the Communists. In the 1983 book *A Distant Challenge*, the staff of *Infantry* magazine wrote:

> Who won the battle of the Tet Offensive? It is a hard question to answer. Certainly the Communists were deprived of every major goal, with the exception of publicity. It certainly was no military victory; 27,706 enemy soldiers died in the Tet fighting. For this, the Communist high command had not one single prize to show.[15]

But the offensive represented something else entirely in the United States. If the size, scope, and time of the attacks came as a mild surprise to MACV leadership, they were a shock to a public in the United States that had been fed a steady diet of rosy reports from Saigon, the Pentagon, and the White House. Tet put the lie to claims by generals and politicians that South Vietnam and the United States were on the verge of winning the war. Instead, it exposed a cruel reality, that for all the enemy bodies that had been counted, and all the American bodies buried, the enemy could still wage war, and that victory in Vietnam would require a long slog, if it could be won at all. Davidson accused an unsupportive US media of recasting a stirring tactical victory into a strategic defeat through coverage that included CBS News anchor Walter Cronkite's proclamation that Vietnam had become a "stalemate."[16]

The North Vietnamese wouldn't realize until later that their failure had actually set them on a path toward final victory. After Tet, the depleted communist forces didn't emerge for another major offensive until after the United States' complete withdrawal five years later. Instead, they fought the war on their own terms only, with ambushes and booby traps, and avoided direct confrontation with the Americans' superior firepower and command of the skies.

But as January of 1970 dawned, the Currahees of Bravo Company had a rare opportunity by the standards of US combat in Vietnam. They had been placed under the operational control of the 173rd Airborne Brigade as part of Operation *Washington Green*, a pilot program for the transition from a body count standard to "Vietnamization," the process of transferring the burden of defending South Vietnam from the Communists from the United States to the ARVN – the Army of the Republic of Vietnam. The objective of *Washington Green* was to pacify Binh Dinh province, the second-most populous region of Vietnam. With Vietnamization, the US staff in Saigon went from focusing on the number of enemy dead to the percentage of population under US and South Vietnamese control, as measured by the Hamlet Evaluation System, which itself was controversial because it was difficult to distinguish citizen farmers from enemy soldiers, not least because the two were often the same.[17]

"You always had to treat just about everyone as, 'I'm not sure just who you are for most of the time,'" said Bravo Company soldier Richard Freeling.[18]

Davidson, the chief US intelligence staff officer, reported that roughly three-quarters of South Vietnam's hamlets were under control of the Americans and their allies.[19] However, even that figure has been contested by historians, such as former US

Department of Defense analyst Kevin Boylan.[20] The pacification tactic employed 59-member revolutionary development teams trained in both defense and psychological operations assigned to "win hearts and minds" and defend the villages militarily against the North Vietnamese. However, Boylan said there weren't enough revolutionary development teams to carry out the mission throughout Binh Dinh province. The teams had some success in Operation *Washington Green* soon after it was initiated in April of 1969, but North Vietnamese assassination campaigns and threats against hamlet officials made those gains tenuous. In many cases, those officials simply supported the Americans during the day and attacked them at night.[21]

Even more ominous from a Vietnamization standpoint was that the South Vietnamese had been particularly ineffective when not supported by the Americans, and sometimes even when they were. ARVN was, like the central government overall, corrupt and rife with nepotism and cronyism. Most of the troops in any given South Vietnamese territorial unit turned up for duty only sporadically because they had to work second jobs to support their families. For one operation in October of 1969, a US revolutionary development team was supposed to have been supported by an ARVN company of more than 100 men. Only 14 South Vietnamese soldiers answered muster.[22] The North Vietnamese, conversely, were getting material support not only from the Ho Chi Minh Trail logistical network, but from as far away as China and the Soviet Union.

After one operation during the siege of Hill 474 during Operation *Washington Green*, Bravo Company trooper Ron Gooch added his name to the list of those frustrated with the South Vietnamese allies. "We were a blocking force with the Vietnamese, but when the shit hit the fan, they leave."[23]

The pacification effort suffered another setback in August and September of 1969, when the People's Army of Vietnam's (PAVN) 3rd Division started filtering into Binh Dinh. Dating back to 1965, the unit, nicknamed the Yellow Star Division, had been engaging the Americans and South Vietnamese in the Central

Highlands so often that journalist Neil Sheehan would call it "the real phoenix of Binh Dinh."[24]

In response to the newfound enemy presence, command in Saigon diverted the 506th Infantry Regiment, including Bravo Company, to oppose the incursion. Those troops were no longer available to work on Operation *Washington Green*'s pacification action, which was already short on resources. But the shift in manpower was unavoidable. With the appearance of the 3rd Division throughout the fall and into December of 1969, the staff of US commander General Creighton Abrams began to worry about a 1970 Tet Offensive repeat.[25]

That notion wasn't altogether irrational. The North Vietnamese had launched small offensives the previous year around the North Vietnamese New Year at the end of January on the American calendar. In 1969, US troops throughout South Vietnam were on high alert in the expectation that the North Vietnamese might try again to use the holiday as a cover for a large-scale attack. At that time, the 3rd Battalion, 506th Infantry Regiment was stationed at Landing Zone Betty near Phan Thiet. The usual procedure was for the Currahees to radiate in platoon strength, combing the jungle for enemy soldiers. But with the alert on, all of the troops manned guard posts at the landing zone. By February 22, battalion and regimental officers believed the danger was past, and ordered Bravo Company back into the field. They hadn't gone more than a few miles beyond the razor wire when the North Vietnamese launched an attack and, with little more than the battalion's headquarters company manning the base, breached the perimeter and destroyed an ammunition depot. Three US soldiers – Sergeant William John Allen, 22, of Greenville, Michigan; Private First Class Kevin Edward Tweedle, 22, from Wharton, Texas; and Captain Gerald Wrazen, 27, from Buffalo, New York – were killed, and 29 Americans were wounded. The enemy lost 21 killed and one captured.

"I could listen to the chatter and a lot of people got hurt, injured, and killed," said Bravo Company trooper Richard "Dick" Freeling, who was in the second month of his combat tour when he saw and heard the ammo dump explosion from less than 5 miles off. "It bothered me a great deal that I wasn't in a position to do anything."[26]

Elements of the North Vietnamese 3rd Division's 22nd Regiment were dug in on an unnamed mountain within a system of tunnels, both natural and man-made, just west of Bong Son village in Binh Dinh province. The North Vietnamese were now based in a fortress that was also a trap. Even though Westmoreland had been reassigned by that time to a place on the Joint Chiefs of Staff and replaced by Abrams, this represented the former MACV commander's ideal scenario.

The enemy was "found" and "fixed." It would now fall to Bravo Company to help "finish" them.

CHAPTER 3

How's Mom and Dad are they in Florida now, I hope so because that's why I didn't write them. Did Roe tell [you] about the two 1st Lieutenants I was hanging around with the day before they sent me to my unit. They were both nice guys, they took me to the NCO club for a beer and gave me a Playboy. Earlier a lifer sergeant who was ahead of our weeks training taped my tapes and gave me a Wes Montgomery tape. I better get some sleep now, there's a 12-hour time difference you know.

Leslie Sabo letter to his brother, George, and George's wife, Olga
Sent November 26, 1969 from Ban Me Thuot

When the 101st Airborne Division was deployed to Vietnam, it was no longer used primarily as an airborne unit, but rather as an air assault unit. Instead of parachuting from troop-carrying airplanes at thousands of feet in altitude, the Screaming Eagles made their combat jumps from the skids of helicopters that hovered over drop zones just long enough to disgorge a squad of troopers before cruising skyward.

During Vietnam, the UH-1D, known popularly among the troops as the Huey, was the workhorse for air assault and evacuation operations. One Huey commonly carried a squad of about 12 men and three were enough to transport a platoon in most cases. Soldiers rarely hesitated about exiting the helicopters in a hot zone – military-speak for a landing zone that was under fire. Just the opposite, in fact. Any trooper who balked at making the leap would be pushed out by his comrades anxious to evacuate the large, hovering target and get on the ground where they could fight back. Koziol, like the rest of his comrades, didn't waste time getting out of the helicopter.

"If I was on the ground, I could run. If I was in the water, I could swim. But if the helicopter gets shot down, I'm gone."[1]

When going in for an attack, the machine gunners, armed with .60 caliber automatic weapons, would typically be out first, because success in a firefight depends on which side can sling the most lead the fastest. In a hot zone, a squad could be on the ground and fighting in a matter of seconds.[2] After only a few weeks in country, Leslie Sabo was assigned to an M-60 crew to temporarily replace a Currahee who was pulled off the line after he sustained a leg injury. He would remain on the machine-gun crew into March, when the injured man returned to duty and Sabo returned to his rifleman duty as a squad leader.

Medical evacuation was more complicated and took longer because the wounded men would have to be brought – usually carried by two or three other troopers – from a concealed area into the landing zone. During the entire time, which could be a minute or more, the Hueys were often taking fire. While a durable craft as helicopters go, the Huey was still vulnerable to ground fire. The chopper pilots' willingness to risk being shot down in the service of airlifting wounded won the admiration of ground troops like Bravo Company's Norm Friend.

"Those guys were good. To put it bluntly, those pilots and crews had gorilla balls."

That wasn't always the case. During the Battle of Ia Drang in November of 1965, medevac helicopters made only one run at

Landing Zone X-Ray on the battlefield, which was under heavy fire. One of the two choppers picked up two wounded soldiers and the other retreated without landing. Later on, gunship pilot Major Bruce "Snake" Crandall – who would receive the Medal of Honor for flying multiple missions on his own initiative to carry ammunition and reinforcements in, and wounded out – got into an altercation with the medevac squadron commander who objected to Crandall leading medical helicopters into a hot landing zone. Crandall said he nearly decked the commander, which might have landed him in some trouble, and volunteered to pick up the wounded himself.[3]

At that point in the war, policy dictated that medevac pilots land only in "green landing zones," on ground that hadn't been fired on by the enemy for at least five minutes. After the policy changed, journalist Joseph Galloway, who had been on the ground at Landing Zone X-Ray in 1965, said the medevac pilots were more than willing to land in hot zones by December of 1969, when the Bravo Company replacements arrived in Vietnam.[4]

And by Norm Friend's standards, the biggest set of "gorilla balls" might well have been the ones that swung between the legs of his battalion commander, Lieutenant Colonel Joseph "Wildcat" Jaggers, who was starting his second combat tour in Vietnam. Although Jaggers was an aviator, he understood the foot soldier's life – he had been a commander of a rifle company during the Korean War. Under Jaggers' leadership, the 197th Aviation Company received the Vietnam War's first Presidential Unit Citation, after Jaggers planned and executed a large airlift of personnel and supplies in Hau Nghia province. In his ensuing stateside posting, Jaggers helped develop the Army's field manual for helicopter gunship operations, which meant that, when Bravo Company took helicopters into battle, they followed procedures developed by their own battalion commander. In between Vietnam tours, Jaggers served as the Army's special staff officer for development on the Cobra helicopter. He had a reputation as a lead-from-the-front pilot for his willingness to fly combat missions alongside his subordinates. And he quickly proved that the reputation was warranted.[5]

"He didn't just throw us to the wolves," said Bravo Company trooper Jack Brickey. "He put us in the position to do good."

Within weeks of landing in Vietnam, one of the new Bravo Company soldiers had something to brag about. Richard Rios had graduated from the University of Texas less than a year earlier and, on January 1, 1970, his alma mater had wrapped up the NCAA football championship. That one might have been a particularly bitter pill to Bravo Company's Pennsylvania contingent – Leslie Sabo, Joe Honan, Steven Dile, and Dave Soden. Texas might have taken the national football title as much by presidential acclamation as it did by anything it accomplished on the field. The previous November, just as Rios and the other cherries were arriving in Vietnam, President Richard Nixon, an avid football fan, took time out from running the Vietnam War to proclaim that the annual Texas–Oklahoma rivalry game's winner should be the national champion. After Texas won that game to remain unbeaten, national championship voters accepted Nixon's verdict, at the expense of another undefeated team – Penn State University.

Rios, who called himself "a child of the sixties," had planned on going to law school, but was snapped up by his local draft board almost immediately upon receiving his college degree, which is how he found himself celebrating his team's success in Vietnam.

Koziol, Friend, Sabo, and the rest of the Currahee cherries were deemed combat ready by mid-January. The 506th Regiment's 3rd Battalion was inserted along with other elements of the 173rd Airborne Brigade during the third week of January into Binh Dinh province, in the northern region of South Vietnam, as part of Operation *Washington Green*. For most of the next three months, the Currahees made their home at the foot of a lump of ground too small to merit a name, only a number – Hill 474. The objective of *Washington Green* was to pacify the population of Binh Dinh province by dislodging the North Vietnamese Army's 3rd Division, 8th Battalion, eliminating its civilian allies and installing local leadership sympathetic to the United States. The operation had some initial successes, particularly through killing and driving enemy forces from the province. But South Vietnamese forces were unable to consolidate those gains, and more than 1,000 local US-connected officials were assassinated or kidnapped during the second half of 1970, which effectively kept the province under enemy control at the village level.[6]

Binh Dinh province ran from the easternmost fringes of South Vietnam's Central Highlands to the South China Sea's shoreline, and it had been a hotbed of rebellion against both the Americans, and the French before that.[7] It didn't take long before Bravo Company's new arrivals realized they would be fighting a different type of war, and a different type of enemy, than their forebears had faced in World War II, when the Allied armies rolled across Europe with a fixation on claiming landmarks like river crossings or national capitals. Instead, Bravo Company would hit Hill 474 in an effort to dislodge the enemy, primarily by killing as many of them as possible.

"We just stayed put in one area. And we stayed there for weeks on end," Rios said.

Hill 474 sat in what Rios called a "good-sized mountain range in the Central Highlands." During the five-plus months that Bravo Company and its brothers in the 3rd Battalion saw its heaviest action, it spent not a day attached to the 101st Airborne as a whole, which was a pointed irony in light of the division's earliest history during World War II. The division, including the 506th Infantry Regiment, jumped into Normandy during D-Day in the early morning hours of June 6, 1944, and again on September 17, into Holland as part of Operation *Market Garden*. But the Screaming Eagles became best renowned for defending a crucial road juncture in the Belgian town of Bastogne against concentrated attacks from the Germans. For more than a week, the American paratroopers, outnumbered and surrounded, held the town and its crucial five-way road junction. In the Battle of the Bulge, the successful defense of Bastogne turned out to be critical. After that, the press stuck the 101st with the nickname "The Battered Bastards of the Bastion of Bastogne." Bravo Company Vietnam veteran Rios said the 506th Regiment's 3rd Battalion continued to be known as the "Bastard Battalion," more than a quarter-century after its stand in Belgium, albeit for a different reason.

"We were like the red-headed stepchild of the 101st Airborne."

The 101st Airborne Division had cut its teeth in Europe, and so had Leslie Sabo, who was destined to distinguish himself as a Screaming Eagle.

When the previous generation of Currahees was leaping into Europe, the Sabo family – which at the time included Leslie Sr., Elisabeth, and one-year-old George – were plotting to escape from their homeland ahead of the advancing Soviet Army and a likely appointment with a Communist firing squad. As they fled, apparent salvation appeared along the road. A German staff officer who was heading in the same direction, in a display of chivalry, offered the family a ride to Austria, which would give them all the opportunity to eventually throw themselves on the mercy of the Americans or British. Getting into the car would carry the young family to its objective much faster and ensure that they would reach Austria ahead of the Soviets, who were decidedly less inclined toward kindness in their dealings with Hungarians like Leslie Sabo Sr., the child of privilege and a government official in a nation allied with Germany.

But Sabo wasn't having it. He declined the ride offer, and rudely so.

"I can remember my father getting into an argument with the soldier," said George Sabo.

The story of Leslie Sabo Sr., and by extension Leslie Sabo Jr., begs an explanation of how the distinguished Hungarian father of an American who in turn distinguished himself during the Vietnam War brought his family through World War II. It would be unsavory, if a little ironic, if an American Vietnam War hero turned out to be a son of a war criminal who participated, even tangentially, in the Holocaust. As a matter of historical fact, Hungary entered the war in 1941 as an ally of Germany, its army participated in the invasion of the Soviet Union and an estimated 70 percent of Hungary's prewar Jewish population was killed in the Holocaust. By war's end, Hungary was ruled by the Arrow Cross, that nation's Nazi party.[8]

But the matter of Hungary's involvement in the war is far more nuanced than that. Miklós Horthy, the regent of Hungary from 1920 until 1944 when he was deposed by the Germans and the Arrow Cross, used political maneuvering to prevent the establishment of anti-Jewish laws and determinedly slow-footed those regulations he was forced into passing. John Flournoy Montgomery, the US envoy to Hungary from 1933 until a few months before that nation entered World War II as an ally of Germany, surmised that Leslie Sabo Sr.'s homeland was forced by circumstances into a marriage with an evil it couldn't comprehend and a philosophy it didn't share.

Hungary, formerly part of the Hapsburg-ruled Austro-Hungarian Empire, was emasculated by the agreements that ended World War I, and Montgomery stated further that it spent the following years protecting itself against the threat of unfriendly nations in the region, particularly Romania and the Slovak nations. In his view, Hungary lacked an army of any consequence and was surrounded by enemies, with Germany and Austria among its few allies. Nurturing that relationship was a case of Hungary playing a bad hand as well as possible.[9]

Leslie Halasz Sabo Sr. – born Laszlo Halasz Sabo – was a prominent attorney and scion of one of Hungary's wealthiest merchant families, which owned a department store and a large farm. George Sabo, who wasn't yet two years old when the war ended, said his family wasn't complicit in the Holocaust, although he added that his father didn't talk much about that time.

"There are a lot of things I would like to learn. The mystery to me was why my father waited so long to leave."

The answer to that question appears to be that, until late in the war, conditions were at least tolerable for Hungarians, even those who hated both the Nazis and Communists – a characterization that likely described Leslie Sabo Sr. – until the Arrow Cross takeover and the Yalta Conference, which put Hungary under the Soviet sphere of influence once the war ended. It's likely that Leslie Sabo Sr. was like the nation of Hungary itself, in that both consented to Nazi-era edicts in halfway and inconsequential measures. In any event, military authorities would have investigated Leslie Sabo Sr., as they did with other postwar refugees, before allowing him to immigrate. As a government official in Hungary, there would have been an extensive paper trail documenting his activities during World War II. If Sabo had perpetrated war crimes, or even joined the Arrow Cross, it's difficult to imagine that immigration officials wouldn't have been aware of it, and that would have been sufficient to deny him access to the United States.

Furthermore, the majority of Hungary's nobles and well-off citizens were anti-Nazi, Montgomery also wrote. The diplomat posited that the country's strongest Fascist supporters were in its rural regions, those most affected by the post-World War I losses of territories that controlled the water those farmers needed for growing crops. To the Hungarian farmer, allying with the Nazis was a matter of survival.

Until the Arrow Cross takeover, which put Adolf Eichmann in charge of the "Final Solution" in Hungary, the country was an "oasis" for central and eastern Europe's Jews throughout most of the war. Eichmann, perhaps the most famous Nazi fugitive brought to postwar justice, escaped to South America in the postwar chaos and lived there for more than a decade before being captured by the Israelis. He would be tried and executed largely for what he did in Hungary during the final year of World War II. Reports indicate Hungary's prewar Jewish population was 650,000, and that 450,000 Hungarian Jews were killed. But the figure of those killed includes hundreds upon thousands of Jews from less hospitable nations who sought refuge in Hungary and swelled the nation's Jewish population to about 1 million prior to the Arrow Cross takeover.[10]

Under Horthy and Miklós Kállay, Hungary's prime minister before the Nazi takeover, authorities prevented the deportation of Jews to German death camps until March 19, 1944, when Hitler turned control of the country to the Arrow Cross party. Tragically, most of the Hungarian Jews who succumbed to the Holocaust died in the war's final 13 months.[11]

Hungarians had a history of acceptance toward minority religions, a tradition that benefited the Sabo family. Even though Hungary was a Catholic-majority nation in the years before atheist communism held sway, the Sabos' Presbyterian faith didn't prevent them from being political power brokers, according to George Sabo. And in spite of their wealth, the Sabos suffered the privations of war along with their less well-off countrymen. A third Sabo brother, Gabriel, died of malnutrition during the war years.[12]

It's a part of Sabo family lore that one of Leslie Sr.'s brothers, a minister in Kállay's government, participated in secret meetings with British Prime Minister Winston Churchill to lobby for the Allies to open a second front along the Adriatic Sea, in spite of Hungary's nominal bond to Germany. Even though George Sabo admits that account might not be accurate, it's a matter of historical fact that Kállay did send such a request to the Allies, but it was rejected. This flirtation was one of the reasons that Hitler ordered the imprisonment of Horthy's family to force the regent's abdication, which paved the way for the Arrow Cross takeover and, eventually, Communist rule.[13]

While the Hungarian upper class had no great love for the Nazis, they, presumably including the Sabos, despised the Communists. After World War II, according to Montgomery, the US diplomat-turned-author, the Soviet Union demanded, unsuccessfully, that Horthy and Kállay be returned to USSR-controlled Hungary, probably with the intent of trying and executing the two leaders.[14] George Sabo said his father left Hungary to escape that fate.

"Everyone was getting out of Dodge because they would have been killed. They would have shot every official that they could get their hands on."

Leslie Sr., who had a PhD in law, was the wartime mayor of Szeged, one of the country's largest cities, and had a brother who was a high-ranking official in the Horthy/Kállay government, which convinced them that a Soviet-controlled Hungary wouldn't be very hospitable toward the family. When Elisabeth, Leslie Sr., and George Sabo – Leslie Jr. hadn't yet been born – slipped out of Hungary just before World War II ended, they left behind what Olga believed to have been millions of dollars' worth of artwork and jewels, which would never be recovered.

After the Soviets took control of Hungary, they turned the family home, Nicholas Castle in the town of Sentesz, into a home for unwed mothers, she said. The family escaped only with some wartime scrip, which was soon declared worthless. In George's estimation, his father believed that exile from the homeland was temporary, with good reason. Hungary's previous Communist government, in 1919, lasted only 133 days before being overthrown in a revolution led by Horthy.

But Leslie Sabo Sr., who died in 1977, never returned to Hungary. Indeed, the Soviet bloc outlived him.

CHAPTER 4

I received your letter on the 27th, it was really good to hear from you. I also received the card Tony sent me, it was real nice to get it. I'm doing real fine although it's tough being out in the field over the holidays. I've lost some weight but everybody does at first. It is tiring carrying that heavy rucksack up and down mountains. Right now, we're in a valley, we were up on a mountain and in the mornings you would look down at a sea of clouds with mountaintops sticking out all over. What's bad is this lousy elephant grass with razor sharp edges that cut your hands all up. We just got resupplied which means we get three days worth of supplies and I carry 7 canteens of water, which isn't too bad. Before I came they carried 5 days worth and 15 canteens. I'm glad to hear everybody's fine and that George is doing well in school. How many more hours does he need. When I come home I am planning on taking about 12 to 15 hours. I am getting paid today at least I won't be able to spend it for a while. One guy is going to get me some film so I'll send some pictures in after a few more months, I'm starting to get a real nice tan, luckily we missed the rainy season although it can get pretty hot. Your New Year's resolution makes me very happy, it is nice to get mail from people you really care about. Well I've got to mail this now. Say hi to the boys and everyone for me.

Leslie Sabo letter to George and Olga
Dated December 30, 1969

Few in Bravo Company were admired more than the medics, universally nicknamed "Doc," who were often called upon to rush the enemy armed with little more than bandages and courage. While combat medics were best known for rushing out to give aid in the face of withering enemy fire at the urgent cry, "Medic!" they also tended to more mundane complaints, like malaria or other tropical diseases that ravaged soldiers in the jungle.

"There were a lot of guys who are around today because of the hero medics," said Bravo Company trooper Dave Soden.

Soden had struck up a friendship with one of those medics, Joe Honan. The two men hailed from the same hometown of Scranton, Pennsylvania, and arrived in Vietnam within weeks of one another. Honan began his tour in mid-November, only a few weeks after Rick Brown, and just before Sabo.

Honan, who had had a rough upbringing in Scranton, Pennsylvania, was regarded by his comrades as among the best at his craft. His parents had split up at a time when that just wasn't done, particularly in Catholic households – he was a graduate of Scranton's South Catholic High School – and he had few roots, even in his hometown. Honan and Soden, who grew up not far from one another, became close. Years later, Soden would try to find anyone who had known Honan, but was unsuccessful, aside from an encounter with one of the medic's high school girlfriends when the Moving Wall half-size replica of the national Vietnam War Memorial Wall made a stop in the Scranton area. In Honan's obituary, his father and a grandmother were listed as his only two survivors. Both have since died. Before being drafted with the late-1969 Bravo Company class, Honan had been a singer and bass player with a Scranton-area band called the Capris.[1] In the field, Honan regaled his comrades with renditions of Tom Jones songs.

"He did what he could to keep us alive and healthy," said 2nd Platoon soldier Joe Hanks. "Everything from passing out our malaria pills to binding our wounds."[2]

Jerry Nash earned his "Doc" moniker only days after arriving in Vietnam, and more than a month before he saw bullets fly for the first time when a group of 2nd Platoon soldiers got into trouble in their quest for something a little more tasty than canned C-rations. Horace Currin – who went by Ben and was nicknamed "Johnny Cash" for his resemblance, physically and vocally, to the singer – found some discarded steaks and whipped them up for his fellow soldiers. Too late, they discovered that the steaks had been thrown out for a reason. The soldiers, including Currin and Ron Gooch, were wracked with food poisoning.

"I was up all night with guys who had diarrhea and vomiting," Nash said.

The 22-year-old medic had landed in Vietnam only a few days earlier. He had made it through half a year of graduate school at the University of Tennessee before the draft man got him. Nash, the son of a dairy farmer, was studying dairy nutrition. After being drafted in 1969, Nash took his final exams on a Thursday, packed up his things and moved back home on Friday and was inducted on Monday. Nash didn't volunteer to be a medic – he was simply assigned the job.

So it was off to Fort Campbell, nestled along the border of Kentucky and Tennessee, for basic training, followed by advanced individual training at the Army's medic school in Fort Sam Houston, Texas, where he received training in emergency field medicine, not only for combat-related trauma, but also for maladies endemic to jungle warfare – infections from blades of grass nearly as sharp as blades of steel, and the effects of animals ranging from leeches to red ants to snakes. That included the one supremely unfortunate soldier who had a tick attach itself to his testicles and a sergeant who had to be airlifted out of the jungle after an allergic reaction to the jungle wildlife caused his eyes to swell shut.

Nash arrived in Vietnam shortly before Thanksgiving, knowing little more about the country than what he had seen nightly on the 6 o'clock news for more than five years since the United States had begun large-scale involvement in the war.

"You think that when you get off the plane, you're going to get shot at," Nash said.

While medics were better known for saving lives than they were for taking them, they were hardly defenseless on the battlefield. In Bravo Company, the medics were riflemen – they carried M-16s and sometimes explosives like claymore mines into the field – until they weren't, when they were called upon to provide care.

All bleeding stops … eventually, as the old nurses' joke goes. But the medics were supposed to treat wounded soldiers primarily by stopping the bleeding as quickly as possible. After that, they were supposed to control pain and keep their patients from going into shock and stabilize them for a medevac helicopter flight to a field hospital. On the 1969–70 tour, Bravo Company's medics carried a pack that weighed about 80 pounds, which contained a first aid bag with, among other items, enough morphine to dull the pain of combat wounds and a maximum of four bags of intravenous fluids.

"I wanted to make sure I did my job," Nash said. "I wanted to gain respect from them so they would know that, if anyone was wounded, I would be there."

When the time came, and the "Medic!" call went out, Nash and Honan did their jobs, and then some.

Vietnam's monsoon season brings almost-daily heavy rains running from late May through October and only slightly lighter storms through the end of the year. The remaining months from January through early May comprised the annual campaign season. Bravo Company began its 1970 campaign season in January, with the year's first serious combat.

In spite of his rank and status as a squad leader, Steven Dile took on one of the most dangerous duties – walking point – on an almost continuous basis. So it was unusual that he was actually not first in line on January 28, when 3rd Platoon ascended a trail along Hill 474 with the mission of retrieving the bodies of two of the four US soldiers from Delta Company killed three days earlier.

Hill 474 was in the middle of an historic center of resistance against invading powers dating back to the years immediately following World War II, when Vietnam battled against French colonial authority. The Central Highlands, which had been regarded as a key strategic prize since the United States began its involvement in Vietnam, had in fact been a stronghold for the communist insurgency since the First Indo-China War against the French.

As Bravo Company arrived in Binh Dinh province in January of 1970, the United States was in the process of drawing down its involvement in Vietnam from the 1967 high of around a half-million troops. The Currahees, along with elements of the 173rd Airborne Brigade, were given a dual assignment of rooting out the North Vietnamese Army's 22nd Regiment, 3rd Division from the hill and training the South Vietnamese Army to repel the enemy on its own. Hill 474 was located near a semicircular bend on the An Lao River in the eastern fringes of Vietnam's Central Highlands about 15 kilometers (9.5 miles) north-northwest of the village of Bong Son.[3]

When the regiment, nearly 1,000 men, was discovered in Hill 474, US General Hubert Cunningham ordered the Currahees to surround the mountain. Cunningham's decision might single-handedly have prevented a 1970 Tet Offensive in Binh Dinh province to overturn progress being made in *Washington Green*'s pacification efforts. A defector captured later said the North Vietnamese command had ordered an offensive to begin in January of 1970, but the plans were abandoned because of a shortage of supplies throughout the region. Historian Kevin Boylan surmised that the shortage was due at least partly to the Hill 474 operation, and to pacification-based efforts to interdict supplies to the North Vietnamese.[4]

The primary challenge in attacking Hill 474 was in its terrain, which offered ample opportunities for concealing enemy soldiers. The peak was covered with huge rocks, some the size of houses. Several streams – small tributaries of the An Lao – rolled down its slopes and it was honeycombed with caves and tunnels, both natural and man-made. Cunningham – mindful of the 101st Airborne Division's assault on Hamburger Hill in the A Shau Valley eight months earlier, when the Screaming Eagles lost 72 men and had 372 wounded during an assault on North Vietnamese forces entrenched atop a mountain – abstained from a frontal assault in favor of a siege against the enemy's makeshift fortress.[5]

"That's where the enemy was. We could hear them at night," Richard Rios said.

Bravo Company had been assigned to help clear-cut (i.e. remove all trees and foliage in a specific area), with the assistance of armored bulldozers and a strangely-named defoliant – Agent Orange – that would one day become intimately familiar to them, and build a small firebase atop a hill near Hill 474. Over their first couple of weeks on patrols, the Currahees had been targeted by North Vietnamese snipers, but took no casualties. The killing on Hill 474 began in earnest on January 19. After checking out a cave just after noon, 1st Platoon of Delta Company took a break for lunch when, in the words of Mike Dingman, the platoon medic, "All hell broke loose." The Currahees were pounded. Private First Class Benjamin Garcia, Specialist Jeff Miller, Sergeant George Spillers, and Specialist Victor Paulino San Nicolas were killed in the initial exchange of fire and the efforts to secure a landing zone to evacuate the wounded. San Nicolas, nicknamed "Guam" for the US territory where he was born and raised, was wounded in the initial attack and was en route to the landing zone when he was shot again, fatally. Spillers was killed in the initial assault, and Garcia and Miller fell while 1st Platoon was struggling to reach the landing zone.[6]

Later the same day, Alpha Company's 3rd Platoon was ambushed just off a trail along the hill's slopes. Enemy fire killed Private First Class Robert Mitcheltree, who was walking point, almost immediately. Platoon leader First Lieutenant Phil Peters led a tactical retreat to a point where his men could return fire. The platoon made repeated attempts to recover Mitcheltree's body, but was repelled by enemy fire. Even the arrival of Huey helicopters failed to dislodge the enemy from its positions. Instead of withdrawing under withering gunship fire, the North Vietnamese neutralized the Americans' air power advantage by advancing nearly into the Currahees' defensive perimeter, which meant the helicopter crews couldn't fire on the enemy out of fear that they would hit their buddies on the ground.

By that point in the war, the North Vietnamese had been facing off against the Americans for nearly five years in battles large and small, so both sides knew the Currahees would spare no effort to claim Mitcheltree's remains. Jaggers ordered a platoon of Delta Company and Bravo Company into the battle, but night fell before the Americans could get to Mitcheltree.

Just after daylight on January 20, Alpha Company made another attempt, which ended in ambush. One trooper was wounded and exposed, but Sergeant Brent Steere advanced and put down covering fire, which enabled the wounded man to reach safety. Steere was himself wounded, but led his team back to the American perimeter. Alpha Company's commander and radio telephone operator were wounded in yet another effort to reach Mitcheltree. The next day, they succeeded. Under heavy fire from helicopters and artillery, the Americans forced the enemy to withdraw, and recovered the body of their fallen comrade.[7]

With the North Vietnamese moving to flank the Americans, team leader Sergeant David Lindsey tried to place a claymore mine – which spreads shrapnel in a contained area, referred to as the "kill zone" – but he was hit by enemy fire. The shot itself didn't do much damage to Lindsey, but it detonated a smoke pack, used for signaling air support, and left him with burns on his leg. The team leader was able to detonate the mine, and temporarily stopped the North Vietnamese advance. When Lindsey saw a fellow team member lying injured and exposed, the sergeant used his own body to shield his comrade. Meanwhile, Specialist Thomas Cremeens and Specialist Lindsey Ford then took the initiative and stopped an enemy advance that could have overrun the Americans. Cremeens pressed a successful attack even after being wounded by enemy fire, and Specialist Tommy Baker crept up on the enemy lines and used a grenade attack to finish off the North Vietnamese assault.

Sergeant Lindsey received the Distinguished Service Cross, the Army's second-highest award for combat action, behind only the Medal of Honor. Cremeens earned the Silver Star, the third-highest award. Baker and Ford were both awarded Bronze Stars.

Lieutenant Colonel Jaggers, call sign "Wildcat," was in the sky on January 25, while Charlie Company of his battalion was getting pounded on the ground. With Delta Company's troops unable to secure a landing zone, Charlie Company's 2nd Platoon was ordered in to help. Private First Class Oscar Gonzalez of Charlie Company was shot and killed by a North Vietnamese soldier hiding in a rocky cave mouth on Hill 474. Only two weeks earlier, Gonzalez had carried a comrade, Dan Linn, more than 200 yards to a landing zone after Linn had been seriously wounded and, in Linn's estimation, saved his life. Charlie Company came under heavy ground fire as it arrived in helicopters to help out Delta Company. Ultimately, the efforts of both platoons weren't enough to enable helicopters to evacuate wounded. The soldiers from Delta and Charlie companies wounded in the January 25 attack would remain in the field until the following day. Ground troops were able to secure helicopter landing zones only after approximately two dozen air strikes by Phantom jet crews.

It took three days for the Currahees to reclaim their Delta Company comrades killed on January 25. Bravo Company, which hadn't been committed in that day's firefight, would get the recovery assignment, with 3rd Platoon detailed to be part of the operation. For Bravo Company's cherries, it would be their first time getting bloodied. Specialist Frank Madrid walked point, followed closely in the lead element by Specialist Peter Guzman, Specialist Forrest "Jack" Brickey, and platoon leader Lieutenant John Shaffer.

The lead element was packed with experience by the standards of US combat troops in Vietnam. All four soldiers – including Shaffer – had been with Bravo Company for nearly six months. Shaffer's father had been a pilot in the US Army Air Corps – the World War II forerunner of the US Air Force – who reached the rank of major and returned home to become a prominent Syracuse, New York-area attorney. His son had graduated from

Syracuse University in his hometown, where he was active with the Sigma Nu fraternity. During his time in college – Shaffer graduated from Syracuse in 1967, before the largest anti-war protests roiled college campuses across the nation – he believed in the cause of fighting the Communists in Southeast Asia.[8]

Since the previous August, Shaffer had led 3rd Platoon and was in line for a new assignment. In the meantime, though, he was serving as acting company commander, with a replacement captain due in a few days.

"Jack" Brickey, youngest of 15 kids, had lived the first years of his life in Virginia before his father, a railroader, moved to the Detroit suburbs. Jack's oldest brother, Miles, who was 27 years Jack's senior, had joined the Army in the late 1930s and was due to be discharged on December 6, 1941. As the following day dawned, Miles Brickey anticipated the end of his military career – planning to hitch a flight home from Pearl Harbor, Hawaii, and return to civilian life. Unfortunately, most of the flights over Oahu that day were piloted by the Japanese. He was wounded in the December 7, 1941 attack that launched the United States into World War II. Miles Brickey's discharge was cancelled and he served in Europe during the war. Six of the Brickey boys served in the military during World War II, the Korean War, and the Vietnam War. Jack was the last.

While in high school at Allen Park, Michigan, "Jack" Brickey had played football, his best position being defensive back. He was drafted on December 13, 1968 – an unlucky Friday. His advanced infantry training was marred by a quarantine when one of the other soldiers in his platoon died of spinal meningitis. The quarantine didn't stop training, but it did force the Army to isolate Brickey's platoon until the session was over. Then Brickey enrolled in non-commissioned officer (NCO) academy – "shake and bake" school – but dropped out before completion after he was wounded. While Brickey was in NCO school, he took the time to learn everything about jungle warfare, including communications and weapons. Brickey reached Vietnam in late August and was assigned to the 101st Airborne Division, which he thought was a mistake because he didn't have his jump certification.

But when a helicopter reached the base to take Brickey and another soldier to 101st Airborne headquarters, a sergeant snarled, "We're all air mobile. Get on."

Brickey was initially paired up on a 60mm machine gun with Ruben Rueda and the two men bestowed each other nicknames. Rueda, the assistant gunner, wound up with the moniker "Wheels," because he had purchased a succession of high-quality vehicles. Brickey got the name "Woody," a play on Brickey's given first name of Forrest.

Bravo Company hit Hill 474 in the morning on January 28, with the assignment to find the two soldiers from Delta Company who had been killed in the previous nine days, and encountered the enemy almost immediately. After one of the Currahees sighted a cooking fire, evidence of enemy presence, it called down artillery on the location. First Platoon killed three enemy soldiers with M-60 machine-gun fire and 3rd Platoon found documents that contained information on enemy positions and plans in a nearby cave.

After advancing uphill along the slope of Hill 474, Brickey found what Bravo Company had gone there for – the body of one of their fallen comrades. The discovery called for caution – it was common for the enemy to booby-trap fallen US soldiers, because they knew other Americans would return to claim their bodies. As it happened, there was a trap awaiting 3rd Platoon, but it wasn't planted on the body of the fallen Delta Company soldier. Brickey looped a string around the soldier's wrist and flipped him over with sufficient vigor to ensure that a booby trap would be tripped if there was one. There wasn't. They collected the body, wrapped it in Rueda's poncho and put it onto a chopper.

Acting on Jaggers' orders, 3rd Platoon began to withdraw. But instead of retracing their original route, which had skirted a ravine at Hill 474's base, the Currahees went right down Broadway – into the ravine's center, where the enemy, unbeknownst to them, lay in wait. Madrid, who had turned 25 a month earlier and had been in Vietnam since the previous May, was killed immediately, along with Guzman and Shaffer. Brickey, who was with Guzman, Shaffer, and Madrid in the lead group, was raked across the back with machine-gun fire. He fell across the body of Shaffer, who had been hit in the head.

"They just opened up," Brickey said. "That was the fuse and they just lit us up. There were rounds all over. It was like the Fourth of July."

Jerry Nash, the medic who had been in Vietnam a little more than a month and was facing his first combat action, rushed into hostile fire to treat the wounded. "Hungry" Dile – known to his comrades as much for being fearless as he was for his unquenchable maw – came roaring over an enormous boulder in an effort to cover the medic's advance. Dile found Brickey, wounded, unable to stand, but still alive. And still able to fight. In the shadow of the giant rock, facing the enemy, Dile propped Brickey, and, backs to the boulder and shoulder to shoulder, they hosed down the machine-gun nests with their M-16s. At first, they called for Guzman, who had been armed with a weapon that fired buckshot, which sprayed ammunition across a wide area. But Guzman was already dead. So the Currahees yelled for the grenade launcher and its operator. Further back in the column, Rick Brown, armed with the M-79 grenade launcher, was about to face combat for the first time. Not far away from Brown was Ruben Rueda, who understood what Brown was going through because he had experienced it months earlier.

"The first time we took fire, I remember the rounds going over my head and the buttons of my shirt were the only things keeping me off the ground," Rueda said.

January 28, 1970, had been Rick Brown's second brush with death, but not his last. On April 11, 1965, nearly 50 tornadoes had ripped through the Midwest from Iowa as far east as Cleveland and killed more than 250 people in one of the 20th century's three Palm Sunday tornado outbreaks. In Lorain County on the outbreak's westernmost fringe, 18 people were killed by two twisters, rated F4 and F5 on the Fujita scale.[9] When the tornadoes rolled through Columbia Station around 11:20pm on April 11, Rick Brown and his brother were asleep in the basement of his family home.

"Our father was a carpenter and he built our home from the basement up," Brown said.

That meant the boys were safe. The same wasn't the case for Brown's parents and his sister, who was injured by flying glass from the family's greenhouse – his father had a side business operating a nursery. As Brown's parents were tending to the gash in his sister's face, a chimney collapsed and narrowly missed landing on all of them. However, the injury might have saved the girl's life – the tornado dumped a tractor on her bed.

"It got picked up from the field and dropped in our house," Brown said.

A little less than five years later, Brown was fighting for his life and those of his exposed comrades on Hill 474 in Vietnam's Central Highlands. He crawled into the ravine and ducked behind the boulder. On the other side was Brickey, wounded but nonetheless able to direct Brown as he lobbed grenades into the North Vietnamese positions. Brown fired his grenades into the jungle at Brickey's direction throughout the firefight, but it would be 40 years before either man would discover the other's identity.

"He fired every round he had," Brickey said of Brown's work with the grenade launcher. But the North Vietnamese machine guns remained in place and they kept firing on what was left of Bravo Company's lead element.

Nash, the medic who had worried about how he would react when he was called to give aid under fire, moved toward the machine-gun fire without hesitation. Hungry Dile was virtually at his side as they moved toward Brickey, who was severely wounded, and Shaffer, Madrid, and Guzman, who were already dead, although Nash insisted on verifying that for himself.

"Lay down a base of fire for Doc," Dile yelled. "Put out the fire!"

Sitting against the boulder, Dile and Brickey unloaded their M-16s toward the enemy machine-gun nests. In the midst of their shooting, a machine-gun bullet ricocheted off the stock of Brickey's rifle and hit Dile in the head, killing him instantly. The shot also destroyed Brickey's weapon, leaving him to work strictly as a spotter for Brown.

Nash ascertained that four out of the five men caught on the wrong side of that boulder were dead. Having already lost four patients on his first day of combat, Nash worked like hell to save the fifth. He stemmed the bleeding from Brickey's back, left arm, left leg, and torso, and gave copious amounts of morphine. That last measure might have been as important to saving the soldier's life as controlling the blood flow was. The medic slapped a morphine injection onto Brickey's leg. Within moments, the pain from Brickey's horrific wounds – a broken bone on his lower left leg was exposed – dissipated, to be replaced with euphoria and a sense of indestructibility. Brickey was thinking in fluent bravado.

"He just slapped it like that," he said of the morphine dose. "I was like, 'Give me a weapon and I'll dust his ass.'"

Then, with the machine-gun fire continuing, Nash hefted Brickey over that massive boulder. Years later, both men would joke that they made it over the giant rock under heavy fire only because the medic used Brickey as a shield. The North Vietnamese pushed their attack and chased off a medevac helicopter, so the Americans sent in a gunship, which made a single pass over the ravine and riddled the jungle with .60 caliber machine-gun fire.

The enemy machine guns went silent.

"He comes in and makes a pass, and he just lights that place up," Brickey subsequently remembered.

After making that pass, the gunship moved in to retrieve Brickey. Nash and Brown heaved him onto the helicopter – where he landed, back first, on the craft's ammunition stores as the metal ammo box dug into his back wound. The resulting pain penetrated Brickey's morphine euphoria and the soldier thought he had been hit again. But the drug-induced fog and trauma reclaimed him – the next thing he would remember was being at a military hospital in Japan. Back in the ravine, Nash noticed, only after he and Brown got Brickey onto the gunship, that there was blood running down his face. His blood.

Rick Brown thought Nash had been shot, even though that probably wasn't the case. During his struggles with Brickey, the medic's helmet had fallen off and a piece of shrapnel or a chunk of rock slashed his forehead leaving a cut on his face. The physical wound was only superficial, but the emotional damage would linger – Nash would have nightmares for some time to come.

"I remember getting off to myself and being really emotional," he said. "After that, I became really hardened."

With the enemy's machine-gun crossfire silenced, the remaining Bravo Company troopers could retreat out of danger. Dile would receive a posthumous Silver Star. In life, the Chambersburg native had taught the newest Bravo Company soldiers how to survive in Vietnam. In death, his sacrifice set the unit's standard. Dile was one of the first Bravo Company Currahees to die for his comrades in 1970, but he wouldn't be the last.

"He's why I'm here today," Brickey said more than 40 years later. "Him and Doc Nash."

Meanwhile, Brown, who was only 18 years old, was dealing with the death of his mentor, Madrid.

"He just took me under his wing," Brown would say later. "It hurt when he was killed."

Weather and enemy fire prevented recovery of the fallen soldiers' bodies on January 29 and 30. The following day, Jaggers' helicopter took several hits from the ground while the battalion commander was taking a low-altitude reconnaissance view of the area for an upcoming ground attack. The enemy fire wounded a door gunner and co-pilot. Without hesitation, Jaggers, who had been a decorated gunship pilot in his previous Vietnam tour, took over as co-pilot and put his helicopter down to rescue the crew of a downed medevac chopper. He then returned to action a third time to direct the Currahees' attack. Jaggers earned his fourth Distinguished Flying Cross for his actions on January 31.[10]

While the wounded soldiers were successfully evacuated, the bodies of Dile, Madrid, Guzman, and Shaffer remained on Hill 474 until February 4, when a sustained artillery assault finally softened up the North Vietnamese defenses and enabled a recovery operation.[11]

CHAPTER 5

First I'd like to wish Tony a Very Happy Birthday and I hope you got nice presents and plenty to eat. Also I want to thank you for the picture you sent me, it was really nice and very well done. Even though I can't be with you on your birthday, I'll be thinking of you and how much fun we'd be having together. I'm sorry I couldn't get this out earlier, but it is hard to write with it raining every day. We've been kind of busy the last few weeks walking up and down mountains. It is really going to be bad now that the machine gunner hurt his leg and I am going to have to carry it now. Tomorrow I'll be receiving mail and your letter so I'll try and write again as soon as I can. If things work out like they say I'll be at a firebase for about a week so I'll have plenty of time to write. I'm going to close so I can still write Roe. I would also like to thank you for your Christmas present, it will come in handy for Roe when we meet in Hawaii.

Leslie Sabo letter to George and Olga
Dated January 18, 1970

Bravo Company was filled with young men who had grown up hunting – men like Rueda, the kid from Los Angeles, and Sabo, the former Hungarian refugee who grew up in rural western Pennsylvania. Those soldiers had spent time in the woods with a rifle stalking animals, particularly deer and small game. That experience served them well in Vietnam, where war often seemed more like hunting. And 3rd Battalion's long-range reconnaissance platoon included some of its most active hunters. The recon platoons were made up of six-man teams who were sent quietly into enemy territory to find enemy emplacements. Those teams could spend several days in the field and would catch sleep, such as it was, in a circular formation with their feet pointing inward. The man on watch would have the radio telephone receiver, often literally a lifeline. On January 23, Sergeant David Lindsey's recon team was in the field at night when it came under attack by a much larger force. Lindsey pulled his six-man team to cover among the boulders that peppered the slopes of Hill 474. But as day broke, the North Vietnamese force swelled to platoon size and outnumbered the Americans roughly six to one. Worse, the recon team had abandoned its supplies when it pulled back. With his men running low on ammunition, Lindsey crawled into the open, within 50 feet of the enemy advance, to collect additional rifle rounds.

Rather than initiate a frontal assault against an enemy that had the advantage of natural bunkering, the Americans improvised, starting with dropping 55-gallon drums of jet fuel on suspected enemy emplacements in those caves. In a process called "sealing the caves," the Americans would ignite high-octane, highly flammable fuel, either from the helicopters or from the ground with M-60 machine guns. That was usually good enough to move the North Vietnamese out of their emplacements. But just to make sure, they would have helicopters drop a bag of powdered tear gas at the cave mouth and detonate the bag. As a result, the caves were uninhabitable.

"You can imagine these horrendous fires," Richard Rios said. "The enemy would never use them again. And if they were in there, they were dead."

If that seems a bit barbaric, it's also instructive. War, when stripped of its patriotic self-glorifying language, is essentially the practice of finding imaginative ways in which to kill one another, or at least thwart the enemy's attempts at killing.

During those early days on Hill 474, the Currahees expended much of their energy in the exercise of honoring the "leave no man behind" principle. During the effort to recover Robert Mitcheltree's remains alone, the battalion committed three companies, amounting to about 300 soldiers, and sent helicopter gunships against enemy ground fire not for a strategic high ground or to gain territory, but to recover the body of a fallen American soldier.

On its face, that might appear to be a colossal waste of resources – and, worse, a colossal risk of resources. But honoring the Warrior Ethos had real battlefield benefits in terms of unit cohesion. In a nation that was becoming more cynical by the day about whether fighting in Vietnam was necessary to America's security, combat troops weren't necessarily defending "freedom" in Vietnam. Instead, like Steven Dile, they were fighting for their comrades, as Ruben Rueda, who joined Bravo Company in late 1969 and initially faced the enemy on the slopes of Hill 474, explained: "You're not fighting for your country... You're fighting for the guy next to you."

———————

Each soldier in Bravo Company had his own story of how he ended up in Vietnam, but probably none had a more circuitous route than Leslie Sabo. The youngest of Leslie Sabo Sr.'s sons was born in exile on February 23, 1948, to a wealthy refugee family suddenly fallen on hard times. On its second stint in Hungary, communism proved more persistent than it had the first time around. Leslie Sr., who had earned a doctorate of law in his homeland, now worked as an accountant for a dairy farmer near the city of Kufstein in Austria.

While his younger brother was being born inside on a sunny mid-winter day in Austrian ski country, four-year-old George Sabo played outside on a large cannon.

"It seemed like a big castle," he said of the hospital.

During the five years his family lived in Austria, George Sabo matured from a toddler through his preschool years and gained a younger brother. George went on mountain hikes with his father in some of the world's most breathtaking terrain – the Tyrol region is a center of alpine skiing, and Innsbruck, the Tyrol's metropolitan center, played host to the Winter Olympics in 1964 and 1976 – and joined Kufstein's May Day celebrations, when the ever-gallant Leslie Sr. led his older son around their small town with a basket filled with chocolates to give to girls walking along the streets.

"He was a very bright man," George said of his father. "I remember parts of being in Austria, flashes of being there."

But Austria was never home for the Sabo clan. Initially, George said his father set up residence there with the expectation that the Soviet presence in their homeland would be temporary. Instead, the Russians not only consolidated their control of Hungary, but made efforts to apprehend Hungarian leaders outside of Hungary for show trials followed by execution in the Soviet bloc.[1]

It is likely that Leslie Sabo Sr. was on the Russians' wanted list. George Sabo said his family had become nervous about the prospect that wartime officials in the Hungarian government would be apprehended and spirited back to face Soviet justice. That fear spurred Sabo to pack up his family for the second time in five years and move them well beyond reach of the Communists. During the postwar years, Australia had a program offering land to Europeans who had been displaced either during World War II itself or by the geopolitical carving initiated by the United States and Soviet Union, so Leslie Sr., perhaps with an eye toward rebuilding his family's fortune as a farmer, booked passage on a ship to Australia in mid-1949. But fate conspired to bring the Sabos to the United States instead. Both George, who was nearly six years old, and Leslie came down with the whooping cough. They were quarantined, which forced the Sabos to miss their ship to Australia.

For Leslie, who was not yet two years old at the time, missing the boat turned out to have been particularly fateful. Had the boys not got sick, it's likely that he would never have been called to serve in Vietnam. Even though Australia participated in the war and initiated a draft, it contributed far fewer troops than the United States did.

"If I hadn't been down with the whooping cough, we would have been on that boat to Australia," George said. "The boat sailed without us."

CHAPTER 6

Thank you very much for writing to me and thinking of me. I really love my nephews and it makes me feel real good to know that you love me too. Your Christmas presents sound really great, I can hardly wait to come home and race you with your new racing set. I received your letters with Olga's today. I'll write as soon as I can but if I want to get this mailed I have to finish. Write again soon. I hope you had a happy birthday.

Letter from Leslie Sabo to George's sons Tony and Steven
Dated January 25, 1970

The Sabos arrived in Ellwood City after starting out in Central Europe as refugees. They were approved for passage on the *General Harry Taylor*, which was bound for the United States. That crossing was sponsored by a Hungarian-nationality group based in Mars, Pennsylvania, a small town located about 30 miles north of Pittsburgh.[1]

General Harry Taylor arrived in the United States in October of 1949 and was processed. George Sabo, who would have just turned six at the time, said that, even after more than a half-century, he could still recall entering his new country through Ellis Island.

"I could remember the noise of the crowd as I stood in line with my parents," George Sabo later recalled. After arriving in Mars, Pennsylvania, the Sabo family – Leslie Sr., Elisabeth, George, and Leslie Jr. – would greet the 20th century's midpoint in the steel town of Youngstown, Ohio, their first New Year's Day in the United States. Moving to Youngstown – only a few miles on the Ohio side of Pennsylvania's western boundary – gave the family a built-in support system because the city had an active Hungarian community.

Leslie Sabo Sr., who was by then in his early 40s, had earned his training, education, and experience in law, government, and as an accountant in Central Europe and the friends Leslie made in the United States told him it would be difficult to relearn the law in a foreign country and pass an American bar exam. But he had another option. During western Pennsylvania's postwar steel boom, there were plenty of engineering jobs available.

So Leslie Sr. made a career switch, his third since leaving Hungary. By day, he worked as a painter for Isaly's, a now-defunct Pittsburgh-based restaurant chain known for its thinly-sliced deli ham still remembered throughout the region as "chip-chop," to support his wife and two young sons. By night, he earned a degree from Youngstown State University, starting a short-lived family tradition – George would earn his degree from YSU and Leslie enrolled there for almost two years before being drafted into the Army.

Leslie Jr. was definitely his father's son in many ways, George later recalled. Leslie Jr. and Sr. both possessed a sense of decency, and a resourceful nature. Unlike his parents and brother, Leslie Sabo Jr.'s first language was English and he never had any direct memory of the family's escapes from the clutches of either the Nazis or Soviets, although he heard the stories from his parents and brother.

Even before graduating from Youngstown State University, Leslie Sr. got a job working at the Aetna Standard steel mill across the state line in Ellwood City, Pennsylvania. Today, a Youngstown-to-Ellwood-City commute can be made in less than an hour. But in the mid-20th century, before highways were built through the rural regions in the 35 miles between those two towns, the trip regularly took much longer, and when Leslie Sr. had a heart attack in 1951 at the age of 44, his doctor blamed the long daily commute for his heart problems and recommended that Leslie move his family a little closer to work.

"The doctor told him, 'Either quit your job or move,'" George later said.

So for the third time in less than ten years, Leslie Sabo Sr. packed up his family and moved one final time – to Ellwood City, which he would call home for the rest of his life.

George and Leslie arrived in the United States, and Ellwood City, with each other and not much else, which might have been the reason for their closeness. Even when there was a wide gap in their ages, there was never an "annoying little brother" phase in their relationship.

"We always hung around, even when he was a little kid," George recalled.

Hartman School, which then, as now, was next to Lincoln High School directly across Crescent Avenue from the Sabos' first Ellwood City home and a short walk from Christ Presbyterian Church. The Stevenson family, including young Robert, was one of the Sabos' neighbors. Robert Stevenson was younger than George Sabo and older than Leslie, and the three boys became fast friends until a few years later, when the Sabos moved across town to Ewing Park.

"He was one of the nicest guys you'd ever want to meet. I've never known anyone to say a bad thing about Leslie," said Stevenson. "He was a very non-assuming person. He was confident, but not overly confident. Leslie fit right in."

Stevenson graduated from Lincoln High School and joined the Navy, where he served during the Vietnam War era as an intelligence analyst who reviewed photographs taken by U-2 spy planes, but never saw combat. After returning home, he became a police officer, initially in Ellwood City and retired as the police chief in nearby Franklin Township. They also shared those streets, school hallways, and fields with people who were destined for fame. In Ellwood City's

West End neighborhood, across town from the Sabos' house in Ewing Park, Donnie Iris, born Donnie Ierace, was prowling the streets and honing the singing talent that would bring the young Buddy Holly-lookalike fame in the 1980s with hit songs like "The Rapper" and "Ah! Leah!" While George Sabo was a student at Lincoln High School, the Wolverines' varsity football coach was Chuck Knox, who went on to coach the National Football League's Los Angeles Rams and Seattle Seahawks.

Western Pennsylvania is known for its football. While George and Leslie Sabo were coming of age, Joe Namath was growing up a few miles away in Beaver Falls. Not much further away and a few years earlier, Aliquippa native Mike Ditka dominated gridiron competition, and Hopewell's Tony Dorsett would follow Ditka to the University of Pittsburgh. And even in Ellwood City, football was a big deal. The 1925 Lincoln High School team, which played in a national championship game, still had a prominent place in the school's trophy chest nearly a century later.

But Ellwood City is a baseball enclave in football territory. Stiefel Park is named after the man who invented seamless steel tubes, but the park's main drive honors the Ellwood City native who turned in one of the greatest single-season hitting performances in Major League Baseball history. In 1930, Hack Wilson Drive's namesake hit 56 home runs, batted .356 and drove in 191 runs for the Chicago Cubs. His on-base plus slugging percentage (OPS) that year was a mind-bending 1.177, still one of the 15 best performances in National League history. The 56 home runs stood as the National League record until Mark McGwire overtook it in 1997, and Wilson's 1930 RBI total remained untouched into the 21st century, even with the steroid-inflated numbers from baseball's Monsanto – better baseball through chemistry – era. And, while the Sabo brothers were working their way through elementary school, future Major League superstar Dick Allen was tearing up the American Legion baseball circuit just down the road in Wampum.

That passion for baseball filtered down to the kids in the neighborhoods where Leslie Sabo lived as a child.

"We played," George Sabo said. "Sandlot ball was pretty popular."

Among the other games they played, in what would become a tragic irony, was soldier.

———————

By February of 1970, being a soldier was very real for Leslie Sabo. He had been assigned to one of the Army's newest – founded only 28 years earlier – but most distinguished units, the 101st Airborne Division, nicknamed "the Screaming Eagles" for the division's distinctive shoulder patch, which features the head of a bald eagle. In the United States, where the bird is a national symbol, the image is familiar. However, the bald eagle is not among the avian breeds indigenous to Vietnam. So the Vietnamese – both friend and enemy – identified soldiers of the 101st with one of their nation's more common breeds of bird and called them "Chickenmen."[2]

In terms of tactical significance, Hill 474 was no more important than the next hill, or the hill after that. There was no crucial road junction, no supply depot, no antiaircraft battery that necessitated the intervention of Bravo Company. The only thing it had was North Vietnamese soldiers, entrenched on the rocky slopes of Hill 474, tucked in caves and behind massive boulders.

In almost daily contact, the North Vietnamese and Americans clashed, which left the Currahees little chance for a respite. Jaggers, the battalion commander, tried to keep his troops fresh by pulling them back to Firebase Tape for breaks, but the constant action put manpower at a premium.

"It was never a safe place," said "Kid Rick" Brown. "Almost every day in Vietnam, we were in contact with the enemy."

Usually, those contacts were with only one or two NVA (North Vietnamese Army) troopers, like the shootout involving 2nd Platoon on February 8. The platoon's point man caught an enemy soldier from behind and fired the fatal shots before he even knew he was a target. Jaggers ordered the Currahees to advance and collect the body, an order that wasn't obeyed – Lieutenant Alan

Johnson said, presumably outside the battalion commander's earshot, that Wildcat could get the body himself if he wanted it.

During part of the siege of Hill 474, Bravo Company used Firebase Tape, a short distance south of the battle zone, as a staging area. During the Vietnam War, the US military established dozens of firebases, also called fire support bases, throughout the country to provide artillery support for operations in the jungles and serve as headquarters for helicopter operations. Each firebase housed several artillery pieces, with an effective range of 11 miles. The bases were also staffed with battalion support troops, including helicopter mechanics and truck drivers, and the battalion staff.

Just as each company sent a platoon on ambush each night, each battalion in charge of a firebase designated one company, usually on a three-day rotation, to provide security. Nominally, the base security duty was an opportunity for downtime – especially compared with patrolling out in the field. In fact, though, the first day on base was consumed with tasks like getting a non-canned meal and a hot, or at least lukewarm, shower. Another day would be devoted to pulling security duty, and troops always worked to shore up the defenses with sandbags and barbed wire. That left little actual opportunity for leisure, much of which was devoted to various types of gambling, especially craps and poker. Ron Gooch was good at the former and Leslie Sabo – who wrote, "what I win in poker, I lose shooting craps," in a letter home to his brother – was better at the latter. In one late January crap game, Gooch won $40 and Sabo lost $65, but the big winner was 2nd Platoon leader Lieutenant Alan Johnson.[3]

"We had jobs every day when we were in the rear," said Richard Freeling, who finished his combat tour in early January 1970. Bravo Company discovered an enemy tunnel camp on February 11, with bunkers, an ammunition cache, and a food supply in the form of live chickens. Two days later, Bravo Company found another cave, which the men described as "kind of an NVA Holiday Inn." The accommodations were, relatively speaking, luxurious, with high ceilings buttressed by bamboo standards, bunks, and an irrigation system that delivered water from one of Hill 474's multitude of streams to individual enemy positions. Again, the Currahees found a large collection of ammunition and medical supplies.

Outside, meanwhile, Charlie Company's 1st Platoon found itself in a battle with a squad of North Vietnamese. Although they were outnumbered, the North Vietnamese were firing from cover and had caught the Americans out in the open. With one of his men already wounded, platoon leader First Lieutenant Francis Patalano exposed himself to lead a counterattack and direct fire support to force an enemy retreat. Patalano would receive the Silver Star for preventing more damage. A medevac helicopter was shot down on a mission to evacuate the wounded soldier from Patalano's platoon. The medevac crew was rescued, as was the wounded soldier. On the day, the Currahees – along with their air support – claimed seven enemy deaths, including one kill by Bravo Company of a North Vietnamese soldier as he emerged from the "Holiday Inn."[4]

Rios and Sabo got their dose of close-quarter combat on February 17, almost exactly three weeks after the ambush that cost the lives of "Hungry" Dile, Peter Guzman, Frank Madrid, and John Shaffer. On that day, First Lieutenant Alan Johnson was leading 2nd Platoon on a patrol to find and kill the enemy in its entrenched positions. Rios said Johnson was well respected among the enlisted men.

"He was a very ambitious, good kid," Richard Rios said. "He wouldn't ask you to do something if he wouldn't try it first."

The day started with Bravo Company soldiers killing two North Vietnamese soldiers in a short firefight. After that, they backtracked to find three more enemy soldiers rooting through their field packs, which they had left behind before the earlier firefight. The Americans killed two of those enemies, while the third escaped, with the Americans in pursuit.[5] They tracked their quarry into a cave and Johnson, in a violation of protocol, ventured inside. Typically, a commissioned officer would have sent an enlisted man into the danger area. But this wasn't the platoon leader's first venture into the caves. On January 18, Johnson had descended about 15 feet into another cave with Ron Gooch. That time, things went well. They found no enemy soldiers and both made it out of the cave safely.

A month later, Johnson believed he had softened up the cave by lobbing in a couple of grenades, and entered himself, to fatal effect.

"He went in and there was someone in there and he lit him up," Rios said.

The cave had a steep overhang, around 10 feet down, which prevented Johnson's men from seeing what had happened. Because of the hill's slope, and the overhang, Rios said it seemed as if he was below the surface when most of 2nd Platoon, including Rios, was outside the cave. Inside, Johnson had been hit multiple times by gunfire. While most of 2nd Platoon stayed on its side of the overhang, Joe Honan, the platoon medic, tried to save his lieutenant.

When Honan went into the cave to help Johnson, he got the same treatment. The 20-year-old medic was killed instantly. Rios said the greatest tragedy was that Honan probably sacrificed himself unnecessarily because Johnson was doomed.

"He didn't have to die there," Rios said of Honan. "He couldn't have saved the lieutenant."

Bruce Dancesia, another trooper, echoed Rios's assessment.

"Joe jumped into that tunnel entrance. The man [Johnson] had no chance but he did it anyway."

Johnson, who was dying, but not in fact dead, exhibited the fortitude expected from a Green Beret-trained officer. Mortally wounded, Johnson found the strength to drag himself out of the cave. Dancesia threw together a makeshift stretcher made out of fatigue jackets and tree saplings so Johnson could be carried to a secure landing zone for airlift by helicopter in Jaggers' command-and-control aircraft. Dancesia said Johnson told his men that he would die, a statement that proved to be sadly prophetic. He succumbed to his wounds on February 25 at the Army hospital in Quang Ngai province.[6]

"Everybody is in a very sad and depressed mood because someone who everyone liked got killed," Gooch wrote in his journal.

After the Americans cleared the cave, they found a large cache of supplies, including weapons, rice, and supplies like toothpaste and soap that had been discarded by, or stolen from, US troops.[7]

The helicopter attracted attention from the North Vietnamese, which forced 2nd Platoon to abandon efforts at recovering Honan's body. With Honan dead, Johnson dying, and the North Vietnamese firing from concealed positions behind the enormous rocks, Sergeant Arthur Sherwood, of Shaker Heights, Ohio, took over as platoon leader and led a retreat under fire, which Rios said probably prevented additional casualties.

"He probably saved lives. If we would have stayed there or if we would have tried to get Doc…" Rios said, his voice trailing off. "They were shooting at us."

Sherwood would receive the Bronze Star with "V" device for combat valor. Bravo Company recovered Honan's body the following day, February 18.

Even non-combat troops, like clerks or supply staff, were expected to perform security duties. On February 18, a day after Honan was killed and Johnson mortally wounded, Specialist Manuel Montoya and Private First Class Danny Blevins were pulling security at Firebase Tape. Montoya and Blevins were assigned to the battalion's headquarters company. Montoya was a supply clerk and Blevins worked as a personnel specialist, but that didn't excuse them from base security duties at Firebase Tape. On February 18, the two men had pulled nighttime guard duty in a perimeter bunker at the base when a grenade blast killed Montoya and mortally wounded Blevins, who died the following day. But no enemy attack followed, and it was possible that they had been killed by the accidental discharge of their own grenades.[8]

That day, it was Delta Company's turn in the wringer. The unit was using CS powder and aircraft fuel in a "sealing the caves" operation when it came under fire from one of the caves targeted. Richard Burgess, a specialist in Delta's 3rd Platoon, led a counterattack. He dodged the enemy's rain of lead and reached the cave location. After lobbing grenades into the cave mouth, he entered to see the results of his own counterattack. Burgess was hit with multiple small arms rounds and sustained fatal wounds. Because of his solo assault on the cave, Burgess received a posthumous Silver Star award. Burgess had graduated from high school in Tower, a town of around 700 residents in northeast Minnesota's Iron Range, not far from Duluth. Before he entered the Army, the 19-year-old trooper had been an accomplished brass musician who regularly played "Taps" for the funerals of deceased World War I veterans. Ten days after his death, another trumpet player from Tower would play the song at Burgess's own service.[9]

Bravo Company got a reward on February 20 – it was pulled back, not to a firebase, but to Qui Nhon for a two-day beach party with all the trappings in what was as close to being back in "the world" as the troopers got during the first half of 1970.

"I almost forgot where I was for a little while," Sabo wrote home to his brother.

He and his comrades dined on barbecue and beer, and swam in the South China Sea's tropical waters. In the rear – whether that meant on the landing zone, base camp, or at the beach – alcohol and drugs, mostly marijuana, were present, if not common. Drug use among Vietnam combat troops was regarded as a significant problem, and the military had programs in place to address abuse. But several Bravo Company soldiers said the troops policed themselves to prevent drugs from being debilitating. Norm Friend said soldiers might have lit up in the rear, away from immediate peril, but never in the field where their own lives, and the lives of their comrades, depended on them being clear-headed.

"That was a no-no," Friend said. "Out in the field, the other guys would beat your ass. You have to be sure he would have your back."

Some of the soldiers went for a more traditional soldiers' form of relaxation, the comfort of prostitutes, which were a fixture even on the firebases. In rear-echelon posts, like Qui Nhon, sex was sold with the tacit, and sometimes explicit, approval of Military Assistance Command, Vietnam, with some prostitutes examined regularly by military doctors for venereal diseases. In that, the soldiers of Vietnam were no different than those who had gone before them in Europe during the world wars and back in the United States during the Civil War and Revolution.[10]

During the week between Johnson's injury and death, Leslie Sabo turned 22 years old. Koziol remembered his first impression of Sabo as looking a little clumsy, long-limbed, and gangly, wearing a pair of MIT-style Army-issued eyeglasses. But his "Revenge of the Nerds" appearance a dozen years before its time belied a physical prowess that became evident in combat. More importantly, Sabo possessed the emotional tools of a warrior.

"After the first time we were shot at, Les basically went from being a kid to a man overnight."

Koziol estimated that he and Sabo were involved in about 15 active firefights in the weeks between mid-January and the end of April. The bulk of their combat action also came during helicopter-based assaults. Both men received the Air Medal for meritorious acts while in flight. It was routine for soldiers to get the award after they participated in their first few hot landing zone drops. Because of his high-volume combat experience on Hill 474, Sabo, as well as most other members of Bravo Company, received the Combat Infantryman Badge, which is a standard decoration for junior officers and enlisted men with a sufficient amount of time on the front lines. Koziol said the badge was a special source of pride for him and his comrades.

"There were a lot of standard medals for being over there," he said. "[The Combat Infantryman Badge] is the one they cherish the most because it means they are a combat soldier."[11]

When in the field, the Currahees received supply drops every three days, weather permitting, including canteens, ammunition, and food, usually in the form of C-rations. Sometimes the soldiers received dehydrated meals, which some soldiers preferred, not for the taste, but because a dehydrated dinner weighed less than a C-ration equivalent. The 1961-era canned rations weighed about 2 pounds and came in cases of 12 meals with an estimated 1,200 calories each. Each case contained one of each different variety of entrée. Each ration had three cans – a main course, a fruit or cake, crackers, and candy or hot chocolate, and a peanut butter or cheese spread.

"The most popular item was the pound cake," said Ruben Rueda. "You'd do anything for a pound cake."

Finally, the ration box contained an accessory packet, which held instant coffee, cream substitute, sugar, salt, gum matches, toilet paper, and two cigarettes. In 1972, the military ended its long-held practice of including cigarettes in the rations. Soldiers sometimes supplemented their rations with personal touches, such as peanut butter or hot sauce, to make the food more palatable.

Although the food could be eaten unheated, and usually was, the rations also included a fuel tablet, which was used to warm the food. With each meal providing about 1,200 calories, it meant a daily intake of approximately 3,600 calories. That would be more than enough for most people on the home front, but for a soldier humping through the jungle, it wasn't enough to maintain body weight. Rick Brown, one of Bravo Company's youngest men, lost quite a bit of weight during his tour and he wasn't alone.[12]

With the supply choppers dropping in every three days, each soldier had to carry all the food, ammunition, and equipment he would need between drops. That included writing material for letters to home, which most of them kept in the leg pockets of their fatigues. Depending on the soldier's duty, he could find himself "humping the boonies" with more than 100 pounds on his back. A machine-gun crewman could wind up carrying 500 rounds of ammunition in addition to the M-60 hardware. Soldiers wielding the M-79 grenade launcher would have to carry at least 50 rounds. The radio telephone operator headed into battle with a device that weighed at least 10 pounds, in addition to roughly another 9 pounds in batteries for the radio.

Even during the most miserable conditions – like the rainy season of January, February, and March – Sabo never lost his sense of humor. Koziol and Sabo swapped jokes, corny ones, by Koziol's own admission, but jokes nonetheless. The big highlight was mail call, a reminder that the world beyond Vietnam was still going on, and each letter served as notice that there was someone out there who cared about them. Those letters contained food – Ron Gooch once received a 37-pound package from his church back home in North Carolina – news from home, and occasionally, coveted racy pictures of women in the States. Richard Clanton said the recreation and mail calls were key elements in maintaining morale.

"You find your moments over there to try to make a bad situation better. Even when we were in a bad situation, we had each other. You talk of home, you talk of family."

CHAPTER 7

Congratulations on completing a 17-hour semester of night school. I can really appreciate how difficult it must have been. Then to take 18 hours takes a lot of guts and determination. I just hope I can do as good when I come home, I can honestly say I have a big [brother] to look up to and be proud of (just don't let all this go to your head). The film I had was ruined but a guy going to the rear today is buying me some so I'll be able to send pictures home one of these days.

Leslie Sabo letter to George and Olga
Undated, but the letter contains a reference to a letter sent the
same day to George and Olga's sons, so it can be assumed to
have been written January 25, 1970

In the climax of Rudyard Kipling's short story, "Rikki-Tikki-Tavi," the titular mongoose chases cobra Nagaina into her underground burrow, which Kipling points out is never an advisable course of action, even for a cobra-killing mongoose:

Very few mongooses, however wise and old they may be, care to follow a cobra into its hole. It was dark in the hole; and Rikki-tikki never knew when it might open out and give Nagaina room to turn and strike at him.

Ruben Rueda was a mongoose, largely by virtue of being one of Bravo Company's smallest guys. As such, he was picked to go into dark caves and tunnels, without knowing when the hole might open out and give the enemy an opportunity to strike. On Hill 474, the North Vietnamese didn't have to dig many tunnels, a practice common in other regions, primarily because Mother Nature did the job for them. When Bravo Company needed someone to poke around in the tunnels or caves, Rueda often volunteered for the job. And his size wasn't the only qualification.

By the time he landed on Hill 474, Rueda had a serious case of "don't give a crap." After being drafted, Rueda married his high school sweetheart for what he admitted were the wrong reasons – he didn't think he would be coming back and she wanted an excuse to get out of her parents' house. A few of Bravo Company's marriages didn't survive homecoming. Rueda's didn't even make it through the first half of his combat tour.

"I got a 'Dear John' letter, so I didn't care. I took point a lot. If there was a hole to go into, I did it."

One of those holes was a cave that had just been hit with a 5,000-pound bomb dropped from a US jet. The bomb was supposed to have eliminated any enemy outpost. Rueda's job was to go in and clean it up. In the cave's near-total darkness he saw a body. Rueda knew it was an enemy soldier, but he couldn't quite discern whether the man was dead or lying in wait for a careless American. He used a concussion grenade to make sure. The caves were rarely completely dark, because most of them had two entrances, which effectively gave the North Vietnamese a tunnel system. On one occasion Rueda went into a cave and, when he encountered no hidden enemies, proceeded to the far entrance a short distance off. Once there, he was less worried about facing an enemy and more about "friendly fire" from his own countrymen.

"I stuck my head out and shouted," he said. "I was more afraid of my own guys shooting me."

Rueda grew up in post-World War II Los Angeles while it transformed into a metropolis claimed from the western desert. He learned a work ethic from his father, who raised his family up into the middle class by working two jobs, one of which was operating a grocery store. Rueda worked in the store and earned money by shining shoes and hawking newspapers. His father's business ventures put Rueda into college and enabled him to offer his son what was nearly a year's pay for the average American so he could run off to Canada instead of reporting for military duty.

But Rueda rejected his father's offer and reported to fight in a war that he had opposed as a civilian. And he showed a talent for jungle warfare – his father had purchased a ranch outside the city and as a boy he gone there as often as possible, riding horses, hunting deer and other small game, hiking, and learning woodcraft. Those skills served him well in Vietnam, and may have saved his life more than once. Rueda developed a knack for seeing booby traps and feeling his way through caves that carried the risk of danger concealed in a lack of light.

"You don't think about where you are or what you're doing. I would see a light and go as far as I could," Rueda said. "I would see things those city boys wouldn't. My good eyes saved my butt."

––––––––

Other Bravo Company soldiers, including Leslie Sabo, arrived in Vietnam after rural upbringings. Sabo grew up in small-town western Pennsylvania, where hunting is part of the cultural DNA – the Monday after Thanksgiving, which marks the first day of buck season, is considered an unofficial state holiday. Schools close and private businesses are forced to deal with a work force depleted by deer hunting vacations.

When Leslie Sabo Sr. and his family moved to Ellwood City in 1951, they arrived in a thriving town whose future collapse was already assured. In keeping with its motto – "What Ellwood City

Builds, Builds Ellwood City" – the town traced its rich industrial history to a time before it was officially founded in 1892. With its first industrial renaissance, Ellwood City probably did as much to tame the west as the railroads or army, and certainly more than the fabled cowboy. Around that time, ranchers in the far west were beginning to fence in their previously free-range cattle. And lining those ranches was barbed wire, most of which was produced in factories owned by industrialist Isaac Ellwood, a Midwesterner who visited the town that bore his name only a handful of times.

A generation later, Ralph C. Stiefel arrived in Ellwood City to spark another industrial renaissance. The Swiss-born engineer developed a method for manufacturing seamless steel tubing by using a mechanical drill to hollow out the center of steel bars. Stiefel's true creativity rested not in coming up with the idea of boring out the bar, but in solving a key problem inherent in that process: preventing the hot steel cylinder from twisting as the drill spun into it. Stiefel came up with the innovation of turning the bar from the outside to counteract the forces placed on it by the drill within. Because of Stiefel's innovation, US Steel housed its tube division at his mill until 1974. In gratitude, Ellwood City named a park in his honor.[1]

Stiefel's invention turned Ellwood City into an 1800s-style boomtown at its peak, with the precious metal in question being steel rather than gold or silver. By the middle of the 20th century, Ellwood City was part of a Pittsburgh-anchored region that was producing more steel than the rest of the world combined. In 1950, the town had a population of more than 13,000 people.[2]

Over the next half-century, it would decline to little more than half that number, and the forces that would rob Ellwood City of its industrial base already were under way before the Sabos arrived. The town was created and grew during a time when railroads were the primary method of moving goods and people. When Ellwood City was originally founded, railroad-based tourism was the big draw. Pittsburgh Circle, which runs past the town's Hungarian social hall, was once a bicycle-racing track. In the late 1800s and early 1900s, across the Connoquenessing Creek from the Ellwood City train station, was Rock Point Park, which was established by the Pittsburgh and Erie Railroad to give people a reason to ride the rails on weekends. The former Rock Point Park site is now a nature preservation area, although hikers can still find some of the amusement park's structures if they know where to look.

Fittingly, Ellwood City had a railroad station, but not a direct exit to any highway – including the region's interstate expressways designed and constructed during the 1950s. As the United States morphed after World War II from a nation that carried people and goods on trains into one where cars and trucks were the main form of transportation, Ellwood City became increasingly irrelevant as a center of production. US Steel, as a prelude to becoming USX and de-emphasizing its steel-making operations, shuttered the Ellwood City Tube Mill in 1974, a catastrophic closure that all but destroyed the town.

But that would be years off, and the Sabo brothers grew up in a town that actively bustled. Even years later, locals old enough to remember the 1950s and '60s regularly say, "You could barely walk down Lawrence Avenue on a Friday night."

During the years that Leslie and George Sabo were growing up, the tube mill, Ellwood City Forge, Blaw-Knox Steel, Mathews Conveyor, and Leslie Sabo Sr.'s employer, Aetna Standard, fueled the local economy. The town had two movie theaters, the Majestic and the Manos. Depending on the season, high school students and younger adults attended local varsity football and basketball games or enjoyed dancing at the Sons of Italy club or in Ewing Park. The Sons of Italy dances were regularly attended by more than 500 people and drew top-shelf stars such as Louis Prima.[3]

Those weekend throngs on Lawrence Avenue often included the family of Leslie Sabo Sr., who, like Ralph Stiefel, had emigrated to the United States from Europe, bringing little more than a work ethic and intellectual brilliance. In spite of his privileged upbringing and position in Hungary, Leslie Sr. carried those qualities, first to Austria, then to the United States. Even more than 30 years after his father's death, George expressed admiration.

"He was a very bright man," George said of Leslie Sr. "He came here with nothing and became an engineer."

And, while the Sabos never fully regained the wealth they lost in their escape from Hungary, Leslie Sr. moved his family from Ellwood City's working class downtown section to Pershing Street in the town's upper middle class Ewing Park neighborhood. As it meanders toward its mouth at the Beaver River, Connoquenessing Creek winds into a horseshoe-shaped pocket that contains most of Ellport Borough, just outside Ellwood City. The creek then cuts a gorge, which divides Ellwood City in two. On the north bank are the neighborhoods of Ewing Park, where Leslie Sabo Sr. eventually settled his family, and North Side. Ewing Park is regarded as one of the better neighborhoods of a decidedly middle-class town – Ellwood City residents still talk about people who live in "the Park" with the same tone that New Yorkers might use to describe condo-dwellers in Manhattan's Upper West Side or Los Angelenos describe people living in Beverly Hills.

Then, as now, Ellwood City had a large Italian Catholic population. Both Sabo sons, who were born into a Presbyterian family in the Catholic nation of Hungary, would marry Italian women from Ellwood City and convert to Catholicism.

Ellwood City was carved out of plots that were once family farms and Indian tribal ground before that. The earliest immigrants were from central France who arrived in the area to cut limestone out of the numerous mines that lined the area, and the Italians who emigrated to work in the mills. Their numbers were bolstered by Eastern Europeans. There was an active Hungarian community, which lived near an iconic structure built by a daughter from the royal family of Hungary's old enemy, Romania. The Orthodox Monastery of the Transfiguration, in the Wurtemburg neighborhood of Wayne Township near Ellwood City was established in 1977 by Mother Alexandra. Before becoming an Orthodox nun in the 1960s, Alexandra was known as Princess Ileana of Romania – the sister of King Carol II, who engaged in figurative fist-shaking with Hungarian Regent Miklós Horthy over control of Transylvania during Leslie Sabo Sr.'s youth.[4]

The Sabos attended Christ Presbyterian Church at the intersection of Fourth Street and Spring Avenue. During those formative years, Leslie Sabo Jr. learned what can be best described as small-town values, not only from his father, but also in his church and community. Pam Powell grew to know the Sabo family in Sunday school classes with Leslie Jr. She recalled that Sabo, even from his earliest days, was a selfless person who looked for the good in other people.

"I remember him as being a very ethical person with very high moral standards," she said of her friend. "I never knew him to say a bad word about anyone."[5]

Thanks at least in part to a comfortable upbringing in the United States, the two boys grew up healthy and strong. A photograph, taken shortly before Leslie Jr. was drafted, indicated that both sons were at least 4 inches taller than their father. In 1961, when Leslie was in seventh grade at Ellwood City Lincoln Junior-Senior High School, George graduated. He married Olga Nocera soon after, who gave birth to their first son about a year later. As George focused on his new and growing family – he and Olga had three sons by the time Leslie graduated from high school – Leslie, still at home, forged a close relationship with his parents, particularly with his mother, who would be especially frantic at the notion that her younger son was in a combat zone.

Had she been fully aware of the intense action Leslie faced on a near-daily basis, Elisabeth Sabo would likely have been even more distraught. But she might have taken some solace from the unspoken pact that existed among the men of Bravo Company. Between the rain, the attacks, and the lack of any tactical mission outside of killing the enemy, the soldiers wound up taking on the mission of seeing as many of their comrades as possible make it back home.

"Those bonds are so strong because you put your life in the hands of your fellow soldier, your fellow grunt," Richard Rios said. "You're not going to find that in some college frat house."

CHAPTER 8

All I do is think about the future but here you have nothing to look forward to except R&R and leave. It is really nice to get letters from you so keep up the good work. I wrote the kids a letter today so I hope they get out. I received your letters and enjoyed hearing from you. I still have a chance to get this off today so tell everyone I said hi. I just hope for the day I can do it myself.

Leslie Sabo letter to George and Olga
Undated, but assumed to have been written January 25, 1970

The battle on Hill 474 sometimes resembled nothing so much as two blindfolded boxers swinging wildly, hoping to land a blow. During the day, the Currahees' 3rd Battalion would venture forth, searching behind those boulders and in those caves. While there was still plenty of jungle around, the Americans also crept along rocky dry riverbeds in search of the enemy. At night, each of Bravo Company's three platoons would establish their own nighttime defense perimeters, and send one squad of about 12 men to venture beyond the camp perimeter and set up an ambush, with remote-detonating claymore mines and overlapping .60 caliber machine-gun fire designed to destroy any enemy soldier who ventured into the kill zone. The process went on a rotating basis – 1st Squad one night and 2nd Squad the next, followed by 3rd Squad. Those ambush zones gave the unit a second layer of protection in addition to the main perimeter defenses.

Occasionally, though, there was time for relaxation, even in the field. Part of the Operation *Washington Green* mission had been to persuade villagers who had supported the Viet Minh against the French and, more recently, the Viet Cong to cast their lot with the United States, which sometimes required interacting with those villagers. Often, the point man in that effort was Donald Smith, a 21-year-old trooper from Rantoul in Central Illinois. Before being drafted in early 1969, Smith worked at a shoe store. He had been in Vietnam since mid-July of 1969 and was especially popular with young Vietnamese – nearly every photo of Smith from his tour in Vietnam shows him surrounded by children.[1]

"He loved the children over there," Rick Brown said of Smith.

The close quarters both at the firebase and in the field forced the men of Bravo Company to forge a friendship in combat and solidify it by relaxing over beers. In early February, while Bravo Company was slugging it out on Hill 474, it picked up a couple of new officers. Captain Jim Waybright, a native of Williamstown, West Virginia, tucked hard against the Ohio River in the state's northwestern region, took over command of the company. A baseball player through his teens – partly because his father wouldn't let him play football – Waybright had been an Eagle Scout and valedictorian of his high school class before attending West Virginia University. Lieutenant Teb Stocks was assigned to be leader of 3rd Platoon as a replacement for Lieutenant John Shaffer, who had been killed on January 28. They joined Lieutenant John Greene of 1st Platoon and 2nd Platoon's Lieutenant Lawrence Neff as platoon commanders, with Lieutenant Thomas Scarboro assigned to Bravo Company as a forward artillery observer.

Waybright, who was commissioned as an Air Force officer in 1966 after he graduated from college, planned on being a pilot, but his 20/200 vision scuttled that plan. Rather than spend the war flying a desk, he filed for an Army commission to serve out the last two years of his military commitment. That arrangement worked well for both the Army, which was desperate for junior officers, and the Air Force, which had more than it needed.

"I couldn't fly and I had a four-year obligation and I wanted to be a part of history," Waybright said.

He completed a wide range of infantry officers' training – parachute jump school, survivor classes, Ranger training – and had been a company commander in the 82nd Airborne Division during stateside training before assignment to Bravo Company.

Under the military's rotation at the time, a company combat commander would be in the field for six months at a time. Earlier in the war, American leadership defined success by body count – the number of enemy soldiers killed – and a junior officer's future career in the military could hinge upon the score his men racked up under his leadership. Officially, the US military strategy had transitioned by 1970 from "body count" to "Vietnamization." However, lieutenants and captains were still encouraged to provide North Vietnamese scalps, figuratively speaking, and therefore the enlisted riflemen were urged to rack up kills as well. In early March, a group of Bravo Company soldiers received three-day passes to another beach party. The passes went only to troopers who had killed at least one enemy soldier. Captains with high body counts could find themselves promoted to major and lieutenant colonel, and eventually colonel or general. Those who failed to produce sufficient numbers were nudged off the career officer track.

The relationship between soldiers and their officers in wartime has always been prickly, but never more so than it was during the Vietnam War, known, perhaps unfairly, for a practice called "fragging," killing troublesome or ineffective officers.[2] In any war, officers are given the unpleasant task of ordering young men to their deaths. But the Vietnam War was different because there was no clear objective beyond killing and dying. James Milliken, who grew up in Leslie Sabo's hometown of Ellwood City and had served a Vietnam tour approximately one year earlier, was drafted after his graduation from Grove City College, a few dozen miles from Ellwood City, and so was eligible for Officers' Candidate School. Milliken dropped out of OCS and decided to serve out his hitch as an enlisted man after he asked an instructor how to handle being ordered on a mission that he knew would cost American lives to little effect. The instructor told Milliken, effectively, "Follow the order, we'll send more bodies."[3]

But the situation was sometimes different on the ground, where junior officers, counting on more experienced non-commissioned officers – sergeants, often in their second combat tour, and battle-hardened corporals and specialists more than halfway through a first tour – knew some orders had very little purpose beyond impressing the REMFs – rear echelon motherfuckers, in the parlance of Vietnam combat soldiers.

And even the Currahees' celebrated World War II forebears weren't above ignoring an order they felt unnecessary and dangerous. On February 15, 1945, about 20 soldiers from the 506th crossed the icy Moder River from Hagenau, in the Alsace region of present-day France, behind enemy lines and captured two German sergeants for interrogation. But they also lost two of their own men in the process. Regimental command had been so pleased by the results that they ordered another one for the following night. But conditions had changed during the daylight hours of February 16 – a fresh snowfall had frozen, leaving an icy crust on the ground surface that would have alerted the Germans of any approaching patrols. Also, while the evening of February 15 had been cloudy and moonless, February 16 was well-moonlit under a clear sky. The legendary Major Richard Winters, battalion commander, told the team to stay in its barracks and falsely reported that the patrol infiltrated German lines but didn't capture any prisoners.[4]

Like Winters, Waybright understood the difference between completing the mission and Completing the Mission. By the time he was assigned to Bravo Company with one year to go on his military commitment, he didn't care about body count numbers or what they meant to him professionally. Instead of throwing infantry into the jungle against larger enemy forces, Waybright preferred to use artillery fire when he knew the enemy was present.

"I wasn't a career officer," he said. "My mission was to keep the men alive."

After their six-month combat leadership stints, officers in Vietnam generally were bumped to a staff job – "Assuming you were still alive," said Greene, who joined the Army in March 1969, after graduating from the University of Houston, where he was in the ROTC (Reserve Officer Training Corps) training program. Greene had been deeply involved in outdoor activities, not unlike a lot of other soldiers in Bravo Company. The lieutenant said hunting and fishing helped transition young men into warriors, up to a point.

"I think you will find that background in those who saw action," Greene said. "But it's a little different when bullets are flying. Rabbits and deer don't shoot back."

For Waybright, the new command came with a taste of home in the form of Private First Class Gary Weekley, who grew up in Middlebourne, West Virginia, not far from Waybright's hometown. Weekley was an avid outdoorsman and had two sisters in grade school. He was one of the more popular soldiers in Bravo Company.[5]

"I'll always remember Gary as the guy who wanted to please anybody and was liked by everybody," Waybright said.

Bravo Company's officers had earned the respect of the men under their command, not least because getting as many of those men back home was a primary – if not the most important – objective. Waybright quickly developed a reputation as an effective company commander. Lieutenant Teb Stocks, who hailed from Georgia, had a reputation as a "soldier's officer." Unlike the vast majority of Army officers, he hadn't graduated from any college, but had a knack for getting the job done with a minimum of casualties. However, even a respected officer like Stocks wasn't immune from the jokes and good-natured insults that are part of life and bonding in any gathering of men.

More often than not, the jokes would focus on Stocks' syrup-thick Southern accent. Dick Bowling and Allen McCulty sometimes set Stocks up by singing lines from Three Dog Night's classic song, "Eli's Coming," which would draw a scolding from the lieutenant.

"He'd come on and say, 'Shut the fuck up. You're going to get somebody kilt,'" said Lee Paterson, who joined Bravo Company in late April. "I was new, so I asked, 'What does kilt mean?'"

Waybright would later quip that he assigned Frederick Harms, another of the late-1969 replacements, as Stocks' radio telephone operator because Harms was the only person in Bravo Company capable of decoding Stocks. In the field, a platoon leader and his radio telephone operator were inseparable – "You were supposed to be right on the lieutenant's ass," one Bravo Company veteran said about the radioman's duty. Harms, an Illinois native, had a touch of the hippie about himself. His rebellious nature took the form of unauthorized insignia like medals commemorating St Christopher and decorations from the Montagnards – mountain people who were allied with the Americans and, before that, the French – alongside peace beads. Stocks and his radioman became fast, if sometimes antagonistic, friends.

"We fought the War of Northern Aggression every day," Stocks said jokingly.

While Bravo Company had an executive officer – who would have overseen paperwork and logistics while the company commander carried out operations – in early January, the position was eliminated during at least part of the tour, which meant much of the coordination of platoon actions fell to First Sergeant Willie Nickleberry, who had been in the Army since 1965. Waybright said Nickleberry was a non-commissioned officer who not only wanted the right thing to be done, he wanted things done the right way, but he also worked to protect and prepare the company's soldiers.

"He was the soldier's best friend when they came into the firebase," Waybright said.

Outside the firebase, Bravo Company's objective was to root out enemy soldiers and kill them. Second Platoon was scouting a cave on

March 14 on Hill 474 when it encountered and killed a North Vietnamese soldier. Rather than continue down into the hole and risk the fate that befell Lieutenant Alan Johnson and medic Joe Honan, Richard Rios tossed a tear-gas grenade down the cave. The irritant drove an enemy soldier out through the cave's far entrance, about 50 meters away from Rios and another soldier, Jim Hurst, who had arrived in Vietnam a few weeks earlier.

"The bad guy comes out of his hole and Jim hit him," Rios said.

The Currahees' assignment was to drive the 7th Battalion, 22nd North Vietnamese Army Regiment, 3rd Division off Hill 474, and by early February the effort was showing signs of progress. Aerial reconnaissance indicated that small team-sized groups of about five North Vietnamese soldiers at a time were slipping away, primarily by filtering past the US siege line. The enemy was leaving, slowly to be sure, but leaving all the same. In the meantime, though, they were determined to make the Americans pay as hefty a price as possible for the remote mound of rocks and dirt. The Americans ruled the air and had the hill encircled, which meant supplies – particularly food – were difficult to come by. So difficult, in fact, that the enemy ventured forth from its caves, tunnels, and rock cover to forage, which left its troops vulnerable to ambush.

"We were just working, finding where the enemy is," said Richard Rios. "There was always something to do."

After the firefight on February 17 that took the lives of Joe Honan and Alan Johnson, Bravo Company settled into a routine of daylight patrols and nighttime ambushes. While it crossed paths with the enemy almost every day, Bravo Company didn't sustain any more fatalities during the last ten days of February and the entire month of March. The rest of 3rd Battalion, however, didn't get off as easily.

By mid-March, hunting for the enemy became an exercise that yielded diminishing returns. Bravo Company's search for the enemy came up mostly empty for several days as the Americans killed time by playing pinochle rather than killing the enemy with their weapons. The only communist soldier Bravo Company encountered during that stretch might have been a mercy killing – 1st Platoon saw the man lying on a rock, possibly dying of starvation, which itself might have been caused by the siege.[6] By April, they followed the enemy out in favor of better hunting grounds. The official count indicated that 101 enemy troops were killed, 47 weapons and about 12,000 rounds of ammunition were seized, and more than 3 tonnes of supplies and documents captured.[7]

Those documents revealed the Americans' action to have been a mixed success. The North Vietnamese intelligence reports indicated that they realized the Americans would battle in the remote jungles and mountains with determination and skill, but also that the enemy saw US troops as "sloppy and lazy." The Americans often threw out still-functional equipment and weapons with their trash, which offered aid and comfort to the North Vietnamese. Even acts of kindness benefited the enemy – C-rations given to village children sometimes wound up nourishing enemy soldiers. The captured files also revealed a tactical problem. North Vietnamese troops monitored unsecured US radio transmissions, which meant that Americans in ambush positions were revealing their locations just by communicating with one another.[8]

By late March, 3rd Battalion was moved to the Crow's Foot region southeast of Pleiku. The Kim Son river valley was given that nickname by the Americans because, from the sky, three streams that merged into the Kim Son resembled a bird's footprint. The Currahees did a tailgate jump – they were transported from Landing Zone North English, 5 kilometers north of Bong Son, to Landing Zone Uplift about 12 kilometers south of the city in the Kim Son Valley by truck.

When Bravo Company moved from the makeshift North Vietnamese fort on Hill 474 to the thick tropical jungles of the Crow's Foot, it faced a greater challenge in finding the enemy. Nighttime tactics remained the same, with one platoon venturing outside the defensive perimeter each night on a rotating basis to set ambushes because the enemy moved at night – "The night belonged to the enemy," Waybright said.

The North Vietnamese stayed put during the day and set their own ambushes while trying to avoid the Americans and their tactical superiority, particularly with indirect fire – artillery and air strikes. On most days, the Americans adopted a different procedure than on Hill 474. Each platoon, even the one that had been on ambush the previous night, would venture into the jungle, separated by about 1 kilometer to prevent US troops from firing on one another out of confusion. When daytime patrol duty fell to 1st Platoon, Greene would advance with one squad, with the remaining two squads held in reserve.

"I felt that it was better to have two squads back because it eliminated the possibility of friendly fire," Greene said.

As the patrol squad went forward, the lead two soldiers would move in a semicircle to one side, returning to the main squad force from behind a short time later. The second two soldiers would travel in a semicircle to the other side. The maneuver, which new arrivals in Vietnam learned as part of their in-country final instruction, was known as a cloverleaf formation because it would resemble the small plant's leaves if viewed from above. Bravo Company had used the cloverleaf on Hill 474 when the terrain permitted, but it became an everyday go-to tactic after the Currahees moved to the Crow's Foot.

The North Vietnamese rarely opted to exchange fire with US patrols, because they were usually outgunned and outmanned. But it was fairly common for the Currahees to be fired upon by the enemy as they cloverleafed through the jungle. Early one day shortly before Sabo and the other early 1969 draftees joined the unit, one of Bravo Company's platoons took fire. One trooper dropped onto the ground, face first. His reaction wasn't quick enough to save him, but the canned food in his backpack was. His C-ration cans stopped the enemy gunfire. The food, however, did not survive.[9]

Historically, the Crow's Foot region had been a Viet Cong hotbed, even after the enemy irregular force had been virtually eradicated in the 1968 Tet Offensive. North Vietnamese raiding parties had made routine forays to harass traffic on National Route 1, which ran within ten miles of the Crow's Foot. The enemy enjoyed broad support in the region, primarily in recognition of the corruption and neglect Saigon's government directed toward villagers.

"The central government has never shown its people anything but tax assessments, and popular feelings run close to 100 percent with the insurgents," war correspondent Howard Moffett wrote of the region's denizens in a 1967 wire service article.[10]

Bravo Company rarely crossed paths with those villagers, at least not in the field. Most of their operations were in what were known as free-fire zones, where soldiers could shoot first in the hopes that they would live long enough to ask questions later. Outside the free-fire zones, generally in populated villages, troopers could shoot only if they witnessed someone with a weapon, or if they were fired on first.

"They would tell you when it was free-fire. If it moved, you could shoot it," Bravo Company soldier Norm Friend said. "To me, that was a better deal."

Bravo Company got into a firefight with two enemy soldiers on April 2, in one of its first operations that month. The North Vietnamese troops got away, but the Americans found a small North Vietnamese outpost with a wide range of medical and personal gear, including a camera, bloody bandage, glasses, wallet, rat poison, and a fortune-telling board. Two days later though, the enemy would hit back. While on daylight patrol, 1st Platoon encountered an overgrown, little-used trail and advanced in search of enemy troops a short distance before the path suddenly widened out. A squad, with 20-year-old Private First Class Gary Weekley walking point, headed forward.

The trail itself would have raised an alarm for the Currahees who, like most American combat units, usually avoided the beaten path with good reason. It was far easier to simply saunter up the trail than it was to slog through the jungles and rice paddies. But in Vietnam, cutting corners was an offense potentially punishable by death. The booby traps and mines, particularly when planted on well-used trails, were a constant hazard. Back on Hill 474, a Bravo Company column was advancing up a trail when Rick Brown, who had been fifth from the front, found a landmine. Miraculously, the first four men had each stepped over, but not on, the mine. Had Brown not seen the device, he or another of the Currahees would surely have trod on it. His keen eyes certainly saved some of his comrades' lives.

Smaller booby traps rarely killed many soldiers, but they performed a tactical purpose for an enemy who was usually outgunned and forced into hit-and-run attacks. At worst from the North Vietnamese point of view, the practice would slow the Americans down by forcing them into the heavy terrain and cover the "run" part of "hit-and-run." The devices, usually triggered by contact with a tripwire or contact plate, were decidedly low-tech and ranged in size from small explosives known as "toe-poppers" to full artillery shells rigged for detonation.[11]

During the early part of 1970, Bravo Company ran into several booby traps. Occasionally an observant trooper would see a trip wire and warn his comrades. But just as often, luck proved to be their salvation – 2nd Platoon tripped an explosive device on March 26, but it didn't detonate.[12] In early February soldiers from Bravo Company found a relatively large booby trap comprised of 2 pounds of explosives packed in a mackerel can with an electronic trigger device after capturing an underground bunker.

As Weekley led 1st Platoon down the trail on April 4 he tripped another large booby trap, a mortar shell set to detonate. He was killed instantly. Two other soldiers – including Sergeant Curtis Casey, who would lose a leg – were badly wounded. Greene, immediately behind Casey, was knocked cold by the blast, but otherwise unhurt. Greene had good reason to expect that the booby trap was a prelude to an ambush.

"That's what they were supposed to do," Greene said. "But they were not highly organized."

The follow-on attack never came. But four days later, on April 8, 2nd Platoon would not be as fortunate. The platoon, under the leadership of First Lieutenant Lawrence Neff, was up to its usual business – hunting down and eliminating enemy soldiers. Before settling in the previous night, platoon observers had seen enemy activity on a nearby hill, so Neff, as platoon leader, decided to divide his group so it could cover more ground in searching for the nearby North Vietnamese.

Neff took one group, which left a second element that included Sabo and radio telephone operator Richard Clanton, under the command of Second Lieutenant Thomas Allen Scarboro, a forward artillery observer attached to Bravo Company. Scarboro's official assignment was with Delta Battery of the 101st's 320th Artillery Regiment, but he was also serving as assistant platoon leader for Neff. The 22-year-old officer had earned a degree in drafting from Asheville-Buncombe Technical Institute and worked at Barbour-Cooper and Associates architectural firm before enlisting in May of 1968. He took officer training at Fort Sill, Oklahoma, and landed in Vietnam on September 28, 1969.[13]

Ron Gooch, who had been promoted to sergeant and designated as a squad leader in late February after being named the battalion's soldier of the month, was also in the lead element along with Bruce Dancesia and Bill Sorg. Gooch hailed from Archdale in the North Carolina Piedmont region. He had attended and played baseball at Appalachian State University in the Blue Ridge Mountains along North Carolina's northwestern fringe. Dancesia played football and took part in track in high school at his hometown of Binghamton, New York but, like Gooch, wasn't nearly as serious about his studies.

"I tried to get out of high school," Dancesia said. "I was smoking and joking on the corner."

Scarboro was within days of returning to his primary assignment as an artillery officer in 3rd Battalion. As Bravo Company's forward artillery observer, he was not a full platoon leader, but Lieutenant John Greene – 1st Platoon's leader – said he was capable of the job.

"Tom was an outstanding platoon leader," Greene said. "He had the confidence and friendship of all the people in the platoon and in his company."

Scarboro's team took a scout dog, trained to locate enemy troops by scent, into the jungle. As the lieutenant led his team through the heavy jungle cover, the scout dog took lead, which indicated that enemy soldiers were near. In response to the dog's scent "hit," Scarboro sent out Dancesia and another soldier as a scout team, but they found nothing. As the column advanced, the dog played insistently out to the end of its long leash. A short time later, as the platoon crossed an open rice paddy, the dog again caught a scent trail belonging to the enemy. This time, however, there was no time to react before the North Vietnamese soldiers detonated a claymore-style landmine and opened fire.

"When we saw movement in the tree line, we dropped to the ground just as the VC blew their ambush," said Rick Clanton, Scarboro's radio telephone operator.

Of the first ten men in line, Clanton was the only one not wounded.[14] Among those hit were the scout dog and his handler, who sustained a hit to the leg and survived. The dog did not. Bill Sorg, Ron Gooch, Crandall Simpson, Lee Richards, and John Ivey, one of the company's M-60 machine-gun operators, were also wounded. Scarboro was killed in the attack's opening seconds. But Leslie Sabo likely prevented a full-on massacre. After the mine exploded, there were at least eight wounded soldiers in the kill zone, along with the uninjured Clanton and the dying Scarboro, and all were exposed to enemy fire. At that point, instead of obeying the self-preservation instinct, Sabo went forward and helped out.

"With pretty much no hesitation at all, Les went up and gave them covering fire," Clanton said of the April 8 firefight. "It does go against your natural instinct to hide. But he didn't, because he knew they needed him."

Additionally, Sabo offered medical assistance. He ran to Sorg – whose first impression of Sabo had been that he didn't belong in combat – and helped stem a serious head wound, which might have saved his life. Meanwhile, battalion commander Lieutenant Colonel Joseph Jaggers, watching the action from his command-and-control chopper, ordered helicopters to extract the wounded. Sorg, Simpson, Ivey, and Dancesia were pulled off the line temporarily, but all returned to Bravo Company after their wounds healed. Gooch faced months of recovery from his wounds.

Because of the ambush, Bravo Company sent out another patrol to sweep the area of North Vietnamese soldiers as daylight waned. This time, the task fell to First Lieutenant John Greene's 1st Platoon, which also had that evening's night ambush duty. As the Currahees set up their perimeter, it came under attack by 60mm mortars that centered on the platoon's first squad, led by Sergeant Vernon Bruner and Richard Calderon, his radio telephone operator. Like Sabo, Horace "Johnny Cash" Currin, Richard Rios, and the other late-1969 cherries, Calderon had matured from an inexperienced soldier into a battle-hardened veteran while facing nearly daily combat during the first four months of 1970. The North Vietnamese never ventured within small arms range of 1st Platoon, but their mortar attack, less than 10 minutes in duration, was tragically effective. Calderon was killed in a direct hit and other soldiers were wounded.

During his combat tour in Vietnam Sabo received the Bronze Star, the military's fourth-highest award for combat bravery, although it isn't clear if he received it for his action in the April 8 firefight. Sabo also received the Purple Heart, Air Medal, Good Conduct Medal, National Defense Service Medal, Vietnam Service Medal, Republic of Vietnam Gallantry Cross with palm, Republic of Vietnam Campaign Medal, Republic of Vietnam Outstanding Civil Action Medal, and Republic of Vietnam Wound Medal.

"Les was dependable," Rios said of Sabo. "He had a great sense of honor."

––––––––––

Sabo's closest childhood friends remembered him the same way. But most of his other high school classmates knew him by name only. To everyone except those close friends, Sabo moved through Lincoln High School like a ghost. He wasn't involved in many activities. According to the 1966 high school yearbook, Leslie Sabo – who possessed a long, lean body ideally suited for basketball – played the sport during his freshman year, but didn't continue onto the varsity team.

While in his teen years, Sabo occasionally displayed the same ingenuity that marked his father's rise from refugee to white-collar professional. An early 1960s copy of the *Ellwood City Ledger* featured a photograph, titled "Seven Cents Profit," of a then-teenaged Sabo and another boy bent over a storm grate. The duo were using a wad of gum to fish a dime out of the storm sewer. The gum cost three cents, hence the photograph's title.[15]

That photograph might have been about as close to notoriety as Leslie Sabo would get while growing up. At Lincoln, he wasn't particularly active either in sports or student organizations. Leslie participated in the bowling club, Spanish club, and Hi-Y, a youth auxiliary for the YMCA. George said his brother possessed some athletic talent – he was a very good bowler and a strong tennis player, about 20 years before tennis was added as a varsity sport at Lincoln High School.

"He was the good son," George said of Leslie. "My dad was a good tennis player so Leslie wanted to be a good tennis player."

There is absolutely no bitterness or jealousy in George Sabo's voice when he says his younger brother had a closer relationship with his parents than himself. Leslie was barely a teenager when George graduated from high school in 1961. Within two years of graduation, George was getting on with his life – he was married with the first of his three sons. And even before George got out of school, he caused his parents a few sleepless nights, by his own admission. Until Leslie shipped out to Vietnam, they never had that issue with him.

"He never gave them any problem, which was a blessing because I did," George said. "His personality was that of a much more caring person. My brother was much more like my father, very caring. He understood my mother much more than I did. He was always the one who was catering to and caring for my mother's wishes."

Until George Sabo graduated from high school in 1961, he and Leslie had been extremely close, in spite of an age difference of more than four years. But life – in the form of the older brother's responsibility for a new family – got in the way. George headed out of school and established his family, his brother moved into his teenage years, a time that can be turbulent for many young men. Olga Nocera Sabo married George, but she admits that Leslie was the gentler soul – she says her husband was a "hardass" in his younger days, and George never disputed that. Within five years of their wedding day, Olga and George had three sons – Anthony, Steven, and Michael – and George was working during the day and attending Youngstown State University at night, just as his father had. During

George's absences, Olga said Leslie helped out with the three young children and was less like an uncle than an older brother to them. During that time, Olga recalled that Leslie made a promise that, in time, would become tragically ironic.

"He told me that if anything happened to George, he would marry me because he didn't want anyone else to take care of our sons," Olga said.

"I could hardly remember my brother getting mad," George said. "I'm sure he was mad a number of times with me, but he never would have shown it. He was such a mild – not mild, but a gentle person."

George might have been overstating any rifts he had with his brother. Even though he was on his own and Leslie was still at home, the two brothers remained close and they, along with their parents, took the oath of US citizenship on March 25, 1964, during Leslie's sophomore year at Lincoln High School, in a ceremony at the Lawrence County Courthouse in New Castle.

During those years after his brother left home, Leslie more or less pampered Elisabeth Sabo. He took his mother on vacation – including a weekend-long trip to Atlantic City, more than eight hours' driving time away from their home in Ellwood City, on one occasion – and saw to her needs in a way that her older son and husband rarely did, said Olga Sabo, George's wife of more than 50 years.

"She was high maintenance and she always needed lots of attention," Olga said. "And he knew how to give it to her."

Before long, though, there would be another woman in Leslie Sabo's life.

CHAPTER 9

Yesterday I received your letter and was very happy to hear from you. Unfortunately, I had to stop here but am now able to continue your letter. Today is Friday the 13th. My 5th month being married and completing my 3rd month in Nam. You asked what a fire base is, well it usually consists of about 2 or 3 105mm cannons with one platoon to secure it. It gives artillery support to us whenever we need it. My third week in country I spent on a fire base but I haven't been on one since then.

Leslie Sabo letter to George and Olga
Dated February 11, 1970

During the majority of 1969, most of Bravo Company trained for combat in Vietnam, starting with basic training, then going through advanced individual training and finally Screaming Eagle Replacement Training School – SERTS – to get them acclimated to jungle warfare once they arrived in country. But no one taught them how to fight a monkey. For one soldier in Bravo Company, that turned out to be an unfortunate oversight. That soldier was slogging with Ruben Rueda when they heard a noise high up in the triple-canopy jungle.

"I'll get it," the guy said, just before he fired into the trees and, amazingly, found his mark. Within seconds, a male bonobo monkey descended from the trees looking for vengeance. Rueda thought the soldier, whose name he couldn't remember, had shot the male bonobo's mate, but it was more likely the mother. Bonobos of both genders are notoriously indiscriminate about their choice of sexual partners, and bond much more closely to their mothers than they do with mates. In any event, the male bonobo initiated a vicious attack.

Because the primate and the human were fighting in close quarters – and close enough to Rueda that he could hear the soldier's bones snap – he couldn't try to shoot the bonobo without risking his comrade's life. After beating the soldier, the animal eventually scampered away. When the soldier regained consciousness, he asked, through a broken jaw, what had happened.

"I said, 'You just got beat up by a monkey.'"

The soldier was immediately transported out of the jungle for medical treatment.

Even under ideal situations, jungle warfare is an unpleasant enterprise. The soldiers of Bravo Company consistently encountered weather that was either too cold or too hot or too wet along with red ants, snakes, deadly beasts, and "wait-a-minute" vines, which would catch on the soldiers' already unwieldy backpacks as they marched through the jungle, which forced the wearer to call out, "wait a minute" to those ahead of him, all of which made maneuvering a difficult slog. The jungle was filled with large foliage – bamboo trees with trunks 6 inches thick and 50-foot tall mahogany trees reaching for sunlight above the jungle canopy.

Jungles, with their moisture and shade, teem with animal life, and the rainforests of Vietnam's Central Highlands were typical. The soldiers of Bravo Company commonly crossed paths with large snakes – pythons and boa constrictors 20 feet and longer. Rueda had spent a lot of time in the woods back in the world, but he was accustomed to deer or small game. Not tigers. Bravo Company encountered one of the big cats, a female around 400 pounds, which had been wounded in a North Vietnamese booby trap. One of the Currahees had to put the animal out of her misery, Rueda said. He quipped that the tiger's mate was going to be out for the blood of her killers, just as that bonobo exacted vengeance on the other soldier. But as exotic and dangerous as jungle wildlife could be, it still wasn't as daunting as the two-legged predators hiding beneath the triple canopy.

"There were a number of times snipers shot at us," George Koziol said. "We were stressed out every day. Being out there in combat position is pretty scary."[1]

When a platoon stopped on patrol for breaks or meals, it would establish a few two-man outposts to keep watch for the approach of enemy soldiers looking to catch the Americans with their guard down. Occasionally, the troopers, already on edge because their comrades a little further back were depending on them for security, might hear a noise and prepare for a firefight, only to discover to their relief that their perimeter was threatened not by the enemy, but by a jungle creature.

"Nothing is quite as funny as being scared half to death and then finding out there's nothing to be afraid of," Bravo Company trooper Dick Freeling said. "The worst thing in the world is being scared half to death when there is something to be afraid of."[2]

During April, Bravo Company got a new sergeant. Staff Sergeant Onorio Romo was brought in as the top-ranking non-commissioned officer in 1st Platoon under First Lieutenant John Greene. A well-seasoned soldier, Romo, 32, was in his third Army combat tour – he had earned a Silver Star in Hue during the Tet Offensive. He had a young daughter and wife waiting at home for him. She planned to re-enter school upon his return from Vietnam.

Before joining the US Army, he had been a police officer and served in the army in his native Mexico. Romo learned most of his English in the Army, which meant he had a rich vocabulary of four-letter words, and Greene regarded him as a valued and smart non-commissioned officer. So did 1st Platoon trooper Norm Friend.

"If it hadn't been for him, there would have been a lot more guys whacked," Friend said of Romo. "He came in and helped to get everyone tight."

In the field, Romo was particular about unnecessary noise – such as the sound of loose C-ration cans banging around in his soldiers' backpacks. Friend dealt with that issue by discarding most of his C-rations. When the supply chopper came in every three days, he would sort through his share of the shipment, keep enough of his favorites for one meal a day and toss the rest so the house on his back would be a less oppressive burden.

"I'd rather lose that extra weight than have the food," he said.

For the first half of April, the battalion hunted North Vietnamese in the Crow's Foot. The Currahees found and destroyed several bunkers. The enemy was able to put a bigger dent in the Americans' helicopter fleet in the Crow's Foot than it could on Hill 474. After going through a well-fortified but mostly abandoned hamlet on April 11, Bravo Company had a helicopter pick up when the landing zone came under attack. Koziol was in the lead helicopter when a rocket-propelled grenade detonated directly under the second chopper. Sabo's 2nd Platoon squad was in the helicopter.

"When I looked back and saw Les, I thought right then and there, 'All your buddies are dead,'" Koziol said.[3]

As it turned out, a total of four crew members and soldiers in Sabo's squad were wounded, but no one was killed in what had been the second US helicopter brought down in three days. The Americans found an extensive North Vietnamese cave and tunnel outpost on April 12. Rather than explore it, the Air Force bombed the caves, followed by Army helicopter strikes. Those gunship crews reported seeing secondary explosions along with the smell of burning human flesh, which indicated that the enemy had been storing ammunition in the facility and that the enemy casualties could conservatively be estimated in the dozens.

The following day – while thousands of miles above Vietnam, the moon-bound Apollo 13 spacecraft sustained a massive malfunction that put the lives of three astronauts at risk and forced them to abandon plans to land on the Moon – parts of Alpha, Charlie, and Delta were all involved in heavy skirmishes, with two Americans killed. Charlie Company's 3rd Platoon saw the most significant action when it ran into a North Vietnamese company. Outnumbered roughly three-to-one by an entrenched adversary, the Americans routed the enemy with air strikes from helicopters and fighters. One of the aircraft involved was 3rd Battalion's command helicopter, the vantage point from which Major Marvin Larson, the battalion's executive officer, viewed the battle, where he clearly saw that Charlie Company's wounded were in trouble. Twice on April 13, Larson ordered his chopper to land to evacuate wounded. On both instances, Larson exited the helicopter under fire and helped load wounded. He would receive the Silver Star for braving enemy fire to assist in evacuations.[4]

During the company's last three weeks in the Crow's Foot, contact with the enemy decreased, but the Currahees lost two soldiers, both of whom were Philadelphia natives with connections to Bravo Company. First Lieutenant Tony Clough, a platoon leader from Alpha Company, was killed in an enemy attack just as the platoon was taking a break. His Vietnam tour had begun in September, when he was assigned as a platoon leader in Bravo Company. In January, before Bravo Company went into action on Hill 474, Clough was transferred to Alpha Company. After the initial grenade attack that killed Clough, the North Vietnamese were driven off by fire from Alpha Company troopers.

The day after Clough's death, a similar scenario played out when Bravo Company, 2nd Platoon, on patrol in the Crow's Foot, stopped to take a break and came under attack. The North Vietnamese strike came as a surprise and broke off quickly. But it cost the Currahees one of their comrades, Bobby Koehler. Koehler was regarded as an easygoing amiable soldier.

"Bobby got hit twice and I caught him, and he died in my arms," Rick Clanton, 2nd Platoon's radio telephone operator, said.

The difficult and diverse conditions didn't bother Leslie Sabo much. By the time he reached the age of 22 in February of 1970, he had lived on three continents and worked at some of the most dangerous occupations short of soldiering. In some places, college kids get jobs waiting tables, stocking shelves in supermarkets, or helping sweep floors at the local high school. In the steel towns that dotted western Pennsylvania in the 1950s and '60s, those kids often would pick up shifts in the mill, particularly – as was usually the case – if they had a father already working there. The sons of World War II veterans were often the first in their families to attend college, thanks in no small part to union efforts to win white-collar wages for decidedly blue-collar workers. For the fathers, bringing the kids into the mill served a double purpose by giving the kids money for tuition and living expenses while they were away at college, and by reminding them of what they were trying to escape by earning a college degree.

With a college-educated father who had a white-collar mill job, it might have been expected that Leslie Sabo would have taken that route after graduating from Ellwood City Lincoln High School in June of 1966. But he had a different plan. Before heading off to college at Youngstown State, Sabo took a summer job working on a Great Lakes cargo freighter. George said he recalled Leslie taking the job and being away nearly all of that summer.[5]

Although George Sabo couldn't recall many details about what his brother did, it is safe to assume he was an Ordinary Seaman, the lowest rank in the US Merchant Marine. An Ordinary Seaman is an unlicensed crewman and generally serves as an apprentice to an Able Seaman, the lowest-ranking licensed worker on a ship. Typically, an Ordinary Seaman must work three years on a ship before applying to be an Able Seaman. Likewise, it can be assumed that Sabo's duties included such menial labor as swabbing the deck, securing cargo, and repainting the boat's superstructure.[6]

Leslie Sabo's three-month stint on the Great Lakes had been the longest time he and George would spend apart since the day Leslie was born. And until Leslie shipped off to Vietnam, it would be the longest separation the two brothers would ever experience. The sailor's life had changed Leslie, and had given him an opportunity to develop himself, physically and mentally.

"I can remember him leaving as a scrawny kid and coming back as a muscular young man," George said.

While Leslie thrived on board the heavy freighter, things were different at Youngstown State. In his freshman year, the two brothers got together regularly in the early evening, after Leslie had finished his classes for the day and as George was arriving for his night courses. Even though they had been close growing up, these conversations represented the closest the two young men had been, or would ever be, to interacting as equals rather than as big brother and little brother. In late September of 1966, George turned 23 years old and Leslie was almost 19, so their relationship could be that of just two young college students.

George and his younger brother talked about almost every topic, including the Vietnam conflict, which was then still escalating. In 1969, a year after Leslie dropped out of college, the US military had more than a half-million servicemen and women in country.[7] While the war had yet to divide the nation, the Sabo brothers, and Leslie's friends, had passionate discussions about the war. They didn't always agree on the subject.

"My brother was very much in favor of being there because of the effort to stop communism before it came here," George said. "Not all of his buddies would agree with that."

It wouldn't be long before Leslie would have to back up those words in the most profound way possible.

One trait Leslie didn't inherit from his father was an ability to focus on schoolwork. In Hungary, Leslie Sr. earned a bachelor's diploma, a law degree, and a doctorate, and then, as a refugee, he obtained a bachelor's degree in engineering. George was going the same route, also in the engineering curriculum. But although George said his brother was no dummy, Leslie Jr. wasn't much interested in studying.

"He was not somebody that wanted to be in college," George said. "He was just there because it was kind of expected. I can remember trying to help him to get motivated to study. I told him that if you drop out, you'll get drafted." But George's motivational tactics didn't work. It's possible, in fact, that the threat of being drafted might have backfired.

According to Sabo's military file, he completed 45 credits at Youngstown State University before leaving school and went to work at the Babcock and Wilcox steel mill in Beaver County, a short distance from Ellwood City. After dropping out of college in early 1968, Leslie Sabo adopted the traditional western Pennsylvania occupation. But he wouldn't face the steelworker's life alone. During the previous fall, he went to a Lincoln High School varsity football game at Helling Stadium, not far from his parents' house, where he met Rose Buccelli. Even though she was only a few months younger than Sabo, the two hadn't previously crossed paths when they attended Lincoln High School at the same time.[8] But their meeting at the football game wasn't entirely an accident. Rose worked as a babysitter, and had looked after George and Olga Sabo's three sons. While at George's home she found a photo of Leslie in her high school yearbook, and was smitten. When Rose saw Leslie at the football game, she made the first move.

"I still can't believe I walked up to him, because that's not me," she said. "We stood and talked and we were together ever since. It was just like we clicked. It was like love at first sight, if you believe in that.[9]

"Something told me to walk up to him and I did, and I'm glad I did."

Leslie was a devoted boyfriend.

"He worshiped the ground I walked on and I worshiped him," she said.

With that meeting, the teenagers began a romance that endured through the following year.

CHAPTER 10

You also wanted to know what I do. We are put in an area like where I've been for the last two months has been our area of operation. At first we did a lot of walking, now we are spending maybe three or four days in one place, then move up not very far and set up again. After we set up, we send a squad or two out to check out the surrounding area. This is called a cloverleaf. That is about the extent of what we do, it isn't too bad because we don't carry those rucksacks as much as we did earlier also they've been flying us more in helicopters which is really nice. George sure is taking a lot of hours but I know he can handle it. When he finally completes school, I hope you both get a chance to relax a little and enjoy yourself. It will be ironic that when I'm out of the army and George will be out of school, things will be reversed. You can help prepare Roe for the future. One good thing I hope I can complete school in about three or four years of night school.

Leslie Sabo letter to George and Olga
Dated February 11, 1970

For Vietnam combat soldiers, one of the greatest joys was the prospect of getting letters from home, which George Koziol called, "our lifeline to the world." Norm Friend might get pictures of his nearly one-year-old son, born the day his father was inducted into the Army. Sabo, one of the company's few married men, often talked about his family, and particularly the wife he left behind following his and Rose's eventual marriage. In March of 1970, while the 506th Regiment was still participating in the siege of Hill 474, a British band named Edison Lighthouse released its only US hit, an earworm ditty called "Love Grows (Where My Rosemary Goes)." Because the song had Sabo's wife's name in it, he sang it almost incessantly, Koziol said. The song could be described charitably as infectious. Uncharitably, it could be described as annoying.

And that's when it was sung well, which Sabo most decidedly did not.

"[His voice] was kind of scratchy," Koziol admitted.[1]

When preparing to propose to his future wife, Leslie Sabo might have envisioned getting engaged in a candlelit dinner, perhaps at a nice restaurant in Pittsburgh, 30 miles or so from his hometown of Ellwood City, or maybe at one of the many romantic overlooks that lined the Ohio and Beaver rivers near his home.

Instead, it happened at a red light in Beaver Falls.

On June 13, 1968, less than a year before he was drafted into the Army, Leslie Sabo sat in his car at a traffic intersection. Rose was in the passenger seat. The couple, who had been dating since the previous fall when they crossed paths during a football game, were returning from a jewelry store, where Rose had picked out her own engagement ring.

"He said, 'You want to put on the ring now,'" Rose Sabo Brown said. "He put the ring on me at the red light."

With that, they were engaged. Rose said they set the wedding for Saturday, September 13, 1969, because she wanted to be wed on the 13th, just as she had got engaged on the 13th.

By the time Leslie put the engagement ring on Rose's finger, they had been dating for less than a year and their courtship would continue for more than another year before their marriage. Rose remembered that she and Leslie had a rather typical dating life, with trips to the movies, dances, or dinners.

"He just was such a special person," Rose said. "We'd go to movies and do what everyone did."

After Leslie left Youngstown State in January 1968, midway through what would have been his sophomore year – his brother, George, said Leslie left for academic reasons, but military records indicate that he had 45 credits, which would have put him on pace to graduate in four years – he went to work at the B&W steel mill in West Mayfield, about a 15-minute drive from Ellwood City. Rose said her family – especially her younger brother – accepted Leslie as a member of the family, even before the couple was engaged. Rose said her mother would throw together what Leslie would call "garbage sandwiches," composed of whatever was in the refrigerator.

"My mother and dad loved him so much," Rose said. "He was so skinny and he'd eat and eat and eat."

Leslie developed an especially close relationship with Carmen "Butch" Buccelli, Rose's brother. At the time, in 1968, there was a pool hall in a walk-down off Lawrence Avenue, Ellwood City's main business district, and Leslie spent a lot of time there, said Butch.

"He liked playing pool and he was good at it," Butch said.

At that time, Buccelli was 17, while Leslie had just turned 20, which would have been a significant age difference. By the time he entered his third decade, Leslie had been a professional sailor, college student, and steelworker, and a proficient athlete in tennis and bowling. Butch, meanwhile, was still enrolled at Lincoln High School. Even so, Leslie never treated Butch like the girlfriend's annoying kid brother, but more like his own older brother treated him.

So when Butch asked to go along on one of those trips to the pool hall, Leslie told him to go ask his father, who also was named Carmen. Given the unsavory reputation of pool halls in those days, the younger Buccelli wasn't hopeful.

"He was very protective of all of us kids and I was sure he would say 'no,'" Butch said. "But my dad trusted him that much. He said [to Leslie], 'As long as he's with you.'"

"I learned a lot from him and not just about pool."

More than four decades later, Buccelli still treasured those days in the pool hall, where Leslie tried to teach him the game, although Butch, by his own admission, never became as proficient at pool as his teacher. But he did get to know Sabo as well as anyone could have. At the pool hall in Ellwood City, Leslie Sabo was one of the best around. And as often happens in pool halls, there was often money riding on the outcomes of those games. But even when gambling at pool, Sabo was still the model of compassion.

Butch remembered several occasions when they would be at the pool hall as Sabo was dominating the competition. Sometimes, though, he would look at his girlfriend's kid brother and say, "this guy's having a bad day." Buccelli knew that meant Leslie intended to make "this guy's" day a little better, even if no one else in the pool hall did.

"I knew enough about the game to know when Les would miss a shot on purpose," he said. "It meant he would lose money but he didn't care.

"He would give you his left arm if he thought you needed it."

To Buccelli, those pool-hall days always ended too soon. On one of those trips, he was just getting into shooting pool and hanging out when Leslie said it was time to leave, because he had to go meet Rose. Butch, who said both he and Leslie were having a good time, suggested they stay a little longer and tell Rose that they had car trouble.

"He said, 'That's tempting, but it's not honest,'" Buccelli said. "You need to be honest with people until they're dishonest with you, then you need to make an adjustment."

Leslie apparently inherited industriousness – the capitalistic, if not the academic, kind – from his father, who had been a political official in Hungary, an accountant in Austria, and a housepainter and engineer in the United States. Leslie Jr. even supplemented his steelworker's income by running vending machines that dispensed pistachios. The machines, which dispensed about ten dyed-red pistachios for a nickel, were all located in bars throughout the Ellwood City area. On weekends, he would drive to Pittsburgh to get the nuts and load the machines. Butch often accompanied him and even took over the route when Leslie was drafted.

"The one thing I blame Leslie for is my addiction to pistachio nuts," Buccelli said. "Even today, in my office at work, I don't run out of pistachio nuts."

Buccelli wasn't the only person to succumb to the addictive nature of pistachios. On one of those trips, they went into a bar where the patrons complained about how many nickels they had pumped into the machine, so Leslie told Buccelli to open up a bag of nuts and hand out a few to each person at the bar. En route to the next stop, Leslie asked for the rest of that bag, and Butch told him it was empty – "I tried to cover up the fact that I ate all the nuts," he said – and that he had given out all the nuts at the previous stop. Unfortunately for Butch's attempt at chicanery, the next bar was brightly lit, which exposed, in the form of red dye on his fingers, evidence that he had eaten most of the pistachios. As was Leslie's tendency, he handled it with humor.

"My hands were as bright red as could be," he said. "Les said, 'I enjoy your company, but I don't know if I can afford it.'"

Leslie drove that pistachio nut route in a bright yellow Dodge that, by Butch's recollection, had a 393-cubic-inch engine, making it a snazzy muscle car. "Leslie adored that car," Butch said.

On one of those Saturdays, Rose remembered that Leslie ordered out from Johnny's pizza shop, an institution in Ellwood City. But when the order was ready, Leslie and his future brother-in-law and father-in-law were still working, so Leslie tossed her the keys to his car and sent her out to pick up the food. To her horror, she sideswiped a tree and dinged up the car while pulling into a parking space. In those less enlightened days, Rose said some men might have reacted angrily to her carelessness. An entire strain of popular culture at that time was devoted to comedy based in the inept woman driver cliché and her efforts to hide accidents from the men, who were certain to be angry about the damage. Rose feared that very reaction, especially when she considered how her fiancé felt about his beloved car.

Instead, Leslie turned it into a joke. "He said, 'Are you OK?'" Rose said, remembering the conversation. "I said 'Yeah.' He said, 'Then what's the problem? Did the tree jump in front of you?'"

"The entire time we dated, we never had one argument. Not one argument."

———————

While the couple was focused on their budding relationship, events more than 12,000 miles away set in motion the circumstances that would land Leslie Sabo in Vietnam, and eventually in Cambodia. From the first days of the Vietnam War, the military top brass expressed concerns to President Lyndon Johnson that the North Vietnamese were moving Viet Cong insurgents and supplying them through Laos and Cambodia over what was known as the Ho Chi Minh Trail, but was actually a network of paths carved out of the jungles outside the US-defined area of engagement. The Chiefs' recommendation was ignored, and in January of 1968, those routes provided North Vietnamese an open door for the Tet Offensive.

For the troops already in the country, and those like Sabo still to arrive, Tet changed the way they carried themselves. George Koziol, who would arrive in Vietnam along with Leslie Sabo, Richard Rios, Rick Brown and the other Bravo Company newcomers in November of 1969, said US soldiers had to be on constant alert, even when well behind the front lines or off duty.

Even after Tet, the North Vietnamese continued to use Cambodia as a staging ground and supply line for attacks behind the front lines into South Vietnamese-controlled territory, because the United States military and civilian leadership prohibited personnel from entering Cambodia.

But even while the Tet Offensive raged and home front opposition to the Vietnam War intensified, the conflict had yet to personally affect Leslie Sabo and Rose Buccelli as 1968 became 1969. One of the last things the couple did together in 1968 was to attend a Christmas event where the well-known 1960s-era folk duo Chad and Jeremy, who had seven US Top 40 hits and appeared on the *Batman* and *Laredo* TV shows – were performing.[2] If they hadn't already got engaged in the front seat of his car, it would have been the perfect atmosphere for Leslie to have popped the question.

"We went and we danced," Rose said. "I just remember that it was a special night."

CHAPTER 11

I'm glad everyone enjoyed their birthdays, and especially Tony liked his blue jeans. Tell your dad I'm looking forward to sampling his wine and I really would like some of your mother's cooking. I wouldn't mind some of your delicious cooking either, I can still remember how good those Raviolis were. Well say hi to the boys and everyone for me.

Leslie Sabo letter to George and Olga
Dated February 11, 1970

Rose didn't have the wedding day she had planned 14 months earlier when Leslie Sabo had proposed to her in the front seat of his fast yellow car at the stop light in Beaver Falls. At that time, they hadn't anticipated that their engagement would be interrupted by the US Army. When their scheduled wedding day approached, Leslie – then Private Leslie Sabo – still had two weeks remaining in his advanced individual training at Fort McClellan, Alabama. It was only through the Army's generosity of a weekend pass that Sabo made it to his own wedding.

Because there was no time to rent a tuxedo, Sabo wore his Army dress greens to the wedding, which was held at Purification of the Blessed Virgin Mary Church. The day after their wedding, Leslie Sabo was on an airplane back to Fort McClellan for the completion of his advanced individual training. A month later, he returned for a 30-day leave before shipping out to Vietnam. The couple's activities during Leslie's time at home included a honeymoon in New York City. They spent their days doing the tourist itinerary, with trips to the Empire State Building, the Statue of Liberty, the United Nations building, and the still-under-construction World Trade Center. They also had an encounter that wouldn't have been in their tourist guide. Rose said a prostitute accosted them and tried to do business with the newly-wedded soldier during one of their sightseeing journeys.

"I almost died of shame at that time," she said. "He turned red as a beet."

After the honeymoon, the couple returned home, which presented a problem. They didn't have a house of their own. Although Rose still lived with her parents, and Leslie was only weeks away from having a field pack as his only home, the newlyweds were able to set up a household for their one month together, thanks to an elderly woman they didn't even know. The senior citizen offered Leslie and Rose a vacant space to set up their temporary household in a neighborhood just outside Ellwood City. Rose forgot the woman's name, but not her generosity.

"I just thought that was the nicest thing," she said.

During those few weeks, the couple had a household and was able to live pretty much as any other husband and wife might have. Rose said she tried – unsuccessfully – to get pregnant.

"I couldn't have asked for anybody better," she said. "I just wish I could have had children with him."

Their domesticity during October 1969 was more than just an extended honeymoon. It was a taste of the life they expected to have together when Leslie completed his military commitment. However, it would be all the time they would have as husband and wife.

The Sabo Boys: Leslie Jr., Leslie Sr. and George Sabo, from left to right in back, stand on the back steps of George and Leslie's childhood home along Pershing Street in Ellwood City in this photograph from the late 1960s. In front are George's sons, from left, Steven, Michael, and Anthony.
(Photo courtesy of George Sabo)

Leslie Sabo, in his dress greens, with his brother, George, on the morning of his wedding day. (Photo courtesy of Rose Sabo Brown)

Leslie Sabo and Rose Sabo Brown walk down the aisle after their wedding on September 13, 1969, at Holy Redeemer Catholic Church in Ellwood City. Less than nine months later, Leslie would be buried in the church's cemetery. (Photo courtesy of Rose Sabo Brown)

Leslie and Rose on their honeymoon in October 1969 to New York City. The World Trade Center towers, then under construction, can be seen in the background. (Photo courtesy of Rose Sabo Brown)

Leslie Sabo Sr. and his wife, Elisabeth, have a champagne toast about the time of Leslie's wedding. Leslie Sr. would die in 1977 without ever knowing the accurate account of his son's battlefield death. (Photo courtesy of Rose Sabo Brown)

Former classmates at Ellwood City Lincoln High School, Leslie Sabo, left, and Mark Gretchen, cross paths at Fort Gordon, Georgia, during military training in June of 1969. (Photo courtesy of Rose Sabo Brown)

Soldiers from Bravo Company's 2nd Platoon, 3rd Squad catch a few minutes' relaxation during the siege of Hill 474 in early 1970. In the front, from left, are Tom Powell, Rick Clanton, Bill Sorg, and Leslie Sabo. In the back are Bruce Dancesia, Lee Richards, Randy Schlachter, and Crandall Simpson. (Photo courtesy of Rose Brown)

Weapon in hand, cigarette in mouth, Jack Brickey slogs through the Central Highlands. (Photo courtesy of Jack Brickey)

Jack Brickey, left, and Ruben Rueda were on one of 3rd Platoon's M-60 teams in 1969. Brickey was wounded on January 28, 1970, and sent to recover in the United States. Rueda narrowly avoided being wounded himself – he was walking point during the Mother's Day Ambush on May 10, 1970. (Photo courtesy of Jack Brickey)

With water containers and C-rations packed around him, Rick Brown departs for the combat zone in a Huey. (Photo courtesy of Rick Brown)

Rick Brown holds a Soviet-made SKS rifle captured during the Cambodian campaign. (Photo courtesy of Rick Brown)

Jungle shadows obscure Rick Brown's face as he prepares for action on May 9, 1970, in Cambodia. This picture was taken on Brown's 19th birthday. (Photo courtesy of Rick Brown)

"Kid Rick" Brown clutches a newly-dropped supply of C-rations. (Photo courtesy of Rick Brown)

With a wan smile creasing his face, "Kid Rick" Brown, who marked his 19th birthday in Cambodia, prepares to leave Vietnam. (Photo courtesy of Rick Brown)

Steven "Hungry" Dile, seen here front left, earning his nickname. Dile was killed in an ambush on January 28, 1970. He was awarded a posthumous Silver Star. (Photo courtesy of Jack Brickey)

From left, Norm Friend, Onorio Romo, and Mike "Tex" Bowman pose for the camera in 1970. Romo, who was in his late 30s and had earned a Silver Star two years earlier during the Tet Offensive, had been a soldier and police officer in his native Mexico before joining the US Army. (Photo courtesy of Norm Friend)

Pete Guzman, with his home on his back. (Photo courtesy of Jack Brickey)

Pete Guzman, who was killed on January 28, 1970, pens a letter home. (Photo courtesy of Jack Brickey)

Frank Madrid, foreground, was killed on January 28, 1970. (Photo courtesy of Jack Brickey)

Combat medic Jerry Nash, foreground, sits down for a breather in late December 1969 or early January, 1970. Frank Madrid and Pete Guzman, who were killed on January 28, 1970, are in the background. (Photo courtesy of Jack Brickey)

At Camp Holloway near Pleiku, Bravo Company prepares on May 5, 1970, for its combat assault into Cambodia. Rick Brown is seated in the foreground smoking a cigarette. On the far right is Brown's closest friend in Bravo Company, Charles Wicks. (Photo courtesy of Rick Brown)

Although Sabo was a rifleman during most of his time in Vietnam, including during the Mother's Day Ambush, for a time in early 1970 he was on an M-60 machine-gun team after another soldier sustained a non-combat leg injury. (Photo courtesy of Rose Sabo Brown)

Lieutenant John Shaffer, facing away from camera, confers with Frank Madrid. Both would be killed by the North Vietnamese on January 28, 1970. (Photo courtesy of Jack Brickey)

Lieutenant Teb Stocks, 3rd Platoon leader, center, enjoys a cold Budweiser with Mike DiLeo, left, and Lee Paterson, right. (Photo courtesy of Rose Sabo Brown)

Rose Sabo Brown preserved some of the medals her late husband earned during the six months he served in Vietnam, including the Bronze Star, Purple Heart, Air Medal, and Combat Infantryman Badge, but not the Medal of Honor. (Photo by the author)

Forty years later: from left, Jim Waybright, Rick Brown, and Richard Rios, at the 2009 reunion in Waybright's hometown of Marietta, Ohio. (Photo by the author)

Sabo's hometown of Ellwood City built a monument, which was dedicated on September 30, 2012. The front includes the text of Sabo's Medal of Honor citation and the names of all eight soldiers killed in the Mother's Day Ambush are listed on the back. (Photo by the author)

Call to attention: about 30 members of Bravo Company stand at attention as President Barack Obama leads the crowd in applause during the Medal of Honor ceremony for Leslie Sabo on May 16, 2012 in the White House East Room. First Lady Michelle Obama can be seen, in red, facing away from the camera. (US Army)

An emotionally moved Rose Sabo Brown accepts the Medal of Honor in place of her late husband, Leslie Sabo, from President Barack Obama. (US Army)

Leslie Sabo's family – by marriage, blood, and blood shed – gather with President Barack Obama and First Lady Michelle Obama at the May 2012 Medal of Honor ceremonies. Seated, from left, are Bruce Dancesia, Ron Stone, Teb Stocks, John Greene, Frances Buccelli, Rick Brown, Richard Lane, Rick Clanton, Mark Rogers, and A. J. Moore. Standing, from left, are Ronny Beasley, Ray D'Angelo, Jack Brickey, Ron Gooch, Richard Rios, Collin Lindsay, Bill Sorg, Ed Dunlap, Mike DiLeo, Kathleen Starkey, Ben Currin, Olga Sabo, George Sabo, First Lady Michelle Obama, Jim DeBoer, Rose Sabo Brown, President Barack Obama, Bill Watling, Ruben Rueda, Dave Soden, Lawrence Neff, Norm Friend, Jerry Nash, Larry Stefan, Tony Krizinski, Doug Lange, Tom Lautzenheitzer, Don Baker, Lee Paterson, Joe Hanks, Bobby Garnto, and James Waybright.
(Photo courtesy of the White House)

George Sabo, left in front, and his wife, Olga, pose in the White House Blue Room with their children and grandchildren after the Medal of Honor ceremony for George's brother Leslie.
(US Army)

Rose Sabo Brown, center, is accompanied by First Lady Michelle Obama and President Barack Obama during a Memorial Day ceremony at the National Vietnam War Memorial in 2012. The President's speech marked the beginning of a 13-year-long recognition of the war's 50th anniversary. (Photo courtesy of Rose Sabo Brown)

Rose Sabo Brown meets actor Tom Selleck during ceremonies at the National Vietnam War Memorial on Memorial Day 2012, a few weeks after Leslie Sabo's Medal of Honor ceremony. Selleck, a California National Guard veteran who serves as a spokesman for the National Vietnam War Education Center, played a Vietnam veteran on the *Magnum, P.I.* television series. (Photo courtesy of Rose Sabo Brown)

HARLES R WEST · LARRY C YOUNG · JAMES A BLACKMO
LAWRENCE N DE BOER · JAMES E DEBREW · TIMOTHY
FREDERICK W HARMS Jr · RONALD W HOLT · TERRY LEE
MURPHY III · CLIFFORD F MACOMBER Jr · JOHN S MELI
AN · EDDIE MOLINO Jr · ERNEST L MOORE · GERALD J L
· ESTILL R McINTOSH · LESLIE H SABO Jr · PHILLIP N SC
H · DONALD W SMITH · GARY A TURNBULL · LESLIE JO
CHARLESWORTH Jr · WILLARD D O'BRIEN · RAYMOND
GLEMAN · BRYAN T KNIGHT · DAVID M KOZAK · ALBERT
· · ROBERT L O'CONNOR · JAMES R OLSON · JERRY W
ULBEE · DANIEL J VAUGHAN · JOHN A VERNO · MORG
ADAMS Jr · GLENN A ADAMS · JAMES V B

Moving Wall: Leslie Sabo's name is visible on Panel 10W of the Moving Wall, the one-half size
replica of the National Vietnam War Memorial, during its July 2009 stop in Ellwood City.
(Photo by the author)

Leslie Sabo's Medal of Honor lists
his rank as specialist, as does his
Medal of Honor citation. While
that was his correct rank when he
performed the acts of valor that
earned him the nation's highest
military honor, Sabo was
posthumously promoted to
sergeant. (Photo by the author)

This stone, provided by the Army, marks Leslie Sabo's grave
at Holy Redeemer Cemetery in North Sewickley Township,
just outside Ellwood City. (Photo by the author)

"We just enjoyed spending time together. We didn't care what we did," Rose said. "That was my blissful month."

But for that entire month, the clock was running on Rose's bliss. And when October ended, so did their time together. After the 30-day leave Leslie's orders called for him to report for deployment to Vietnam. Leslie's parents drove him to the airport in Pittsburgh for a flight to San Francisco. And from there, to the jungle and war.

"I stayed home and cried that whole day," she said.

Then she packed up, physically and psychologically, from her one month as a housewife and returned to her parents' home. The following day, Rose went for a walk. When she returned, her parents said Leslie had called from San Francisco just before his plane left for the Far East. As it would turn out, she had missed the last chance to hear her husband's voice. "I missed his phone call," she said. "To this day, I can't forgive myself for that."

———

Rose, like everyone else connected to the soldiers in Bravo Company, worried for their loved ones in the combat zone. But even with nightly news reports bringing the war into their living rooms – a situation unprecedented in history – few of the people back home knew the exact danger those troopers faced. Since hitting Hill 474 in mid-January, the unit had tangled with the enemy almost every day – "Kid Rick" Brown said he had lost count of the firefights he had been involved in. In one of those skirmishes, on April 8, Leslie Sabo advanced into enemy fire to provide covering fire so his wounded comrades could withdraw and even bandaged up one of their head wounds. Of the first ten soldiers in the column that day, nine were wounded.

"I started thinking I was a lightning rod," said Rick Clanton, the only man in that lead column on April 8 to escape unscathed.

The Army, as a matter of routine, moved to take advantage of the frayed nerves of soldiers who had experienced too many close calls. Recruiters would report to combat units and offer a deal to combat-weary soldiers – sign on for an additional four or six years in the Army and be transferred out of combat to join the REMF ranks. Some soldiers accepted the offer, including one Bravo Company soldier who was almost killed when a North Vietnamese mortar exploded a few feet from his foxhole.

"The guy was scared to death," said Ben Currin. "He re-upped for six years and went to clerk school."

Lawrence Neil DeBoer, whose tour had been scheduled to end on May 21, made the opposite arrangement – he took an extension of his combat tour in order to get an early discharge. The typical draftee's Army two-year hitch started with six months basic and advanced infantry training, followed by the one-year combat tour, and a final six months, mostly on stateside "busy work." Some of the servicemen who fought for their lives in the Tet Offensive finished their combat tours in time to supplement the Chicago police during the 1968 Democratic National Convention during anti-war protests that erupted into violence. DeBoer, a Grand Rapids, Michigan, native who had been working on his master's degree in microbiology at Western Michigan University when he was drafted, was due for discharge near the end of December. He received an early release that would allow him to resume studies in the fall semester at the price of extending his combat tour. DeBoer's focus wasn't entirely on the enemy – his field pack often included textbooks. He was among several soldiers assigned to Bravo Company as replacements for troopers wounded or killed, and for those who had made it to their own DEROS.

Sergeant Thomas Merriman had been reassigned to Bravo Company at about the same time, in late March or early April. He had initially been assigned to the 1st Infantry Division, the legendary Big Red One, which was redeployed back to the United States as part of the troop drawdown. In 1971, it would be the Screaming Eagles' turn. Those soldiers with significant time remaining were redistributed to other units. Merriman, 21, was sent to Bravo Company. A native of Paulding, Ohio, a small town south of Toledo, he had been drafted in 1969 while working for Oakwood Oil Company. During his time in the 1st Infantry Division, Merriman earned the Bronze Star for combat valor and the Purple Heart after being wounded.

James DeBrew, of Whitakers, North Carolina, near the Virginia state line, had been added as a replacement in Bravo Company along with DeBoer a month earlier. The 20-year-old arrived in early March and was only one month into his tour as of late April.

Another new arrival, Ernest Moore, of Grand Haven, Michigan, also was only a few weeks from the end of his tour. Moore's wife, Candace, was in Grand Haven, Michigan, not far from his home of Spring Lake, on the state's western shore. That part of the state is known for its sand dunes and the paper mills in and around Muskegon, where Moore was born. Moore was devoted not just to his wife, but also to being a gearhead. Before being drafted in early 1969, Moore, 21, spent much of his downtime tinkering with and racing his red 1962 Chevrolet Impala.[1]

After chasing the enemy, first on Hill 474, then in the Crow's Foot, Bravo Company might have expected a well-deserved rest. Instead, President Richard Nixon undertook the most controversial action in the most controversial war in US history – a move that would ultimately press the luck of everyone in Bravo Company.

CHAPTER 12

Today I wrote my wife, parents and now my brother and sister. First I'd like to thank you for the Valentine's cards. I really like the one George sent me. In the other two letters I wrote all about us going to the beach to swim in the S. China Sea, drink cold beer and sodas, playing poker and having a lot of fun and relaxation. ... They even provided some of the other kind of relief but I still am true to my wife although I must admit it gets a little tough out here but I think I can hold out until Hawaii. We had a lot of fun at the beach, I almost forgot where I was for a little while. We had a good poker game too, tell George I am getting really good at it. What I win in poker, I lose shooting craps. How are the boys doing I hope they're all doing fine and doing good in school. I liked their Valentine's card very much and I hope they enjoyed their Valentines. Tell Louise I received her letter and it was very nice of her to write me. I'll try to write her, but sometimes it's hard for me to find the time. Tell Louise, Frank and their kids I said hi and I am doing very well.

Letter from Leslie Sabo to George and Olga
Dated February 22, 1970[1]

Almost without exception, every North Vietnamese success in its four-decade-long war against the western powers was a victory not of tactics, firepower, or unit cohesion, but of logistics. At Dien Bien Phu in 1954, French General Henri Navarre calculated that Giap, the Viet Minh general, would not be able to move and supply enough troops and artillery pieces to threaten his garrison, and that even if the North Vietnamese could surround the base, he would be able to supply his soldiers by air. Navarre was proven wrong on both counts and France was evicted from Southeast Asia as a consequence. In a country where the roads were few and in poor state of repair, Giap established a network of porters to supply his soldiers, often primarily by foot, which proved barely efficient enough to keep them fed and armed – the North Vietnamese Army needed four times as many porters as soldiers. Over great distances, the porters would eat almost all of the food they carried.[2]

But that primitive system proved to be sufficient for winning a modern war, especially after the North Vietnamese opened business on the Ho Chi Minh Trail, which ran about 1,000 miles from North Vietnam's border with Laos into Cambodia and back into South Vietnam. The trail traced its origins back decades, to a footpath that ran the ridgeline of the mountains that separated the three countries from north to south.[3]

From the time US advisors first arrived in Vietnam during the Eisenhower administration, the Viet Cong insurgents and North Vietnamese Army used trails in Laos and Cambodia along the western border of Vietnam. Those paths were used most famously to move men and supplies prior to the Tet Offensive in January of 1968. But the North Vietnamese used those trails with impunity because they knew the Americans had a policy that prohibited them from officially entering either country. By early 1970, in the view of President Richard Nixon, Hanoi was displaying so little respect for Cambodia's neutrality that the country was effectively a base for the North Vietnamese. As early as 1964, the Joint Chiefs of Staff had urged President John Kennedy, and his successor,

Lyndon Johnson, to invade Cambodia and Laos to disrupt those supply and troop routes.[4]

MACV knew the North Vietnamese were using the path, but couldn't do much about it. The United States' rules of engagement, which prevented troops from crossing South Vietnam's western border, allowed the Communists to use Cambodia and Laos as a refuge and strike with impunity before retreating to the relative safety of their facilities in nominally neutral nations. With much of the trail under double- and triple-canopy jungle, it was invisible to American fliers from the air. Even when aerial bombings managed to strike the trail and do significant damage, access would be restored within days, and sometimes hours.

In this, the North Vietnamese primitive logistics system – even on the Ho Chi Minh Trail, many supplies moved on foot or bicycle – proved an advantage against the most technologically advanced, well-armed, and well-trained force in the history of warfare. The Communists didn't have to maintain a highway for heavy trucks or a field for aerial supply flights, only a trail sufficient to bear ox-drawn carts, which transported the Ho Chi Minh Trail's heaviest loads.

Prince Norodom Sihanouk, Cambodia's ruler, had publicly balanced both US and North Vietnamese interests. In fact, though, Sihanouk's sympathies were with the North Vietnamese, and he made no effort to stop them from using his country as a staging ground for the war against South Vietnam and the United States. Sihanouk, who played a major role in Cambodian politics for more than 60 years from the 1940s to the 2000s, had a passion, and some apparent talent, for the arts. He was an accomplished musician with multiple instruments, and a busy filmmaker. His movie *Spellbound Wood* was included at the 1967 Moscow International Film Festival. Like the Sundance Film Festival in the United States, Moscow's is a juried festival, which means Sihanouk's inclusion indicates his work had some artistic merit, at least for the Russian judges.[5]

A second Sihanouk-produced movie, *Shadow over Angkor*, that was accepted to the Moscow International Film Festival two years later, would prove more prescient. The movie's plot focused on a US-backed coup against the leader of Cambodia – which, at the time, was the filmmaker himself.[6]

Elements of the plot from *Shadow over Angkor* came to life in March of 1970, when pro-Western Prime Minister Lon Nol led a coup while Sihanouk was away in France. Nol ousted the flamboyant leader and closed North Vietnamese access to the port at Sihanoukville, which deprived it of sea access in the south. Nol then prohibited the North Vietnamese from using the Ho Chi Minh Trail, even though he lacked the firepower to back up his demand. Instead, the North Vietnamese launched an invasion of Cambodia and threatened to smash the weaker, untested Cambodian Army.

The long-term effects of Nol's coup would be an eventual takeover of Cambodia by the communist Khmer Rouge, but the immediate effect would be to give US President Richard Nixon, who had been in office for all of one year, a rationale to do what the country's military leadership had recommended for half a decade – invade Cambodia. Nominally, the attack was to have been for Cambodia's defense, but the actual objective was to deal a killing blow to the North Vietnamese logistical network. About 15,000 men participated in the assault.

Under increasing pressure from people who wanted Nixon to make good on his 1968 campaign promise of a withdrawal from Vietnam, the United States had begun decreasing its troop strength in the country. But on April 30, a Thursday, Nixon announced what amounted to an escalation of the war – an incursion into Cambodia, a nation previously deemed off limits, in what MACV dubbed Operation *Binh Tay*.[7]

Between Nol's overthrow of Sihanouk and *Binh Tay*'s May 5 D-Day, the 4th Division found itself in a scramble to develop logistics and intelligence on the incursion area – which hadn't been on the standard maps US military personnel used during the war up to that point. Lieutenant John Greene, leader of Bravo Company's 1st Platoon, said he didn't get maps of his operation area until a few days after the insertion.[8]

On April 27, with the invasion of Cambodia only days away, a helicopter that carried the entire command staff for the 3rd Battalion, 12th Regiment of the 4th Infantry Division, took off from an airfield in Pleiku to scout landing zones for its part of the assault into Cambodia. Pleiku, about 50 miles from the Cambodian border, was one of the westernmost heliports safely controlled by the United States or South Vietnamese. It also was the region's largest US-friendly base.

As the helicopter flew over the North Vietnamese-held territory west of Pleiku, a ground battery took aim on the chopper and brought it down. The crash killed battalion commander Lieutenant Colonel Gerald McKay, operations officer Major James Russ, the battalion's ranking non-commissioned officer Sergeant Major James Palmer, and artillery officers Captain Roy Gray and Captain Carl Fisher. Also killed were three of the four crewmen, pilot Chief Warrant Officer Robert Gardner, co-pilot Warrant Officer Stanley Miller Jr., and crew chief Specialist 5 (equivalent to a sergeant) George Tom. The sole survivor was Specialist 4 (equivalent to a corporal) Gary Fields, who leapt from the helicopter from a height of about 200 feet when the crash became inevitable. Fields landed in a rice paddy and was badly wounded, but lived.[9]

The destruction of that helicopter was the final twist of fate that sent Bravo Company to its destiny in Cambodia. At that point in the war, the 4th Infantry Division was a relatively inexperienced unit. Army brass decided not to compound that handicap by sending in an inexperienced battalion with an entirely new command staff. The 506th Infantry Regiment's 3rd Battalion, including Bravo Company, was selected not just to replace the 12th Regiment's 3rd Battalion, but to be lead element for its area of operation. The Currahees were among the most battle-hardened troops in Vietnam and Jaggers, the battalion commander, was in his second Vietnam tour. He not only understood air assault warfare, he had helped to develop some of its principles as an advisor on the next generation of assault helicopters.

Bravo Company got the word in early May, while Greene's 1st Platoon had a North Vietnamese unit "found" and "fixed," and were in the process of "finishing." Greene was ordered to break off the attack, which convinced him that something big was up. American bombers had been intensifying air raids along the Ho Chi Minh Trail in Cambodia and Laos since the beginning of April. Even though nobody told them, Bravo Company knew this assault would be unlike any of their previous actions. The first US troops began landing in Cambodia on May 1, and the US media were reporting on the incursion. Considering the urgency with which Bravo Company was pulled off the line, the Currahees reasoned, correctly, that they would soon cross the border themselves.

"We put two and two together and we sort of knew where we were going," Greene said.

Fourth Infantry Division's command was already familiar with the 3rd Battalion, 506th Infantry Regiment, having served alongside the airborne battalion earlier in the year on Hill 474 during Operation *Washington Green* in Binh Dinh province. By May of 1970, the company – including the soldiers who had arrived as raw recruits in October, November, and December of the previous year – were battle tested. Even though many of the men in Bravo Company had been in country for only about six months, it had been an eventful half-year.

As a result, the 3rd Battalion, 506th Regiment was among thousands of soldiers participating in Operation *Binh Tay*, loosely translated as "Tame The West." While most of the 101st Airborne Division was still stationed around Khe Sanh near the border between North and South Vietnam, the Currahees had been "op-conned" – military jargon for "operational control" – to the 4th Infantry Division.

Those circumstances were fitting with a characterization by Bravo Company trooper Richard Rios, of the 506th as being the "bastard" regiment. Even today, the 506th is known as the "Currahees," a nickname that comes from the name of a small mountain near the now-closed Camp Toccoa, which served as a training outpost when the regiment was founded. But the name has a second meaning. The Native American word "Currahee" is translated as "We stand alone."

During its previous four months in Vietnam, Bravo Company had maneuvered not as a company, but in platoon strength. That would change for the incursion, when the company would operate as a single entity for the only time in the late-1969 arrivals' entire combat tour. Like most combat units in Vietnam, Bravo Company was understrength when it went into the field. The company's assigned strength was 143 troopers, historically typical. At any time, a company could be missing soldiers who were on their two-week rest-and-relaxation leave, and a portion of each company would be assigned to fire support bases for security or supply duties. For *Binh Tay*, most of those support soldiers who had been held out of combat were moved back into operations, to give each company something close to maximum manpower, albeit at the cost of having soldiers who were inexperienced and possibly out of condition for the rigors of infantry operations. Companies typically went into action with about 80 to 100 soldiers, about two-thirds of their assigned strength. As a result, the Currahees would rarely see their counterparts from other platoons, even within their own company.

When the Americans entered Cambodia, the 506th Regiment's 3rd Battalion would join two 4th Infantry Division battalions – 3rd Battalion, 8th Regiment and 1st Battalion, 14th Regiment – in the incursion task force's 1st Brigade, which would land in the northernmost area of operation. During the incursion, Bravo Company's 3rd Battalion would operate out of Fire Support Base Currahee, well within the Cambodian border. Currahee would be one of three 1st Brigade fire support bases, which were a source of artillery and logistical support, with supply and ammunition caches. Infantry troops would radiate outward from fire support bases and call back to the base for indirect fire support from its 105- and 155mm artillery weapons if they ran into an overwhelming enemy force. Preparations for the operation included new communication codes for radio telephone operators because commanders expected that the enemy force would include Americans who defected to the other side.[10]

In the US Army, a combat company would have around 140 to 150 soldiers, with a commanding officer (usually a captain), an executive officer (a first lieutenant), and three platoon leaders, often first or second lieutenants. In Vietnam, though, some companies lacked an executive officer, and those that did retain one usually kept him back at the fire support base handling paperwork and logistics, no small consideration with the transportation by helicopter of manpower and supplies into the field, and manpower, wounded and well, back to the fire support base. During at least part of its 1970 tour, Bravo Company did not have an executive officer, although some of their platoons sometimes had two assigned officers.

An Army company's ranking enlisted man is typically a first sergeant – followed by sergeant first class, each platoon's top enlisted man. Platoons would have an approved strength of around 40 soldiers. Staff sergeants usually led a squad, with a listed strength of about 12 soldiers – the number typically carried into combat by one helicopter. A sergeant generally leads a team of around three or four soldiers. Based on that rank structure, Bravo Company's non-commissioned officer roster would have had a first sergeant, three sergeants first class, nine or ten staff sergeants, and more than 25 sergeants.

In fact, according to a company roster from July of 1970, Bravo had one first sergeant, one sergeant first class, seven staff sergeants, and 23 sergeants. That meant soldiers like Staff Sergeant Mike DiLeo were pressed into duty as platoon sergeants, and sergeants like Richard Rogers into the post of squad leaders. The resulting backfill meant that some of Bravo's specialists – including Ben Currin, Roger Cope, and Leslie Sabo, all of whom were among the December 1969 new arrivals – would become team leaders. That wasn't uncommon in Vietnam, where non-commissioned officers were often enlisted men or draftees on their second combat tour after completing the Army's non-commissioned officer school back in the US.

Each of Bravo Company's three platoons had a Vietnamese "Kit Carson" scout, named for the famed military leader in the pre-Civil War American West. The real-life Kit Carson fought against and alongside Americans, Native American Indians, and Mexicans, and married two American Indian women. Whether deliberate or accidental, there was a distinct irony in evoking Kit Carson's name for the Vietnamese scouts. Just as Carson himself shifted his loyalty back and forth across multiple factions, most of Vietnam's Kit Carson scouts were former Viet Cong or North Vietnamese Army soldiers who had been taken prisoner and turned to the American side. The Kit Carson scouts would serve as interpreters and provide information about the terrain and jungle.[11]

On rare occasions the Kit Carson scouts could be undependable. In at least one instance, a Bravo Company scout disappeared just before his platoon was ambushed. Jim Waybright, who led Bravo Company during its period of heaviest combat, said the scouts – just like the South Vietnamese Army – were sometimes absent in times of trouble. But usually the scouts worked well with their American allies.

Less than 24 hours before D-Day for Operation *Binh Tay*, the Currahees' Kit Carson scouts informed commanders en masse that they would not be accompanying the Americans into Cambodia on the grounds that they weren't being paid to perform interpreting duties outside South Vietnam.

"The scouts were generally loyal and brave allies," said Bravo Company soldier Joe Hanks. "But if they were so frightened to go into Cambodia, we figured we were in for some bad times."[12]

Like Hanks, the rest of Bravo Company bore no illusions about the operation's impending danger. They were heading into uncharted ground, literally and figuratively, where the enemy had worked for five years to build a jungle fortress, where it stored its supplies and its ordnance, and based much of its manpower. Unlike the daily jungle patrols, the Currahees were heading into Cambodia wondering when – not if – they would encounter the enemy. A couple of Bravo Company troopers also wondered whether they had exhausted the good fortune that had kept them alive through four full months of heavy action, and two of them refused to accompany their comrades in Cambodia. There's an old Army saying, "The Army can't make you do anything. They can just make you wish you had." One of the two dissenters did wish he had gone, and joined Bravo Company a day after its initial landing in Cambodia. The other continued in his refusal to enter Cambodia, Waybright's entreaties notwithstanding, and was court-martialed.

"I told him, 'You're screwing up the rest of your life,'" Waybright said, but to no avail.

After Bravo Company was pulled out of the Crow's Foot, the troops were transported by trucks to Pleiku, site of the Central Highlands' largest base and capital of Pleiku province. The US had built a military airfield and maintained a base in the city until 1969, when the Nixon-initiated policy of Vietnamization enabled a handover of the facility to South Vietnam. Bravo Company slept outdoors – which the soldiers were somewhat accustomed to in the first place – because there was no place for them in the barracks, and spent the layover accumulating anti-tank weapons because they heard reports that the North Vietnamese had armored vehicles on the Ho Chi Minh Trail. Pleiku, along with Plei D'Jereng, a former special forces training facility, were used as staging areas for the push into Cambodia.

The soldiers also got as much rest as possible and they would need it. Their supply loads would double, with additional ammunition, food, and water. Additionally, every platoon would be packing mortars, which would pose an additional burden as they humped through Cambodia. During operations in Vietnam, the 81mm mortars were often left behind, either with a reserve force, or at the firebases and landing zones.[13] Each member of each platoon would take turns carrying parts of the weapon, which consisted of three elements weighing from 30 to 45 pounds each.

In response to Nixon's decision to expand a war that he had pledged to de-escalate, war opponents on college campuses throughout the nation howled in protest. And few students howled louder than those at Kent State University in Ohio. On May 2, protesters burned down Kent State's ROTC building, which prompted Governor James Rhodes to order the Ohio National Guard to restore order on the Kent State campus. The following Monday, May 4, under circumstances that still aren't completely clear, the guardsmen opened fire on the students, killing four and wounding nine. The weekend of protests and tragedy was triggered by the US march into Cambodia, even as Leslie Sabo and the rest of the 506th Infantry Regiment crossed Vietnam's western frontier.

CHAPTER 13

Roe wrote to me how well you are getting along and how much she likes you. She also wrote me about her starting to smoke so I wrote and told [her] that she's old enough to think and act for herself and to do what she thinks is right for her. Well anyway she wrote me another letter, before I think, she received mine that she quit for good, which makes me very proud of her also for quitting that mill and finding a new job makes me very, very happy, I really couldn't stand having her work there but I never wanted to say anything since that's all there was, so having her go out and get that job at the newsstand is really great. How is everything with you at your job. I'm really glad that you found such a good job. Well, I must finish for now. Say hi to everyone for me.

Letter from Leslie Sabo to George and Olga
Dated February 22, 1970

While Elisabeth Sabo might not have known about the 101st Airborne Division's historical status as a beyond-the-tip-of-the-spear unit, she was aware that her son was facing combat – and was aware of exactly what that meant, having seen the devastation of her homeland during World War II.

"She said, 'We have to do something to get Leslie out of the front lines,'" Olga Sabo, George Sabo's wife, remembered of her mother-in-law.

Perhaps no one benefited from Leslie Sabo's generous spirit more than his mother. When George, Leslie's older brother, was born, he joined a family that had lost another son in infancy and was trying to survive in Hungary, just as it fell under the grip of Nazism. By the time Leslie came into the world in 1948, the family had achieved some degree of normalcy in Austria and was considering emigration to the west to stay out of the Soviets' reach. Then, George married and set up his own household shortly after graduating from high school in 1961. By the older brother's own estimation, Elisabeth and Leslie forged a close relationship during the next five years until Leslie enrolled in Youngstown State University. And Leslie's unselfish nature must have been a special point of pride to his mother.

But Elisabeth wasn't the only person who was feeling Leslie's absence. As April drained away, he continued to write letters nearly every day to Rose and both of them anticipated Leslie's two-week rest-and-relaxation furlough, scheduled for that summer. As with many other married soldiers, they planned to spend that time together in Hawaii. Rose said Leslie wanted his furlough to be toward the end of his combat tour, which was scheduled to end in November.

"He said, 'That way I won't have that much time to go when I get back.'"

While Leslie Sabo's loved ones fretted about his well-being, they were part of a home front that was becoming increasingly hostile to the war he was fighting. The Tet Offensive and massacre of Vietnamese civilians by American troops at My Lai within the span of a few months in 1968 combined to erode support for the action in Vietnam. Even though the North Vietnamese achieved exactly none of their tactical objectives in Tet, and the enemy's battle deaths outnumbered the US killed by a ratio of more than 20 to 1, the clash served as an indication that the United States was much further from final victory than Americans had been led to believe.[1]

When news of the My Lai atrocity broke in April of 1970, it left a blot on the military's reputation. Even while her husband was in the combat zone, Rose Sabo Brown remembers hearing the slurs directed at the soldiers.

"It bothered me when [people] called them baby killers," she said.

But if the war was unpopular on college campuses, the disapproval was even more pronounced around the Sabo family's dinner table, where Elisabeth was frantically trying to get her son out of harm's way. At Elisabeth's urging, Olga contacted the US Department of Defense to see how they could get Leslie transferred to a non-combat – or even a stateside – post. Improbably enough, staff at the Pentagon told Olga such a thing was possible. After the intervening 40 years, Olga said she couldn't remember the Army's possible justification for moving Leslie out of the front lines, but she knew that Leslie had to apply for the reassignment himself. And by the time Olga and Elisabeth obtained that information, it was already too late for them to free her son from his military commitment.

The battalion briefing on May 3 confirmed what Waybright and the rest of Bravo Company already suspected. They were headed into Cambodia, in a region that was reasonably flat with few trees. Along the ridges, there were some single-canopy jungles, comparable to the wooded areas in and around Ellwood City where Leslie Sabo played as a youth. By the prior experience of Bravo Company, which had fought in double- and triple-canopy jungles inhabited by tigers and monkeys, western Pennsylvania forests qualified as light vegetation. The tallest of those ridges would have been just under 1,100 feet in altitude, with the lowest point in the regiment's attack area being around 300 feet.[2]

They landed along the Se San River in Cambodia's Rotanah Kiri province. Then, as now, the river ran through one of the most isolated, impoverished regions of Cambodia tucked up against the nation's northeastern boundary, where Vietnam, Cambodia, and Laos meet. The Se San River originates in the mountains that divide Vietnam and Laos. From there, it runs south to form a small portion of the border between Vietnam and Rotanah Kiri province around the 14th Parallel before flowing into Cambodia. Bravo Company would launch its assault just west of the river border, about 35 miles northeast of Lumphat, the provincial capital.

North Vietnamese activity along the Ho Chi Minh Trail and US bombings – particularly in the run-up to the incursion – had driven much of the populace out of the Se San region, not that the area was densely populated to begin with. Bravo Company's invasion area was dotted with a few small villages, with huts on stilts as a precaution against monsoon-swollen rivers and streams. The farmers who lived in those villages practiced a form of crop rotation known as "slash and burn," where they would clear a field and use it for a number of years until the soil became depleted. Then, they would move onto a new area and clear it for the process to start again.[3]

The Se San River flows westward to the city of Stoeng Treng, where it meets the larger Mekong River, which runs through Phnom Penh, Cambodia's capital, then back into Vietnam down through the Mekong Delta into the South China Sea. Commanders in the 4th Division selected the 506th's 3rd Battalion to spearhead its wing of the operation, and, on the morning of May 5, the Currahees boarded helicopters at Camp Holloway in Pleiku. Even though Pleiku was one of the westernmost secure airfields in that region, it was still more than 50 miles from the landing zone, which meant that the choppers had just enough fuel to fly in, make the drop, and return. Getting the entire 3rd Regiment of the 506th to its landing zones would require 60 helicopters.

US Air Force bombers had flown dozens of sorties into Cambodia every day for a month leading up to the assault. But the bombs they dropped had little effect on North Vietnamese troops and their facilities concealed beneath jungle canopies.

"Each morning, the B-52s would fly in from the Philippines and Okinawa and we could feel the earth shake," Waybright said. "We couldn't see the planes, we couldn't see the bombs, but we could feel things shake."[4]

The helicopter landings were met with stiff resistance. On D-Day, heavy ground fire forced the Currahees to employ an alternative landing zone. Lieutenant Colonel Joseph Jaggers earned the second Silver Star of his command tour when he used his own helicopter to draw fire in an attempt to determine whether a landing zone was safe. In the manner of George Washington, renowned for changing horses when previous mounts were shot from under him, Jaggers had to adopt a second helicopter after his first sustained severe damage.[5]

In spite of their commander's valor, the Currahees were unable to secure a landing zone after trying the primary location and several alternatives. So, low on fuel, the helicopter fleet retreated to Plei D'Jereng, about halfway between Pleiku and the Cambodian border, for refueling before another attempt. Around 1pm, on the helicopters' second run, the battalion's Alpha Company secured a landing zone in a clearing – to be named Fire Support Base Currahee – about twice the size of a football field after softening up the perimeter with heavy fire from gunships. Fire Support Base Currahee was about 9 miles west of the Vietnamese border near the Stoeng Ta Pok River. Bravo Company went in with the second wave.[6]

As the choppers roared in, Sergeant "Little John" Roethlisberger, a squad leader in 3rd Platoon, regarded the men in his helicopter. He turned to Allen McCulty, armed with an M-79 grenade launcher and about to face combat for the first time and yelled, "Do you know how to use that thing, Cherry?"

After McCulty answered in the affirmative, Roethlisberger yelled back, "I sure hope so!"[7]

The entire 3rd Battalion was established at Firebase Currahee, about 30 miles west of Plei D'Jereng and about 60 miles west of Pleiku, by mid-afternoon. But plans called for the unit to be on the ground hours earlier and the impending arrival of a storm – monsoon season was just getting started – meant no other US forces would land in Cambodia on D-Day. However, the Currahees did earn a historical distinction on May 5. Their successful insertion into

Cambodia marked the first time an entire battalion was taken into enemy territory by helicopter.[8]

For five years, the North Vietnamese Army had been able to stage its war from along the Ho Chi Minh Trail running through Laos and Cambodia at American and South Vietnamese strongholds. That impunity ended quickly, when Bravo Company's 1st Platoon captured a weapon and radio after encountering two enemy soldiers carrying supplies along the trail on bicycles. The use of bicycles to transport supplies on the Ho Chi Minh Trail is well known, but it conveys an inaccurate image of a man pedaling along a mountain path with hundreds of pounds of supplies on his back. In fact, the Ho Chi Minh Trail bicycles were modified slightly to carry loads and for two-man teams to push the bicycles using handles attached to the two-wheeler.[9]

The Americans killed one of the North Vietnamese soldiers, wounded the other, and captured a radio and other supplies. That was the exception though. Lieutenant John Greene said Bravo Company's orders were to destroy supplies that the North Vietnamese had painstakingly moved into more than a dozen staging areas along the Ho Chi Minh Trail and these staging areas as opposed to individual enemy combatants were to be the primary focus. Almost immediately after getting down to work, the Americans realized just what a complicated task it would have been to "cut" the Ho Chi Minh Trail by aerial bombing – and just how intricate the path network actually was. In most areas where the Currahees and 4th Division soldiers found footpaths, they were "braided," with individual trails weaving back and forth through one another sometimes miles apart and as little as just under 1 mile between trail junctions. In linear measure, the route was only about 1,000 miles long. However, the Ho Chi Minh Trail wasn't a single trail, but a labyrinth of nearly 10,000 miles in intersecting, "braided" paths. The arrangement allowed the flow of supplies to continue even if the US aerial bombing managed to make a lucky strike and destroy a section of trail, which was all but concealed in most places beneath a thick jungle canopy. If one segment were rendered impassable, the North Vietnamese would merely move traffic to another segment. The enemy built bridges, strong enough to carry an ox cart and load of a half ton, largely out of items found in the jungle like bamboo and vines.[10]

In terms of supplies, Bravo Company found the early hunting rather fruitless, but they had no shortage of encounters with the enemy. On the three consecutive days after the May 5 landings, the company swapped lead with North Vietnamese soldiers, including a firefight on May 7 involving Bravo Company's 2nd Platoon, including Sabo. During the ensuing firefight, First Lieutenant Lawrence Neff, leader of 2nd Platoon, and Ray D'Angelo, Neff's radio telephone operator, were wounded and four North Vietnamese were killed. Although D'Angelo was seriously wounded, it could have been far worse. An armor-piercing bullet had gone into his hip and came out his backside, tearing a furrow in the soldier's backside all the way through. Once hit, D'Angelo scurried behind a tree and hid until the firefight was over and a helicopter could take him and Neff to hospital facilities.

"If it had been an M-16, I'd have bled to death," he said. "I laid out behind a tree for an hour or two before a helicopter could take me out."

D'Angelo's war was over, but his ordeal was only beginning. As he was being flown off the battlefield, hidden North Vietnamese soldiers fired on the Huey medevac. D'Angelo could hear enemy rounds "pinging" off the chopper's body, and thought that the death he had narrowly avoided on the ground would catch up with him in the air, but his pilot managed to navigate the danger and return to a base hospital, which was promptly hit by a North Vietnamese mortar attack. A couple of soldiers piled a mattress on top of D'Angelo, where he languished for about another hour until the attack ended.

At the other end of D'Angelo's trip – the Army hospital at Cam Ranh Bay – his 13-inch-long gaping wound was packed with gauze and he was sedated. He remained in the hospital for a few days before he was transferred to an Air Force treatment facility.

The gauze packing was supposed to have been replaced every few hours, but doctors at the Air Force hospital realized, much to their disgust and to D'Angelo's eventual horror – that no one had performed that task. As a result, the soldier's flesh had grown into, around, and through his bandages. The Air Force doctor remedied that situation the hard way, by physically tearing the gauze out of D'Angelo's perforated cheek. It began when the doctor grabbed a pair of forceps, got a good grip on the gauze, and pulled it out of the wound.

"You know how they have that one to ten pain scale?" he said, years later, referring to the standard used by medical professionals to gauge physical discomfort. "That's wrong, though. There is no limit to the amount of pain you can have."

D'Angelo nearly passed out from the agony, in combination with the weakness stemming from his own wound. But after much struggling by the doctor, and much screaming by D'Angelo, the gauze came free, along with a sizeable chunk of his gluteus.

As it did, the doctor said, "That's one. Fourteen more to go."

Painful though it was, that injury to D'Angelo's backside on May 6 might have saved his life. With D'Angelo and Neff off the battlefield, Bravo Company was ambushed again the next day. After a short firefight, both sides broke off the assault, with no American casualties. During skirmishes on May 6 and 7, the Currahees killed eight North Vietnamese and captured one. Delta Company discovered and destroyed a large collection of food supplies, with an estimated 30 pigs, 50 chickens, and more than 500 tonnes of rice.

As Bravo Company was preparing to set up its defensive perimeter on May 9, it picked up signs of a large enemy outpost. Greene said he could see a large hut – called a hooch in GI parlance – probably one of many in a North Vietnamese facility about a half mile from the Americans' position. A large clearing, about 300 yards long, separated Bravo Company from the enemy facility. Waybright contacted battalion command back at Fire Support Base Currahee with news of the discovery and a request for supplies, especially desperately needed ammunition.

Waybright's request was met with battalion command's order for an immediate "kick-out" supply drop and a promise for a full supply delivery the following morning. The kick-out drop, being exactly what it sounds like – crates of supplies ejected from a helicopter as it hovered over the American soldiers – attracted fire from an area near the hooch prior to a mass evacuation by the North Vietnamese.[11] As the North Vietnamese set off, it was Bravo Company's turn to hear the enemy's operations. The sounds of large-group movement and barking dogs broke the twilight.

"You could hear them moving through the jungle," Greene said. "There were a whole lot of people, hundreds of them, in the jungle."

Bravo Company's orders for the next morning were to overrun the enemy facility and destroy any supplies found within. In the meantime, though, there was the small matter of a celebration for "Kid Rick" Brown's 19th birthday. A year earlier, he had been a standout high school athlete in Columbia Station who celebrated with shouts and congratulations upon the arrival of adulthood and looked forward to prom and graduation. On the Saturday night that he turned 19, Brown marked the occasion in whispers alongside comrades who shared in his deadly every-day combat grind, deep in enemy territory. Brown's boonie brothers pooled their C-rations to give him a pound cake with a scrounged candle. As a birthday gift, Brown received another delicacy, a fruit cocktail. Because the enemy could have been anywhere – in fact, might have been watching them – and Bravo Company was on a silence order, Brown's chorus of "Happy Birthday" was a hushed one. Brown then posed for a couple of pictures, taken with his own camera – including one where he is holding a Chinese-manufactured weapon – in what he believes are the only photographs Bravo Company took in Cambodia.

"We were too busy surviving to take pics," he quipped.

The following day, "surviving" would become considerably more difficult.

CHAPTER 14

It has been a little while since I've written so I thought I'd drop you a few lines. I heard you bought another car, from what Roe wrote it sounds real sharp. ... I am looking forward to driving it. How is everyone at home? I hope you and the boys are all fine. Is George having any difficulty with all those courses he took at school. I certainly do admire him for being able to do it. I'm still in the same area I've been the last two months. It looked like we were going to leave but now they started something new so we'll be here for I don't know how long. I was hoping for a change to help my 5 and 6th months go by a little faster. In three days, I'll be starting my 5th month. They say these are the longest months but I hope it won't hold true in my case. It looks like we won't be going back to the beach again unless they have a change of heart but we were lucky to get that one day. Well there isn't much more for me to write about. I hope you and especially the boys have a Happy Easter. Which I can hardly wait for because I'll be that much shorter.

Letter from Leslie Sabo to George and Olga
Dated March 10, 1970

As dawn broke on May 10 – Mother's Day back in "the world" – the US soldiers stirred from a mostly sleepless night marked by an attempt to breech the Currahees' defenses. Responding fire from the sentries turned away the enemy probe. While patrols the following morning failed to turn up the intruder's body, they did find evidence – in the form of a blood trail – that he was wounded by fire from the Americans.

But that didn't do anything to lessen the sense of foreboding in Bravo Company's perimeter. A North Vietnamese force – probably one much larger than their own – was in the jungle not far away, so Bravo Company began May 10 with each man preparing for battle in his own way. Leslie Sabo tied a maroon bandanna around his head and replaced his horn-rimmed "birth control" prescription eyeglasses with a set of dark sunglasses before heading off into the jungle. Among the soldiers of Bravo Company, 506th Infantry Regiment, Sabo stood out for his battle rattle. Sabo, honoring ancient warriors' traditions, had a ritual to follow when he expected to see combat.[1]

"Les was a funny guy and he enjoyed people. He was very fond of his squad mates and platoon mates, but Les was a soldier," said Richard Rios. "The easiest description I can give of him – he was fun and crazy until the time hit when he needed to be a soldier and he became a soldier."[2]

Sabo's 2nd Platoon and 3rd Platoon remained in the nighttime perimeter as the sun rose, as Greene's 1st Platoon advanced to the outpost and found it deserted, but extensive, with dozens of buildings and hundreds of pigs, chickens, and dogs. After being apprised of 1st Platoon's findings, Lieutenant Colonel Jaggers ordered the facility's destruction. Waybright departed the nighttime perimeter just after 9am with 2nd and 3rd Platoons on their mission. Greene's 1st Platoon was left behind to guard the company's packs, collect the full supply drop and remain as a reserve force.

Bravo Company wiped out the facility, used in part as a field hospital. The base included 40 buildings, 150 chickens, 50 pigs, 20 dogs, and two tonnes of rice. The soldiers killed the pigs execution-style – a single shot behind the ear to conserve ammunition, which was in short supply because the Americans still hadn't got their main supply drop. First Lieutenant Teb Stocks, 3rd Platoon's leader, flung chickens into an open fire. Rick Brown was gripped with foreboding from the sheer size of the complex because he knew that its garrison wasn't far away. And wherever it was, it had Bravo Company outnumbered. He knew that the base had been manned by a unit much larger than a 100-man company.

"I can remember there were so many pigs. There were so many chickens," he said. "This was too much livestock."

By way of perspective, that morning the regiment's Delta Company found and took control of seven buildings, captured one North Vietnamese prisoner, and killed three more. The larger, far more copiously stocked outpost captured by Bravo Company indicated that its garrison had left recently and in a hurry. Within two hours of departing the overnight encampment, Waybright reported to Jaggers that the facility was destroyed.[3]

Jaggers, flying above Bravo Company in a command-and-control helicopter, ordered Waybright to check out another collection of hooches, about a half mile to the northwest.[4] Almost immediately after setting out, Bravo Company encountered a small enemy force around 11:15am and exchanged fire in a short skirmish with no casualties on the American side before the Vietnamese broke off the attack.

Bravo Company's 2nd and 3rd Platoons initially traveled in a southeasterly direction, but the trail then doubled back to turn to the northwest into a clearing, which had the two platoons headed back toward the previous night's defensive perimeter, and 1st Platoon.

With Ruben Rueda walking point, 3rd Platoon took the lead, followed by 2nd Platoon, including Leslie Sabo and George Koziol, and it didn't take long for them to find trouble. Just after 3pm, the Americans moved into a jungle clearing with sparse tree cover, and a trail that ran down through the clearing's center. Sabo's second squad of 2nd Platoon had just broken out of the tree line when, in Koziol's words, "the shit hit the fan."

In the lead element, Rueda immediately saw signs that the clearing was in fact inhabited, with punji sticks and hooches along the perimeter. As he neared the huts, Rueda saw enemy soldiers pouring out of them. The instincts that had served him so well in the tunnels of Hill 474 and on the Crow's Foot trails were screaming out a warning.

"A guy came out with a rifle. He ran into the woods, followed by another guy," Rueda said. He began returning fire. "I was standing there like John Wayne until a lieutenant said, 'Stop shooting and get down.'"

That would have been Stocks, who was the only lieutenant in the clearing, with Neff previously having been wounded and lifted out and John Greene's 1st Platoon back down the trail. Rueda complied with the order and went onto his belly in a small depression.

"Every time I went to get up, I could see the rounds going over my head," he said. "Were I a little higher, I wouldn't be here. I couldn't see more than 10 feet and everyone was shooting."

Back in the column, the other Currahees were doing the same.

"We had very little cover. We walked into an open area," Koziol said. "Once we were in the whole middle area, they opened up on us."[5]

The attack started just as Sabo's squad, which was at the column's tail end, entered the clearing. Koziol's squad was about 10 meters ahead of Sabo's when the Currahees were hit from three sides by a much larger North Vietnamese force. The enemy had not only the advantage of numbers, but it also was dug into defensive positions from the cover of a surrounding tree line and able to fire down on the Americans, who were caught out in an open area.

"They were actually in trees and behind trees, and pretty well wrapped around us," Waybright said.

Estimates of the enemy force range from 100 soldiers to 400 or 500. And they were pouring hot lead down on the Currahees, who scrambled for whatever small amount of cover was available. There was little vegetation in the clearing, and the trees and shrubs were no taller than 5 feet, so they offered little protection. The encircling jungle was surrounded by trees upwards of 40 feet tall, and the enemy soldiers were entrenched, behind cover, and even fired rockets and AK-47s down on the Americans from high in the tree branches.

Brown, in 2nd Platoon, tried to find shelter behind a large anthill, but didn't know where to hide because the gunfire seemed to be coming from all directions, which, of course, it was. "For about five seconds (that's an eternity), we were too busy scurrying for cover. I felt we froze just a bit just to get our bearings. [Then we] returned fire with a vengeance. The enemy was everywhere."[6]

For those crucial seconds, Bravo Company was getting clobbered, but, incredibly, no one was killed immediately as the Americans tried to find cover. In the lead, 3rd Platoon encountered fire from two entrenched enemy units on either side of the path that ran through the clearing from southeast to northwest. Roughly at the center of the clearing, Captain Waybright found himself in a small patch of trees along the trail. He called for helicopter gunships and artillery fire.[7]

While Bravo Company was fighting on Hill 474 and in the Crow's Foot, air and artillery support arrived quickly. During those operations, US tactical aircraft had been based minutes away in the Air Force base at Phu Cat, near Qui Nhon. But in Cambodia on May 10, the Air Force flew only one sortie into the clearing during the Mother's Day Ambush, because the North Vietnamese were so close to the US forces that even an on-target bombing would do pretty much the same damage to comrade and enemy alike.

After the crucial hesitation Brown referred to, Waybright gave the order to return fire, which kept the situation from getting worse. There was some light tree cover in the clearing, and the Currahees scrambled to find it in those early seconds.

"We went for whatever cover we could find," Richard Rios said. "With all of the shooting going on and the dust and the guns, everything was a haze."[8]

Toward the column's front, up with 3rd Platoon, that haze concealed much of what was going on. The exposed Currahees were on the verge of being overrun from all directions.

Rick Brown, one day past his 19th birthday, wasn't keen on his chances of ever seeing 20. As he hugged the ground and looked unsuccessfully for concealment, Brown expected the rearguard would be quickly overrun, which would have freed the enemy to finish off everyone who was left. As the fighting continued, Koziol dropped back toward the southeast tree line, which brought him into close contact with his friend Sabo. As Sabo headed for the jungle's relative safety, he led a counterattack against an enemy element that was attempting to close the pocket and completely surround the Americans.[9]

While Sabo would perform more spectacular acts of valor that afternoon, none would be more vital to the Currahees' defense of their position. As he defended the Americans' rearmost element, Lieutenant Teb Stocks, 3rd Platoon's leader, was trying to stabilize the situation and maintain a connection between the two platoons. Stocks was concerned that the North Vietnamese would pour into a gap between the two US elements. He and Sergeant John Roethlisberger moved to shore up the Currahees' defense under heavy enemy fire – an effort that, by Stokes' own admission, succeeded primarily because of Sabo.

"If it hadn't been for him holding his side of the perimeter almost single-handedly so I could reinforce his position, we would have been overrun," Stocks said.

In the rear guard, on the clearing's southeast corner, Sabo was leading efforts to stabilize Bravo Company's rear perimeter and kept the smaller, exposed US force from being surrounded, overrun, and annihilated. While the North Vietnamese took prisoners during the war, they usually were pilots shot down in North Vietnamese territory. American prisoners taken by enemy infantry in the field were often killed, and almost certainly would have been on May 10, if only because the alternative would be marching them through the mountains along the border of Vietnam, Cambodia, and Laos, using their own resources to feed and care for the prisoners. Three days before the Mother's Day Ambush, a 4th Infantry Division company commander and radio telephone operator were captured, tortured – within earshot of their comrades – and executed. A similar fate likely awaited Bravo Company if it had been overrun.[10]

Certainly, Sabo wasn't the only person in Bravo Company to fend off the North Vietnamese flanking element.

In the rearguard, there was no shortage of valor. With 2nd Platoon under a withering attack, one soldier – likely Leslie Wilbanks or Thomas Merriman – exposed himself to provide covering fire until the enemy cut him down, and Donald Smith attacked an enemy machine-gun bunker with grenades. Smith silenced the gun, but the assault cost him his life. James DeBrew and Ernie Moore manned one of 2nd Platoon's 60mm machine guns. The following morning, their bodies would be found, still at the weapon. Larry DeBoer ran into the open field under heavy enemy fire to rescue a wounded comrade.[11] Sabo, Smith, the machine-gun team of DeBrew and Moore, DeBoer, and Wilbanks kept the North Vietnamese out of the clearing.

"If they would have gotten around them, I was easy pickings," Brown said. "They kept me alive."

But Leslie Sabo's actions were outstanding, even on a day when outstanding acts of courage were almost routine. "Leslie did more than any of us," said George Koziol, in what might be the most succinct yet accurate assessment about Sabo's relative contribution to that effort to prevent the encirclement, and probable massacre, of Bravo Company. The brunt of that pressure was borne by 2nd Platoon who sustained nearly 100 percent casualties.

At this point in the firefight, however, by late afternoon, with the North Vietnamese raining fire on Bravo Company from three sides, their success was far from assured and the Americans were still in danger of being overrun.

CHAPTER 15

First I want to thank you for your birthday cards. I especially liked that card George sent me, it was really nice. Tell the boys I liked their card very much. Roe filled me in pretty good on your accident but you did clear a few things up for me. I'm happy you found such a nice car so soon. It sounds like you lucked out in finding that car. We're going to be leaving these mountains soon and are going to new ones about 15 miles from here. Roe sent me a package to fatten me up but I think I'm about the right weight now. I'll be receiving some pictures I took when I do I'll send them to Roe and you'll be able to see for yourself whether I lost weight or not. I'm not a machine gunner any more the old one came back. Now I'm just a regular rifleman. I just finished reading a very unusual and unique book called "Tell Me That You Love Me, Junie Moon," they made a movie of it which I don't know would be as good but the book was quite good and I would recommend it very highly for you to read it. I'm going to start reading a book by W. Somerset Maugham called "Achenden," it should be good. About that, I received it the same time I got the Air Medal but it is different you'll see if the Army puts the Air

Medal in the paper. Well Olga, I have an opportunity to mail this today some colonel is supposed to come out then I can send the letter along with Roe's in with the chopper. Say hi to everyone. I hope your father has recovered completely from his operation and that they are all doing well in your family. Well I'm in my fifth month so I'll be seeing you soon.

Leslie Sabo letter to George and Olga
Dated March 22, 1970

For the only time in Bravo Company's 1969–70 tour, it was outmanned and outgunned. That wasn't how firefights typically worked. Instead, the attacks usually lasted only a few minutes because the North Vietnamese rule was that their potential for survival decreased in direct proportion to the amount of time they spent engaging the Americans – who never were much more than a radio telephone call away from helicopter gunships, reinforcements, fighter sorties, and artillery. On Hill 474 and in the Crow's Foot prior to the Cambodian Incursion, air support was usually swift and effective.

But during the Mother's Day Ambush on May 10, 1970, help from above was almost non-existent and, when it did come, was late in arriving. Captain Jim Waybright, the company commander, said a single F-4 air-to-ground plane made a single sortie, and that might have been strictly for show because Waybright said he didn't see or feel ordnance from the jet's 20mm cannons striking the trees and bunkers where the enemy was lodged.

Around nightfall, a CH-47 made a pass over the battlefield, solely as a monitoring measure. For most of the war, the US military's CH-47 fleet – alternatively nicknamed "Spooky" or "Puff the Magic Dragon" – was a valuable source of air support, thanks to its dual 7.62mm Gatling guns mounted near the plane's tail. The weapon's larger caliber and high rate of fire was devastating, particularly in a jungle battle where the rounds cut through trees and enemy bodies alike. On this day, however, "Spooky" was present for monitoring purposes only, and that single F-4 run was the only airplane support Bravo Company had all day.[1] Waybright said he thought the Air Force, a branch in which he had previously been an officer, might have been stretched too thin providing air cover for the entire Cambodian operation and was unable to spare Bravo Company anything more than a single jet that had already expended its ammunition. A gunship, which Waybright surmised to have been the battalion command-and-control helicopter, provided some fire support.

But other factors were likely at play, as well. In his after-action report, Waybright's battalion commander, Lieutenant Colonel Joseph Jaggers, said communication and coordination of air support had indeed been a problem throughout the entire Cambodian Incursion. Vital calls for air support had been forced to compete with what Jaggers called non-essential radio traffic on the Army's communication grid. The Air Force and Army artillery support were also plagued by poor or non-existent maps – many units, including Bravo Company, that participated in *Binh Tay* operated beyond the range both of the Army's own maps and its radio network. After the Currahees had withdrawn to Vietnam, Jaggers called on his superior officers to improve the communications network prior to similar operations.

"If this is not accomplished then those units might find themselves seriously engaged and unable to obtain the necessary support," Jaggers wrote.[2]

Waybright cited another factor that might have prevented more support from Air Force jets – space, or the lack of it. The North Vietnamese were right on top of the Americans. Anything less than a pinpoint strike would have wounded or killed Currahees.

"That was one of their tactics," Waybright said. "They came in as close as they could get."

As the Americans battled for their lives, they did it from within what amounted to a frying pan. Nighttime temperatures hovered around 70 degrees – comfortable, at least for sleeping in the field.

During the day, that figure increased to between 88 and 100 degrees throughout the *Binh Tay* operation. Koziol said May 10 was a particularly sunny day, so it is safe to assume that the men of Bravo Company were contending with temperatures well into triple figures with humidity only slightly lower than they would have encountered at the ocean's bottom even as they battled an enemy who was entrenched mostly in a shaded area along the tree line.[3]

And as the Americans poured out sweat, they were unable to rehydrate. When Waybright's force left the perimeter, it was traveling light, with no food and little water, and the supply drop still hadn't arrived. By late afternoon, almost completely encircled by a much larger North Vietnamese force and running low on ammunition, Bravo Company's situation was desperate.

"We were all but surrounded and in the end, we had to call in artillery fire to help get us out," Waybright said.

But Bravo Company was hampered on that count. During the Vietnam War, infantry companies typically had a three-man artillery team consisting of a forward observer, usually a lieutenant, with a reconnaissance sergeant and a radio telephone operator who physically called down a fiery rain on the enemy. But Bravo Company's forward observer, Second Lieutenant Thomas Scarboro, had been killed on April 8 while leading part of 2nd Platoon when Lieutenant Lawrence Neff split his force on patrol. Scarboro had not yet been replaced, which left Sergeant Bobby Garnto pulling double duty as the artillery team's forward observer and recon sergeant. By all accounts, Garnto did both jobs more than adequately, but with the North Vietnamese practically – actually in some parts of the battlefield – on top of Bravo Company, the resulting barrage wounded men on both sides.[4]

As the shooting continued, Lieutenant Teb Stocks, 3rd Platoon's leader, and Sergeant "Little John" Roethlisberger moved back toward the rear element to set up a defensible perimeter until help arrived and prevented the enemy from driving a wedge between 2nd and 3rd Platoons.

That action was a matter of instinct for Stocks, who had no communication with the rest of Bravo Company or outside support because his radio telephone operator, Specialist Frederick Harms, was seriously wounded early in the battle.

Stocks regarded Harms as one of the most dependable men in his platoon. Not long after taking command of 3rd Platoon, Stocks, an Atlanta native, said he quickly found himself on the receiving end of Harms' sense of humor. When Harms was assigned as 3rd Platoon's radioman, Stocks said the Bartonville, Illinois, native told him it was because Captain Waybright couldn't understand the lieutenant's Southern twang. But the platoon commander came to depend on Harms until May 10.

"I knew something was wrong when I reached for my radio and it wasn't there," Stocks said.

From his vantage point, Stocks saw that just about everyone was scurrying for cover. For those, like Rueda, who couldn't find any, the lieutenant ordered them to hug the dirt like their lives depended on it, because they did. And everyone complied with that order, with one exception. Under withering fire from the trees, Sabo was on his feet, shooting back. Stocks yelled at Sabo.

"I was cussing at that son of a bitch, telling him to get down and he just looked at me and grinned."

As the battle raged on, the Americans heard and saw their comrades' dying moments. In the column's lead, point man Ruben Rueda was pressing his body into a shallow grassy depression. With bullets flying inches above his head, Rueda had trouble seeing anything. But he could hear everything. And the sound tormented him. Rueda could hear Les Wilbanks, one of his closest friends in Bravo Company, mortally wounded and calling for help.

Wilbanks had been in college in 1969, but his grades fell, which left him vulnerable to the draft, and he was snapped up. Rueda, who was pressed into a small depression at the column's point and couldn't see more than a dozen or so feet in any direction, heard him cry out for help when he was hit. Even years later, Rueda would remember his friend's final moments.

"He was more serious than most of the rest of us were," Rueda said. "I remember him calling for a medic. I was thinking, 'They killed my buddy. This has got to be a dream.'"

Jerry Nash had been 3rd Platoon's medic, but was transferred to Bravo Company's headquarters platoon a few weeks before the Cambodian Incursion. After two other medics became patients themselves when struck by North Vietnamese fire, Nash was the only source of medical care. With enemy fire raking the clearing, Nash moved from one wounded man to another, doing his best with dwindling supplies to offer treatment and hope, even for those beyond hope.

"Don't let me die," a badly wounded soldier cried out as Nash hovered over him. "Please don't let me die."

Nash lied to him.

"We're not going to let you die," the medic said, even as he knew the man wouldn't survive.

As the enemy pushed to surround Bravo Company, the men of 2nd Platoon would have launched their defensive effort with the awareness that not only their lives, but those of their comrades, depended upon their next moves. Alton Mabb, who would serve with the 101st Airborne in Vietnam the following year and later rescue Sabo's story from history's scrap heap, said that responsibility transcended any notions of defending their country or thwarting the spread of communism.

"Those guys were fighting for each other and they weren't fighting for anything but their buddies," Mabb said. "You look out for the guys to the left of you and to the right of you because they're looking out for you. Instinctively, he [Sabo] probably jumped to the front of the line."

Koziol, who had been retreating toward the tree line, had a close-up view as Sabo engaged the advancing North Vietnamese with rifle fire and grenades. When an injured soldier was caught out in the open, Sabo moved directly into the enemy attack. It was the same thing he had done a month earlier at Hill 474 during the ambush in Binh Dinh province, when Scarboro was killed. Koziol said Sabo was motivated by the same instinct in both cases.

"When he saw a guy wounded, he went to help," Koziol said.[5]

While the enemy was attacking his position on May 10, Sabo once again "went to help." The injured man – who had just moments earlier been working with Koziol, Sabo, and the rest of 2nd Platoon to repel the North Vietnamese – was lying exposed when an enemy soldier, from a two-man trench, threw a grenade that landed near the fallen Currahee, who still has never been identified. Sabo moved forward and threw himself over the body of his comrade, absorbing multiple shrapnel injuries to his back in the process.[6]

"What I recall was that Les ran out in the direction of the wounded soldier just as a grenade was thrown in that area and he dove on the guy on the ground when the grenade exploded. I think Les got hit with shrapnel on the back and the wounded soldier crawled to the tree line," Koziol wrote years later on the Bravo Company online message board.[7]

As the unidentified wounded soldier made his way to the relative safety of the wooded area, Sabo, who was by then wounded himself, went on the attack. He rushed the North Vietnamese trench with a grenade assault of his own and killed both enemy soldiers. By this time, late in the afternoon, several of Sabo's fellow 2nd Platoon defenders were already injured or dead, and the beleaguered Bravo Company soldiers were running low on lead to throw at the North Vietnamese. Sabo, already injured from the earlier hand grenade attack, again exposed himself so he could strip ammunition magazines from Americans who had been killed earlier.

"He picked up two or three of them and threw one to me, and one to another guy and ducked behind a tree, and that's when he got hit in the leg."[8]

Even with the additional ammunition and with his M-16 rifle set on semi-automatic, instead of full automatic, to conserve his rapidly dwindling rounds, Koziol's weapon soon ran dry, just as a North Vietnamese soldier, armed with a grenade, rushed him. Koziol used the only weapon – a rocket-propelled grenade launcher – left at his disposal. Both soldiers cut loose their attacks simultaneously. Koziol's grenade was close to the enemy. But as the old saying goes, close counts in horseshoes and hand grenades. The North Vietnamese soldier was killed. The enemy's grenade hit Koziol's helmet and ricocheted a relatively safe distance away before it detonated. He immediately went deaf, and sustained a concussion and extensive shrapnel injuries. The deafness eventually subsided, although Koziol had sustained permanent hearing damage. But he acknowledged that it could have been much worse.

"If I didn't have that steel pot on my head, I'd have been dead."[9]

The clearing stayed open, albeit at a terrible cost, with seven 2nd Platoon soldiers dead or dying. But those men, through their sacrifice, bought the rest of Bravo Company the most precious of all commodities for an outnumbered, outgunned, and exposed military force – time. Around 5pm, several hours after the ambush had begun, an artillery strike forced the North Vietnamese snipers out of the trees. Waybright said even that was fraught with peril. Bobby Garnto, the company commander's radio telephone officer, radioed in the artillery support from Fire Support Base Currahee even though the enemy was so close to the Americans that any effective shelling would fall on comrades as well as enemies.

"He was concerned that he couldn't call it any closer because it ran the risk of hitting friendly forces," Waybright said.

But the artillery brought an end to the North Vietnamese fire on Bravo Company's exposed forces. By that time, with 2nd Platoon decimated and ammunition virtually depleted, Sabo stood almost alone against the North Vietnamese, with Koziol *hors de combat* and serving only as a witness to his friend's heroism.[10]

The air and artillery support didn't settle the issue, it just gave the Currahees some breathing room. And even with Sabo stripping ammunition from his fallen comrades, the Americans were in danger of running out of bullets, an eventuality that would have been catastrophic.

"If they would have run out of ammunition, they [the North Vietnamese] would have shot them right between the eyes," Greene said.

From their reserve perimeter, Greene and the rest of 1st Platoon could hear the sounds of battle. From the radio, which blared forth Waybright's calls for artillery support, they could hear the situation within the clearing continue to deteriorate. The two platoons of Bravo Company still in the fight were still outnumbered and caught relatively out in the open. Retreating from the clearing would have been fatal for most of the two dozen or so soldiers already wounded and unable to move. They couldn't go out. Reinforcements had to go in.

As the North Vietnamese clamped down on Bravo Company, Hanks, in 1st Platoon, suffered and waited. "We were all listening to radios and waiting for the call to go in," he said.

Back in the relative safety of Fire Support Base Currahee, Mike DiLeo was working with company staff and some of the new guys like Lee Paterson, who had arrived in Vietnam less than two weeks earlier, to gather supplies and ammunition for their comrades on the battlefield.

DiLeo was organizing helicopter lifts and agonizing over his wounded and dying comrades.

"There's a little bit of guilt there," he said. "Actually, more than a little bit. You always feel like you could have helped."

But Jaggers wasn't considering mobilizing Bravo Company's base garrison. Battalion command initially sent a platoon from Alpha Company, but a helicopter that was carrying part of the unit into the battle was shot down. Alpha's efforts immediately shifted from rescuing Bravo Company to protecting its own downed comrades. Next, Delta Company was ordered to break the North Vietnamese grip on the clearing. John Greene said 1st Platoon was encouraged because an entire company was being sent into action. But Delta's cautious advance meant it wouldn't reach Bravo Company before nightfall, and traveling by night, with little light and undependable maps, was too hazardous, so it established a nighttime defensive perimeter and prepared to resume the following morning. There was only one thing for it – 1st Platoon would have to mount the rescue mission itself, outnumbered and in advancing darkness.

"We carried as much as we could," Hanks said. "We literally ran to their position. I thought that was the last sunrise I'd see. I thought that we were going to prove our loyalty to our brothers by dying alongside them."[11]

But Greene's force did have one circumstance working in its favor. After destroying the hospital facility a few hours earlier, the Currahees initially pursued the enemy southeast and then swung back to the northwest shortly before entering the clearing. As a result, 1st Platoon was at the opposite end of the clearing from Sabo and the rest of 2nd Platoon, an eventuality that would work to Greene's advantage because it would allow his force of around 25 men to catch the enemy from behind. Speed and stealth were of prime importance because the Currahees had to cover about 1 kilometer – roughly two-thirds of a mile – and traverse an open field.

"It was dark when we went in," 1st Platoon soldier Mike "Tex" Bowman said. "We brought as much stuff as we could carry. We had to go by sound."

Greene readied 1st Platoon for an advance on the clearing in near-complete darkness, and then to immediately attack an enemy that still had the advantage of superior numbers while trying not to shoot any friendly troops. Initially, the troops advanced in a single column, with Bill Watling at point. When 1st Platoon reached the open ground just outside the North Vietnamese ambush perimeter, Greene split them into three columns for the final advance across a stretch where even one North Vietnamese soldier with a machine gun could have wiped out the entire platoon.

But the approach of night provided cover, and sound generated by the continuing battle was an ally to the Currahees. They advanced in three columns, with one squad in the center a few steps in front of the other two squads on the flanks. Waybright thought the North Vietnamese, who probably still outnumbered 1st Platoon by a ratio of more than five to one, likely thought Greene's force was much larger than it actually was.

"I expected we would all be killed," Greene said. "The only advantage is that it was getting dark. We got across the field without anyone shooting at us, which amazed us."

After crossing the clearing, Greene and his men burst through the perimeter near Rueda's position in front of the main element across the clearing from 2nd Platoon. For Richard Rios, seeing 1st Platoon's arrival was like the cavalry arriving just in time in the old American western movies he grew up watching back in Texas.

Greene's men broke the siege, only to take fire from helicopter gunships whose pilots were unaware that the clearing was now being taken by Americans. At a few hundred feet elevation at speeds approaching 100mph, the Currahees pouring into the clearing were indistinguishable from the North Vietnamese who had threatened to overrun it all afternoon. However, the North Vietnamese were able to tell the difference. Soon, 1st Platoon was taking fire from both friendly helicopters and decidedly unfriendly troops on the ground. A radio call by Waybright to the choppers solved the first problem but not the second.

"The bullets started popping over and I realized I needed to be crawling instead of walking," Greene said.

It was up to the very same soldiers who had just spent hours fighting for their lives to secure a safe landing zone for the helicopters to land in near-darkness at the outer end of their fuel range, a task that took on vital importance because there were almost 30 injured soldiers who couldn't wait for daylight for medical treatment. And even though 1st Platoon's attack and the onset of night broke the enemy's opportunity to overrun Bravo Company, the North Vietnamese still posed a real threat to harass any helicopter coming into the clearing. Greene found a suitable landing site near the area where 2nd Platoon, which had absorbed most of the casualties, was still pinned down. While the choppers, popularly known as Hueys, were known for their durability, they were still vulnerable to ground fire as had been shown earlier in the day when North Vietnamese forces had shot down a helicopter that was to have brought troops from Alpha Company of the 506th to lift the attack against Bravo Company.

The landing zone was barely adequate. It was surrounded by jungle and not much wider than the radius of a Huey's main rotor, which meant the medical evacuation helicopters had to descend almost vertically into the landing zone, which in turn meant that each approach and departure would require more time and greater exposure to enemy fire than it would if the choppers could make a more horizontal approach.

Two machine-gun emplacements had the planned landing zone caught in a crossfire. Those machine guns had to be silenced, permanently and quickly. Any delay in securing a landing zone could cost more American lives – as it turned out, Larry DeBoer and Fred Harms would die of their injuries before they could be treated, which would bring Bravo Company's death toll for the day to eight.[12] Already, Greene could hear the voices of his wounded comrades calling out for water to replace some of the fluids they had lost through their own blood and sweat, even before the first helicopter cruised in to pick up Koziol and another wounded soldier at the not-quite-secure landing zone.

From behind the tree line, enemy soldiers began firing on the helicopter. Greene, who was among the troops trying to secure a patch of ground for the helicopter, said the combination of fire from close in and off in the distance thwarted the Americans' efforts even as the first aircraft headed in. One of the helicopter crewmen was hit in the arm while helping Koziol on to the aircraft. The enemy continued to attack the helicopter as it was lifting off.

"I remember someone pulling me into the medevac chopper and then I must have passed out," Koziol said. "When I came to, we were in the air and it seemed like red and green tracer bullets were coming in all directions."[13]

Then Sabo did something extraordinary. Again.

He stepped out from behind a small tree that for hours had been his only cover, and squeezed the trigger on his M-16, which he had set to full automatic. Sabo probably didn't know about the helicopter that had been shot down earlier in the day, but he knew that if this one went down, his fellow Currahees would have been on board. Perhaps he made a calculation – with a 20-round magazine it would be only a few seconds before his weapon ran dry. Perhaps he knew it would be enough. Or perhaps Sabo just acted instinctively to protect his comrades. Whatever the case, Sabo's attack stopped the enemy machine guns and allowed 1st Platoon to eliminate the single enemy soldier in the landing zone. It also gave the helicopter time to carry his injured friend from the battlefield.

"He stood up," Greene said. "Until he did that, we couldn't get up and secure that landing zone. I couldn't believe Leslie stood up like that. It sure made a difference."

Mike "Tex" Bowman, who was in the clearing by that time but missed seeing Sabo's earlier acts of heroism, would later be amazed that Sabo was still able to stand up, much less cover the helicopter landing.

"He got hit two or three times and still kept on going."

Sabo was able to clear the landing zone, but the 22-year-old soldier paid for that real estate in his own blood. For hours, after almost single-handedly preventing the North Vietnamese from wiping out dozens of American soldiers, Sabo was vulnerable while he reloaded. And when the enemy soldiers were able to poke their heads – and their weapons – back into the open, they took advantage of that opportunity. After Sabo stopped shooting, the enemy fired on him, in full view of Koziol, then en route to a field hospital.

"I saw him when he dropped his rifle, dropped to his knees and fell face first into the dust."[14]

After bursting into the clearing and relieving their brothers, 1st Platoon's work still wasn't over. Greene's men helped establish a more secure landing zone that wouldn't require a near-vertical descent. Once that was completed, Bravo Company got a kick-out supply drop of food, ammunition, and water to slake the thirst of men who had spent hours fighting for their lives without enough of all those commodities.

Survivors of the Mother's Day Ambush unanimously reported that 2nd Platoon's counterattack, and particularly Sabo's repeated heroic acts, saved their lives, even if they didn't realize it at the time. All Rick Brown knew as the sun beat down and the enemy rained hot lead on them from all directions was that he expected the North Vietnamese to emerge from the trees at any moment to kill him. But they never showed themselves.

"I couldn't work out why they couldn't get around that corner," he said.

Only later did he find out that the North Vietnamese couldn't get to him because Leslie Sabo owned the corner.

CHAPTER 16

When daylight broke on May 11, it revealed the Mother's Day Ambush's horrific toll. Six Currahees lay dead in the clearing – two more would succumb to their wounds on their way to rear-echelon treatment areas. Leslie Sabo's body couldn't be immediately found. Ernest Moore and James DeBrew, the machine-gun team from 2nd Platoon, died at their post. Rick Brown, one of the few unwounded soldiers from the previous day's battle, took the 60mm weapon from Moore, who died while holding the gun's extra barrel in one hand and the asbestos glove, used to change overheated gun barrels, in the other.

"He was an excellent machine gunner," remarked Brown.

The wounded, dead, and unscathed were scattered haphazardly across the clearing wherever they had dug in to fight for their lives the previous afternoon and the nearby landing zone used a few hours earlier to evacuate the most severely wounded, which necessitated a defensive perimeter that was barely defensible as the enemy made a few attempts to claim more casualties. A North Vietnamese soldier penetrated the Currahees' territory through a 15-foot gap, but was repelled. As day broke, another enemy trooper, having spotted the antenna of Waybright's radio telephone operator, launched a rocket-propelled grenade at the company commander's shallow foxhole, but it fell short. The grenade landed near radio telephone operator Dave Soden, and left him wounded by shrapnel and temporarily blinded.

Sergeant Vernon Bruner returned fire on the enemy position. The "Big Bandito" found his mark and ended the final North Vietnamese assault of the Mother's Day Ambush. By 9am, Delta Company, under the command of Captain William Ohl, arrived and, at long last, the siege was broken.

"I'll never forget the look on the Bravo Company survivors' faces when we entered their perimeter," said Delta Company medic Tony Foster. "It was as though they [had] fought with the devil himself."[1]

With the arrival of relief, Bravo Company could survey the damage. 2nd Platoon all but ceased to exist, with all eight dead and most of the 28 wounded coming from among its ranks. First Lieutenant Teb Stocks, leader of 3rd Platoon, only narrowly avoided being added to the casualty list.

"He took off his helmet and there was a bullet crease," Greene said.

During their combat tours in Vietnam, the soldiers in Bravo Company had to carry packs that weighed up to 75 pounds, which didn't include heavy-duty and heavyweight weapons such as machine guns and mortars. But the greatest burden they would ever have to bear was the bodies of their six fallen comrades, which they had to carry for about a mile on May 11. Lieutenant John Greene, commander of 1st Platoon, said the helicopter pilots, who performed with such gallantry when picking up wounded soldiers a day earlier, required a larger landing zone on safer ground to retrieve Bravo Company's dead.

With the arrival of Delta Company on the battlefield, one of the Vietnam War's longest firefights came to an end. With most of the soldiers in 2nd and 3rd Platoons either dead or wounded, the task of escorting their fallen comrades on the first leg of their journey home fell largely to the men of 1st Platoon, which had joined the battle as darkness fell the previous day and had been relatively unbloodied. That trip required the survivors to trek through hostile territory and rugged terrain – carrying the bodies of their fallen comrades, which had remained in the clearing throughout the previous night, wrapped in ponchos that had been repurposed as makeshift bodybags. But that method of transport quickly became unwieldy. Rick Brown said the bags began to show signs of strain – some of them had ripped open before the journey was completed.

One team was having problems carrying a casualty until Sergeant Bruner stepped in. "Big Bandito" slung the fallen Currahee over his back and carried him solo to the landing zone. Even for its makeshift nature, the funeral procession was made up of men who approached their duty with the same consideration that six pallbearers might have shown during a home front funeral service.

"They carried them with as much respect as they could under the circumstances," John Greene said.

Dave Soden, the radio telephone operator who had been left blind by a rocket-propelled grenade, was ambulatory, but still needed help making it to the pick-up point. For almost two-thirds of a mile, Soden walked through the jungle while gripping the back of another man's pack and following his comrade through the darkness.[2]

When Bravo Company reached its extraction point, Brown and Mike "Tex" Bowman lifted the bags into the helicopter, where, because of the aircraft's limited space, the remains had to be, "stacked like cordwood," to use Brown's description. Sabo's body was last to be loaded into the helicopter. As Brown and Bowman lifted the man whose sacrifice saved so many lives, Sabo's body broke in half – in death, his body was beyond wounded, it was irretrievably damaged. Even the helicopter crew was affected by the loss of life.

"The door gunner, he was really upset," Brown said.

After Sabo's body was loaded, Brown thought the helicopter was so crowded that he feared one of the bags would fall out.

"I said to the door gunner, 'You take care of our bros,'" Brown said.

Before the week was out, Brown and the rest of Bravo Company would follow their "bros" out of Cambodia. After losing eight men and having 28 wounded in the Mother's Day Ambush, the company was airlifted to Fire Support Base Currahee, about 4 miles west of the Se San valley. Based on Waybright's estimate of around 60 men in the two platoons caught in the Mother's Day Ambush, Bravo Company's casualty rate ran above 50 percent and it was assigned the task of garrisoning the base and supporting other units in the field. Alpha Company replaced it in the line until the battalion was pulled out of Cambodia the following Saturday, May 16.

Back at Currahee, someone asked Brown, "How many gooks they killed" – possibly because that was the way the US military and civilian leadership was still defining progress in Vietnam. But Brown wasn't in any mood for providing the score and let the guy know about it.

"I didn't care about that," he said. "What was important to me was that we lost eight guys. I didn't care if we killed 5,000 of them."

The actual number of enemy killed was far less than 5,000. Delta Company, which had tried to reach their fellow Currahees in the clearing a day earlier, spent most of that Monday cleaning up at the battle site. It would report finding the bodies of 47 North Vietnamese soldiers who died in the Mother's Day Ambush, and trails of blood left by enemy soldiers wounded in the fight.[3]

Estimates of the number of North Vietnamese involved in the ambush range from 200 to 500 – a full battalion, which would have made it the largest enemy force any US Army unit would face during *Binh Tay*. And Bravo Company was not only outnumbered, it was caught in the open by a larger force that was firing from bunkers and jungle cover, which made it surprising that the entire American force hadn't indeed been massacred. One day after Bravo Company's dead, wounded, and survivors reached Fire Support Base Currahee, their rucksacks caught up to them, which came as a great relief to the soldiers who had been convinced that the "houses on their backs" had fallen into the enemy's hands.[4]

Nearly 100 percent casualties were sustained by 2nd Platoon in the Mother's Day Ambush, and 3rd Platoon didn't come out of the attack unscathed. Only 1st Platoon had sufficient manpower strength to mount operations. Greene's unit was called out to assist Charlie Company in taking a large weapons cache from a "skyscraper" hooch estimated to be about 20 feet tall. The US troops uncovered an armory with more than 500 Soviet- and Chinese-manufactured handguns, semi-automatic, and automatic weapons. There also were more than 300 various types of rockets, thousands of rounds of ammunition, more than 100 US-manufactured weapons, more than 600 grenades, more than 3,000 blasting caps – used to detonate explosives – and about 300 pounds of explosives.[5]

The captured weapons filled two Chinook helicopters, twin rotor craft large enough to carry a platoon of 35 to 40 soldiers as opposed to the Hueys, which could carry only about a squad of 12 troops. While the Chinooks were larger than Hueys, they were also slower and more vulnerable.[6] As the Currahees were clearing the huge cache of weapons, they came under fire. Once again, Sergeant Vernon Bruner used well-placed rifle fire to drive off the enemy.

"We were the only ones that were still in mental and physical shape to do things," Greene said.

By mid-May, Bravo Company was back in Cambodia. The Currahees were pulled out of Cambodia on May 16, and the firebase named in their honor was dismantled. Everything that couldn't be taken back to South Vietnam by Chinook helicopter was destroyed. Operation *Binh Tay* was cut short by political pressure in Washington, DC. Even before Sabo's family had learned of his death, the US Senate Foreign Relations Committee demanded that the troops be pulled out of Cambodia. "The way out of Vietnam does not lead through Cambodia," US Senator Edmund Muskie said at the time.[7] Initially, Bravo Company was moved to the base at Plei D'Jereng as there was no room for them at Pleiku. Because of the political reality back in Washington, DC, the Currahees spent a day at Firebase Wildcat in Plei D'Jereng.

"The politicians wanted to announce that all of the American troops were out of Cambodia," Greene said. From Firebase Wildcat, the 3rd Battalion was flown to Ban Me Thuot by C-130.

During its 12 days in Cambodia, the 506th lost nine men and had 39 wounded. The majority, by far, of those casualties – 89 percent of the deaths and 72 percent of the wounded – were sustained by Bravo Company on May 10. Overall, 46 US soldiers were killed during the 12-day-long *Binh Tay* operation, with the Mother's Day Ambush being the deadliest single encounter. The North Vietnamese had 80 men killed in the 506th's section of *Binh Tay*, which ran from May 5 to 16. Most of the Currahees' enemy kills came at the hands of Bravo Company and its artillery support in the Mother's Day Ambush.

The Currahees were plagued by inaccurate maps, not enough aircraft, and a base too far from the operations area. The 506th had been launched from Pleiku, more than 50 miles from the Cambodian border, and Plei D'Jereng. This distance and lack of helicopters forced the soldiers to get by on less than 40 percent of its requirement of water.[8]

Communication by handsets across 50 miles of hilly terrain and jungle was another problem. Jaggers proposed establishing communications relays, but virtually all of the territory between the air base in Pleiku and the Cambodian border was enemy-controlled, which would have made any relay facility vulnerable to sabotage. Failing the creation of relays, Jaggers suggested restricting non-essential communications during sensitive operations such as *Binh Tay*. "During the entire operation, communications did not reach the standard they must have. However, the non-essential traffic that would tie up the command net was not reduced," he later reported.

It's impossible to say whether the problems cited by Jaggers contributed to the deaths of Sabo and the other seven Bravo Company soldiers on May 10, but they certainly didn't help.

In spite of the difficulties, Jaggers said the Currahees accomplished their mission to, "find, fix, destroy, and capture enemy personnel and equipment in … Cambodia." The 506th captured or destroyed more than 500 weapons, including 88 Chinese-manufactured assault rifles, 81 Russian-made assault rifles, and 122 automatic pistols manufactured in Russia during the early 1930s. The regiment also captured nearly 3,000 rounds of ammunition, more than 3,500 explosives, and 530 tonnes of rice.

There was a long list of medical items taken, including a blood-pressure measuring device, ten cases of gauze, 24 cases of injection solution, ten cases of penicillin, one case of cobra antivenom, 17 cans of plasma, and 1,000 doses of quinine, a medicine to treat malaria.

The capture and destruction of the medical supplies was an important part of the operation, as those items probably came from the outpost destroyed by Bravo Company on May 10, because it was the most significant medical facility captured.[9]

While the amount of enemy supplies captured and destroyed – especially the loss of food to an army that was already hungry, according to enemy documents captured during the siege of Hill 474 indicated – was impressive, it ultimately delayed, but didn't prevent, the North Vietnamese eventual victory. Political pressure, both in Washington and throughout the United States, in opposition to what pro-peace factions regarded as an expansion of the Vietnam War, kept the US forces from pressing its successes. The objective of *Binh Tay* was to weaken North Vietnam's ability to operate within South Vietnam and give pacification and Vietnamization time to work. But time turned out to be the ally of North, not South, Vietnam.

Even though his combat-related obligations to the Army largely ended on May 10, Koziol still faced one self-imposed duty to one of his brothers on the line. So he sat down and composed a 416-word document, which detailed the actions – specifically Sabo's actions – he witnessed. As he wrote it, Koziol expected that those 416 words would be enshrined in history as the official award citation, to be included on the Army's files. The document got its start in a military hospital, where Koziol recovered from the injuries he sustained in the May 10 ambush.

Most of Koziol's masterwork delves into Sabo's extraordinary actions that day, but it also includes what might be called Medal of Honor boilerplate language, such as the final line, "Spc. 4 Sabo's extraordinary heroism at the cost of his own life are in the keeping with the highest traditions of the military service and reflect great credit upon himself, his unit and the United States Army." Or the opening, which refers to, "conspicuous gallantry and intrepidity at the risk of his own life above and beyond the call of duty."

That piece of paper, which landed on Waybright's desk, would have been personally momentous to Sabo's family and comrades. It was likely the reason the Army was sparse with details regarding Sabo's death, and, when US Defense Department officials never completed that investigation, the reason why the people who knew him best in peacetime were deprived of the true stories about his heroism.

More than 20 soldiers from Bravo Company received medals for their heroism during the Mother's Day Ambush. James DeBrew and Donald Smith were both awarded posthumous Silver Stars, the US military's third-highest award for combat valor. Lawrence DeBoer, Frederick Harms, Thomas Merriman, and Leslie Wilbanks all received posthumous Bronze Stars. Ironically, their names were forgotten precisely because their sacrifice was instrumental in keeping Bravo Company from being annihilated. The Mother's Day Ambush wasn't listed among the Vietnam War's major battles and isn't even mentioned in most accounts of the *Binh Tay* operation. But when the North Vietnamese opened fire on Bravo Company in that clearing on the afternoon of May 10, it could have resulted in the largest mass execution of captured US troops since the December 1944 Malmedy massacre during the Battle of the Bulge in World War II.

Captain Jim Waybright was awarded the Silver Star for his leadership throughout the Mother's Day Ambush, and Lieutenant Teb Stocks, Paul Bieder, Thomas Kirkman, company medic Jerry "Doc" Nash, Ruben Rueda, Reid Schmotzer, and Ronald Stone all earned Bronze Star awards. Ernest Moore received a posthumous Army Commendation Medal with a "V" device, denoting valorous service. Michael "Tex" Bowman, Glenn Guillory, Ronald Leslie, Daniel Maxey, Allen McCulty, and Richard Rogers also received commendation citations.

The name of Leslie Sabo – who did more than anyone else, according to Koziol, the man who saw him fall – was conspicuously missing from the list of those who were awarded medals.[10]

CHAPTER 17

By the time Elisabeth Sabo received her Mother's Day flowers, Leslie Halasz Sabo Jr. – the son who sent the bouquet – was already dead, lying face down in a jungle clearing on the world's far side and 13 time zones in the future. For Elisabeth Sabo, 1970 was the last Mother's Day she would ever celebrate, even though she lived to see 37 more of them.

"We never celebrated it much, but we tried to make it special for her," said George Sabo.

To his mother, Leslie Sabo Jr. was a cause for comfort in a life that unexpectedly became difficult. Elisabeth Sabo was born into privilege and married into it as well. She might have had expectations of a comfortable life before the Nazis, and then the Communists, interfered.

By Mother's Day of 1970, Leslie was a little more than halfway through his tour of duty in Vietnam and his family was looking forward to him being out of the combat zone by Thanksgiving as they sat down to a big meal at Olga's parents' house. Even though Elisabeth, Leslie Sr. and George Sabo were all born in Hungary, they developed a taste for Italian food, fostered initially by their move to Ellwood City, which has historically had a large Italian-American population. When George and Olga Nocera wed just months after he graduated from high school, the Sunday trips to her parents' home became a custom.

Aside from dining at his in-laws' and the fact that Mother's Day 1970 was a beautiful sunny day – coincidentally, the weather conditions were nearly identical to, if perhaps a little cooler than, that Cambodian jungle clearing where Leslie Sabo had died – George Sabo doesn't remember much about that day. It's difficult to imagine nearly 40 years later, in an instant information culture, that news of Leslie Sabo's death didn't reach his loved ones for an entire week, which raised the metaphysical question of whether a tragedy has happened if no one knows about it. Ultimately, that question would turn to whether an act can be heroic if its tale remains secret.

Across town, Rose Buccelli Sabo marked the morning of her husband's death with Sunday Mass at Purification of the Blessed Virgin Mary – better known as Purification BVM, or simply BVM Church, to Ellwood City residents. And as she attended that Mass, she was already a widow, although she didn't know it at the time. Rose would later say she had premonitions about her husband's death. Leslie, she said, was a devoted husband who wrote letters nearly every day until early May.

"I had nightmares for three months," she said of the weeks leading up to her husband's death. "He sent me a letter every single day and I didn't get a letter all week." It would turn out that the participation of Leslie's regiment in the invasion of Cambodia prevented him from writing letters home.[1] Even while she admitted that it sounded difficult to believe, Rose said she had a dream during the early morning hours of Friday, May 15, that her husband had been killed. To her, the dream was so realistic that she was relieved to wake up to a day when her nightmare would become real.

"I sat up and said, 'Thank God it was just a dream,'" Rose said. "And damn if my dad didn't come into my work the next day. My dad was devastated when he got killed."

That Friday, Army notification officers fanned out through Ellwood City to inform George, Leslie Sr., and Rose that Leslie was officially missing in action, a matter of semantics – Sabo and the other soldiers who died on the battlefield had been unaccounted for early on May 11 until their bodies were collected hours later.[2]

The same thing had happened months earlier to the family of Sergeant Steven "Hungry" Dile, who was killed on January 28, 1970. Lee Dile, Steven's brother, was 14 years old when the Army informed his parents that their son was missing in action. Except for fliers – who sometimes were pronounced missing until the North Vietnamese reported that they had been taken prisoner – a missing-in-action report was usually only a prelude to a death notice. It worked that way for Dile's family, which was left in limbo for ten days because his body wasn't recovered for a full week after his death in a mission to recover the bodies of fellow Currahees killed on January 25.

Lee Dile, who was still living at home, awoke on a Sunday morning to the sound of screaming and the voices of soldiers saying that Steven was missing. Their mother, Ann, saw the notification party and knew right away what they were there for.

"You're praying and hoping that everything is OK," Lee Dile said. "Your world just falls apart. I just couldn't comprehend that I was never going to see him walk up onto the front porch."

When Leslie Sabo was killed, George Sabo said the soldiers came to their home. Rose was working at the Ellwood City News Stand. Leslie Sabo Sr. was working at Aetna Standard in Ellwood City, where he was an engineer, when they came for him. After receiving word that Leslie Jr. was MIA, George said he and his family, just as Dile's family did a few months earlier, still held out hope that Leslie was taken prisoner by the North Vietnamese. As unsavory as that scenario was in a nation that already was aware that the enemy tortured its prisoners, it was better than the alternative.

But they got to maintain that hope for only a few days. On May 17, the family received word that Sabo's body had been recovered and was on its final trip home.[3]

The remains of Sergeant Leslie Halasz Sabo Jr. – he had received a posthumous promotion from specialist – traveled to his hometown almost faster than news of his death did. The young soldier's body had been ravaged by the Cambodian heat and humidity, by the multitude of wounds he had sustained, and possibly by the enemy, which rendered his remains, in the Army's estimation, as unviewable, a designation that was sometimes deceptive, said Robert Stevenson, a childhood friend of the Sabo brothers. At the time of Leslie's death, Stevenson was an Ellwood City police officer. When Marine Lance Corporal Joseph Listorti was killed three years earlier – he was the first of six Ellwood City residents to die during the Vietnam War; Sabo was the last – his remains also were classified as unviewable.[4]

Listorti sustained a fatal head injury, but funeral director Howard Marshall needed only a quick look before issuing a different review.

"He said, 'Give me an hour,'" Stevenson remembered.

After Marshall's work, Listorti had an open-casket funeral.

Sabo's family wasn't as fortunate. After a closed-casket service at P.O. Contrucci Funeral Home in Ellwood City, Sabo was laid to rest on May 25, 1970, in Holy Redeemer Catholic Cemetery, on a hill just outside Ellwood City.[5] His plot would serve as final resting place for his father in 1977 and mother in 2008.[6]

Rosemary Sabo turned 22 years old the day after Leslie was buried. That morning, as one of the soldiers who escorted Leslie Sabo's body looked on, she was greeted by a delivery man bearing flowers. According to the card, her flowers were a birthday gift from a husband who had been dead for more than two weeks. She thought it was some kind of sick joke.

"I told the guard, 'Someone's got some explaining to do,'" she said.

The explanation was that when Leslie arranged for his mother and mother-in-law to receive orchids on Mother's Day, the day he was killed, he also had roses sent to his wife for her birthday on May 26, which turned out to be the day after he was buried.[7]

Elisabeth Sabo's last Mother's Day flower was preserved, encased in clear polyurethane by her engineer husband. To Leslie's family, the ability to send flowers from beyond the grave merely cemented his distinction as an extraordinary man.

"That was the kind of person he was," Olga Sabo said.

What they didn't know, and wouldn't know for decades, was that Leslie Sabo was an extraordinary hero. George said the Army reported that he had been shot by the enemy while guarding an ammunition storage facility when it blew up, which was a gross misrepresentation of the facts. Some of his friends were told he was shot by a sniper and Donald Hollerman, one of the organizers of Lincoln High School's Class of 1966 reunions, said he had heard Sabo tripped a landmine.[8]

It's difficult to say for certain why the Army concealed the truth from Leslie Sabo's family, because military representatives declined to comment. The most likely possibility – and this is only speculation – is that Sabo's death was still an open investigation and would likely remain so for months, if not years, because his fellow soldiers had already recommended him for the Medal of Honor. The ongoing Medal of Honor probe might have prevented the full details of Sabo's death from being released, even to his parents, brother, and wife. Had that investigation ever been completed, the full story of Sabo's death would have been revealed in a Distinguished Service Cross Citation or at a Medal of Honor ceremony in the White House. As it turned out, however, the investigation wouldn't be completed for another 40 years, after both of Leslie Sabo's parents had died, and the Army's decision to withhold those facts would ultimately exacerbate the pain experienced by Sabo's family. Because of the Army's misstatement, the loved ones Sabo left behind were thwarted in their effort to find meaning in Leslie Jr.'s death for decades to come.

For Leslie Sr., healing would be particularly difficult. After George and Olga received word that Leslie Jr. was missing in action, they rushed to his parents' home just in time to see Leslie Sr. pull into his driveway after having received the news at work. He stepped out of the car and leveled an oath against the man he blamed for the death of his younger son. On that afternoon, the object of Sabo's wrath was near the height of his prestige. Sabo Sr. would live long enough to see that man be disgraced and hounded from public life under a cloud of dishonor, although there is no evidence that his fall would be associated with any mystical Eastern European hex or even any errors in judgment traced to the Vietnam War.

A distraught Leslie Sabo Sr. cast his gaze into a sun-drenched sky and shouted his anger into the heavens with four words.

"I curse Richard Nixon."

CHAPTER 18

As the company medic, Jerry Nash saw the best and worst of war, alongside men he came to know as brothers. Between January 28 and May 10, 1970, eighteen Bravo Company soldiers were killed in action. Thirteen of them died with "Doc" Nash at their side. The experience took its toll.

"You will do anything to support each other, and protect yourself and each other," he said of his time as a combat medic. "You have a lot of fine days, you have a lot of bad days."

The Mother's Day Ambush amounted to a sad going-away party for some of the Currahees' officers, starting with the battalion commander. Jaggers was promoted and transferred to the 1st Cavalry Division, where he earned the first of his two stars and rose to assistant division commander.[1] Waybright was transferred and finished out his military career as the battalion supply officer. Captain Richard Lane, a battalion logistics officer, who was aware of what Bravo Company had been through even if he hadn't been there for it, assumed command.

"I knew of their reputation," said Lane, who ultimately made a career out of the Army. "They were just a tremendous group of guys, there were kids, 18, 19, 20 years old. The standard was not just doing their duty, but protecting each other. And these guys did this in spades."

Lane, a Special Forces-trained officer, joined the Army while in the ROTC program at the University of California at Santa Barbara. After joining the Army as a Second Lieutenant, Lane was gung-ho about training.

"I said, 'I've gotta go airborne, I've got to go special forces.'" he later recalled.

He had spent most of 1968 commanding a Special Forces detachment along Vietnam's western frontier with Cambodia. Lane returned late that year to the United States after sustaining a leg wound.

After the Mother's Day Ambush, monsoon season arrived and Bravo Company was pulled off the hot burner. The unit had 18 combat deaths in the first five months of 1970 and none in the following six months. But if the enemy became less bothersome, the Vietnam jungle remained a daunting adversary. The country's tropical climate gives it a cool season from November until January, a hot season from March to October. Of course, with Vietnam being close to the equator, cool is relative – the coldest month was January with average temperatures in the mid-60s in the day and the low 60s at night. During June, those averages rose to 91 with a low of 77. The hottest months coincided with the monsoon season, beginning in May and June. Nearly the entire second half of the 1969–70 Bravo Company tour took place during the monsoon season, which added to the general unpleasantness of jungle combat. Heavy rains were basically a daily occurrence, with heavy storms during the afternoon, followed by a sunny period and more rain after nightfall.

In spite of the rain – an average of a half-inch a day during the peak of monsoon season – Norm Friend said thirst, brought on by the oppressive heat and, ironically, a shortage of water, constantly stalked the Currahees.

"You just wanted something cold to drink and you could never get it," he said.

Ruben Rueda said it was impossible to stay dry during the daily rainstorms.

"When you slept, your armpits and your crotch were the only things that were dry because you were folded into a little ball," Rueda said. "After a while, you get used to it."

While Rueda was getting "used to it," the Army broke up some of Bravo Company's leaders after the Mother's Day Ambush. Upon recovering from his wounds – at least his physical ones – George Koziol returned to Bravo Company. Koziol hadn't sustained a million-dollar wound – GI-speak for the kind of damage that rendered a soldier unproductive to the military and resulted in a disability-related discharge – it was more like a $100,000 injury. In spite of his permanent hearing damage, the Army could still use Koziol, and it did, but his combat days were over. When he left the hospital after he had recovered some of his hearing, Koziol was transferred into the 3rd Battalion supply depot.

Once there, he found that, as often happens when small people are asked to oversee large things, people in charge of supply jealously guarded their turf and sometimes disbursed items as if the supplies were their own personal property. And Koziol knew that some of the things that battalion supply saw as luxuries were absolute necessities. Canteens, for one thing.

In a country spider-webbed with wetlands, American soldiers rarely had to walk far before finding a rice paddy or river – albeit not in Cambodia, where the water was, "of such a foul quality that the troops could not be expected to drink it," as Lieutenant Colonel Jaggers, commander of the 506th Infantry Regiment, wrote in his report after the operation. Presumably, those troops wouldn't need many canteens to keep well-hydrated, even on a hot day. But Koziol was an exception. He preferred juice, so that's what he put in his canteens. And there was very little orange juice flowing through the rivers in Vietnam. When Bravo Company headed into the field, each man was expected to carry three days' supplies, including water and C-rations.

"Most guys carried three or four canteens," he said. "I'd carry ten or twelve."

Even though he was no longer a combat soldier, he still had friends out there. And that consideration outweighed any trivial notions of responsibility for the taxpayers' property.

"I'd tell the guys," Koziol said. "'Hey, I'll handle this stuff. I know what the guys in the field need because I've been there.'"[2]

Bill Sorg, the Binghamton, New York native whose head wound was bandaged by Leslie Sabo during the April 8 ambush that killed Lieutenant Thomas Scarboro, returned to the company's supply depot, as did Crandall Simpson, also wounded April 8. Like Koziol, Sorg was transferred into supply after sustaining partial hearing loss.

Teb Stocks found himself in a battalion headquarters after being promoted to captain and appointed as S-4, military terminology for the supply officer, in an 82nd Airborne Division battalion. He continued in the Army after his tour was completed, but was involuntarily discharged during the postwar troop drawdown – Stocks believed he was forced out for his lack of a college degree.

Greene was pulled off the line and sent to his new assignment as an instructor at Screaming Eagle Replacement Training School – SERTS – where he trained newly arrived junior officers to the 101st Airborne Division in the particulars of small unit jungle fighting, which is exactly what Greene was up to when he got his new assignment.

"They pulled me out of a patrol and said, 'A chopper is coming. Be on it,'" he said.

Replacements for the men killed and wounded up to that point in the tour arrived. Lee Paterson had been left at a rear base on May 10 because he had linked up with Bravo Company only a few days earlier. When the company's survivors returned, Paterson, 21, was fully integrated into the unit.

"They joined me, rather than me joining them," Paterson later remarked.

From the end of May through November, when Rick Clanton's tour ended, eight men from the battalion were killed, but none from Bravo Company.[3] During the early weeks under Lane's command, Bravo Company and the rest of 3rd Battalion operated out of Ban

Me Thuot and chased the enemy throughout the Central Highlands, mostly unsuccessfully, although the Currahees exchanged fire on several occasions with enemy snipers. Bravo Company's primary mission was to attack North Vietnamese supply lines and disrupt enemy operations. They were back to cloverleafing and dodging raindrops. And it was back to moving in platoon, or even squad strength, instead of as a company, the way they did in Cambodia.

"They were a pretty tough group of hombres," Lane said of Bravo Company's surviving soldiers. "We did a lot of searching and bumped into some enemy units."

Whenever one of his platoons "bumped" into the enemy, Lane could call in artillery fire or a helicopter.

While the men of 3rd Battalion were fighting for their lives on Hill 474, in the Crow's Foot, and in Cambodia, their fellow Currahees in 1st and 2nd Battalion were doing pretty much the same in the A Shau Valley, on the Central Highlands' western fringe. During early 1970, the 3rd Battalion, 506th Regiment was operating as the tenth of nine battalions in the 101st Airborne Division, so it was a "firefighter" battalion – MACV used it to extinguish enemy flames all over the Central Highlands. In March, the 506th Regiment's other two battalions had landed in the A Shau region with the intent of engaging the enemy and driving him out, just as 3rd Battalion was then doing on Hill 474. But they quickly became the prey of an enemy that outnumbered them ten to one in some instances. For the better part of four months, the North Vietnamese and Americans battled almost daily over a small peak called Fire Support Base Ripcord, but the battle turned white hot in early July. The enemy rained down concerted attacks from higher ground surrounding Ripcord over the next three weeks until the facility was eventually abandoned. The battle of Fire Support Base Ripcord would claim the lives of more than 70 US soldiers, including Currahee Lieutenant Colonel Andre Lucas, who would receive the Medal of Honor posthumously. But Lucas wasn't the most famous person to fall at Ripcord. That distinction belonged to First Lieutenant Bob Kalsu, an artillery officer with the 101st.[4]

Kalsu went to Vietnam in November of 1969. Less than a year earlier, he had been named the Buffalo Bills' rookie of the year for his play at offensive guard. While at Oklahoma University, he had signed on through the Reserve Officer Training Corps – ROTC – and owed the military two years. He could have fulfilled that commitment in a reserve unit without interrupting his promising football career, a practice common among professional sports franchises. But Kalsu opted for a regular Army commission and was sent to Vietnam. He was killed on July 21 in a mortar attack. Two days later, the American forces abandoned Ripcord, the military notified Kalsu's wife of his death, and she gave birth to a son who would never know his father. He would be the only recently-active professional athlete to die in Vietnam.

"A lot of fine guys were killed," Lane said of the Ripcord defense. "They just kept getting chewed up."

Because the 506th Regiment's 1st and 2nd battalions had sustained such heavy losses at Ripcord, commanders at the 101st Airborne Division reintegrated the 3rd Battalion, including Bravo Company. After eight months in the combat zone, the Currahees would, for the first time in the case of many individual soldiers, be Screaming Eagles in the sense of more than just their shoulder patches. The 3/506 was attached to the 101st Airborne Division's 2nd Brigade. By mid-September, they were based at Fire Support Base Pistol into a thick jungle near Phu Bai, with an area of operation running west to the A Shau Valley. During that time, Bravo Company returned to platoon-sized operations with fairly regular hit-and-run attacks by the North Vietnamese. Snipers continued to plague the Currahees – one Bravo Company soldier was lifted out of the jungle after being hit when outside the nighttime defensive perimeter to answer nature's call.

On September 20, a Delta Company reconnaissance squad encountered a North Vietnamese ambush. Specialist Vernon Whitlock, leading the squad, was hit square in the chest with a rocket-propelled grenade. To Whitlock's surprise, the grenade didn't explode and he was not only still alive, but wasn't even injured – the grenade hit a round of machine-gun ammunition, which was flattened, but that bullet, and not Whitlock's chest, absorbed the grenade's force. After regaining his senses, Whitlock returned fire on the enemy. Private First Class Larry Dunham braved wilting enemy fire to unjam the squad's machine gun before he used it to hold off the North Vietnamese attack.[5]

For Bravo Company soldiers like Koziol, Richard Rios, Rick Brown, and Rick Clanton, who arrived in Vietnam the previous November and December, the second half of their tour was much quieter than the first. Through most of October and November, Bravo Company was kept out of action on more than a few days by the weather. While there were no fatalities after the Mother's Day Ambush, there were some close calls.

Clanton, for one, became more cautious as his tour of duty neared its end. A bout with malaria forced him out of the action for a few days in August, and he took part in one firefight in September. Richard Rios, like Clanton, also had a bout of malaria. Unlike Clanton, though, he also had battle scars as evidence of his time in combat. Rios had sustained severe injuries, including a burst eardrum and shrapnel wounds in the back from a rocket-propelled grenade in the Mother's Day Ambush.

Malaria and other tropical diseases were a constant threat to American soldiers throughout the Vietnam War, especially during the monsoon season, when the every-day rain swelled rivers with often-befouled water. Worse, it eliminated the Americans' greatest tactical and logistical advantage – their helicopters. During October of 1969, the company was in the field when heavy rains forced the cancellation of supply runs. Low on water, the men drank from a stream, which infected many of them – Jack Brickey contracted both malaria and hepatitis, which nearly was fatal.

A year later, as the men who arrived in Vietnam with Sabo were counting down the days to their DEROS, the same thing happened and the victims included Lane, who lost his entire rest-and-relaxation leave to a bout of malaria at the end of that month.

Most of the other soldiers were more fortunate with their R-and-R. During their tours, most Vietnam servicemen were permitted two weeks' leave, which benefited not only them, but also their comrades left behind – soldiers going on leave traditionally took hundreds, sometimes thousands, of dollars with them to buy things in "the world" that they couldn't get in the jungle. Many of the married soldiers made plans to use their leave to meet wives in Hawaii, which was Sabo's intent had he not died in the Mother's Day Ambush. Norm Friend and "Kid Rick" Brown were able to keep their dates in Hawaii.

Friend had sent his wife, Ardie, a diamond watch earlier in his tour – "I didn't know if I was coming back," he said. But when he got that chance to finally see his wife, Friend was distant. Guilt, and an obsession with the comrades he left behind, if only for two weeks, prevented him from truly reconnecting with his wife.

Brown would find himself in the same situation. After looking forward to his leave for months, rest-and-relaxation was something of a letdown for Brown. Before he left for Vietnam, Brown was "totally in love" with his wife. By the time of his leave, less than a year after their wedding, he could barely communicate with her.

"She called home and said, 'Rick's got demons,'" he said. "All I could do was think about my buddies… But I did get laid."

Brown was moved out of Bravo Company a few weeks after the Mother's Day Ambush through the practice of "infusion," where soldiers who had been in country for months were transferred into units that had large numbers of inexperienced troops just starting their combat tours. Brown was transferred in July to the 2nd Battalion, 35th Regiment of the 4th Infantry Division, where he became a squad leader in Delta Company. Infusion brought Brown full circle. After learning about war in "the boonies" from Frank Madrid – "He took care of an 18-year-old kid whose mom wasn't around to wipe his nose anymore," Brown said of Madrid – and Steven Dile only a few months earlier, 19-year-old Rick Brown was passing on his own hard-earned wisdom to a new crop of "cherries," most of whom were older than he was. After the Mother's Day Ambush, the remainder of Brown's combat tour was, by his own admission, somewhat foggy, as if he were trying to mentally unplug from the war while his body was still in country.

"I was angry," he said. "I wanted to kill as many of them as possible. I didn't give a damn. I figured I was going to die."

That "going to die" feeling persisted until Brown was down to his last few days in Vietnam. Ironically, those final days brought him to his final brush with death, when he was fired on by a sniper. On October 26, five days before his DEROS, Brown was moving through a creek near Ban Me Thuot, southwest of Qui Nhon, when the sniper took a shot at him. Like most of his comrades, Brown lost weight during his tour, courtesy of all those hours "humping the boonies" carrying their homes on their backs and dining on sometimes-barely-edible C-rations. And that weight loss might have saved his life when the sniper's bullet ripped through his increasingly baggy fatigues and missed Brown completely.

"I was thinking, 'This is bullshit. I want to go home.' I was way too short and I almost bought it."

But he survived, and returned home. One by one – Rios, Clanton, Nash, Bruner, Currin – in September, October, and November, the rest of Bravo Company's surviving late-1969 cherries returned to "the world." Even their company commanders – Waybright was discharged and Lane, who would make the Army his career, was promoted to assistant operations officer for 2nd Brigade in the 101st Airborne Division – were no longer around.

"It was the most rewarding experience I've ever had in my life and it was the saddest at times," Waybright said of his time commanding Bravo Company.

After an anticlimactic second half of their tour, most of them returned home and made an honest effort at returning to their lives, with varying degrees of success.

CHAPTER 19

If Rick Clanton thought he was supposed to have been proud of the year he served in Vietnam, one of the final orders he got before returning to "the world" dispelled that notion. Clanton was told not to wear his Army uniform through the civilian airport in San Francisco. For most US combat troops, homecoming meant arrival in a city that was at the epicenter of war opposition, where protesters were liable to chant taunts at returning soldiers. Clanton said the ferocity of that opposition – and the fact that much of the dissent was directed at the troops themselves – made the adjustment from combat to civilian life more difficult.

The "Band of Brothers" forebears of Clanton, Koziol, and Rios trained together at Camp Toccoa, Georgia. They jumped together in Normandy on D-Day and in Holland in Operation *Market Garden*. They froze together at Bastogne, and they went home together after serving their "duration plus six [months]."

"In most wars, you went over as a unit and you came home as a unit. In Vietnam, you went over and came home in onesies and twosies," Clanton said. "Sometimes you don't know what happened to the guys you spent a year of your life with."

After facing death for a year in Vietnam, soldiers like Richard Clanton returned to the United States with baggage that couldn't be contained in a duffel bag or suitcase in a nation that hadn't yet come up with terms like "post-traumatic stress disorder" (PTSD). When Clanton's year in the jungle ended, he packed his bag and returned home alone.

Clanton, unlikely enough, survived that year physically, if not emotionally, unscathed. During most of his tour, he was a radio telephone operator, which meant being the lifeline from ground troops to air and artillery support back at the firebase. Throughout the Vietnam War, American and American-backed troops hunted for, and were hunted by, an enemy willing to die and kill in service of Ho Chi Minh's famous "You kill ten of my soldiers and we'll kill one of yours and it will be you who tires of it first" proclamation. In the air, however, the United States enjoyed almost uncontested control. The North Vietnamese had no helicopter fleet to counter the Americans' Hueys and Chinooks, and few fighters to prevent tactical bombing from naval aircraft carriers or Air Force jets. Barring damage from ground fire, the North Vietnamese had little response to US air superiority.

That advantage was rarely more than a phone call away thanks to the radio telephone operator, a fixture in every US infantry platoon. And because getting that call through quickly could make a big difference in combat, the radio telephone operator, or RTO, was a prime target for North Vietnamese troops looking to delay a platoon commander's effort to call in an air strike or helicopter gunship support. In spite of that, Clanton, radio telephone operator for Bravo Company's 2nd Platoon, the same unit as Sabo, survived his entire combat tour without so much as being grazed by a bullet.

"It always seemed to be close, but they always missed me," he said. "I had the command to call in artillery or air support and that little antenna sticking up didn't help."

During his one year of combat service, Clanton had apparently lived a charmed life. But in some ways, it also was a curse. He arrived in Vietnam during November of 1969, fought for a year alongside some of the closest brothers he would ever have, and watched many of them, like Leslie Sabo, die, and saw others sustain debilitating wounds. It all left Clanton, who made it through some of the war's bloodiest fighting completely unscathed, wondering if they had sustained injuries meant for him, or if other soldiers had leapt into his grave, figuratively speaking. On May 10, 1970, Clanton was not on the line with Bravo Company. To this day, he doesn't remember why, on the day his closest comrades were getting killed, he wasn't around. But the question haunted him for years afterward.

"That's been part of my own demons," he said. "I was there the day after."

Clanton was hardly the only one who brought home demons from Vietnam. Jack Brickey's war ended on January 28, when Steven "Hungry" Dile died at his side. After sustaining severe wounds to his legs, arm, and torso, Brickey was hospitalized in Japan for more than a month before being transferred to a military care facility in Valley Forge, Pennsylvania. After surviving five months of combat, and severe wounds, Brickey made it back to "the world," just to have the Army put his life at risk in a snowstorm on a helicopter flight from Philadelphia to Valley Forge. He and another recovering soldier were on board the chopper, which flew directly into a late-winter storm that reduced visibility to near zero, so the pilot put down in an eastern Pennsylvania farm only to have the landowner come running out, armed with a shotgun out of fear of an alien, or perhaps communist, invasion.

While at Valley Forge, Brickey had little to do except recover and sleep. So he was surprised and pleased by the deviation from routine on the day that he awoke to find a woman twice touched by tragedy at his bedside.

"Is it OK if I visit you?" Steven Dile's mother asked Brickey. Ann Dile, widowed while her children were still young, had made the three-hour trip from Chambersburg to face the man who had been at her fun-loving, generous eldest child's side when he was killed. Her most pressing question dealt with the fate of Hungry's eternal soul – she asked if he had time to pray before he died.

"We all prayed before we went down in that ravine," Brickey told Ann Dile, and he said it seemed to give her comfort. "I didn't lie. We prayed 24/7."

When Brickey recovered from his wounds, he still owed the Army a few months before his discharge. And the Army planned to collect. He spent that time at Fort Knox, where he had almost nothing to do, before Brickey returned to Allen Park in mid-December 1970 and followed his brothers into railroad work.

Ron Gooch, whose combat tour ended when he was wounded in the April 8 ambush, was discharged in November and was back in left field for Appalachian State the following spring. It turned out to be his salvation with the transition from combat soldier to civilian on a campus where students who knew about his time in combat asked him how many babies he had killed.

"If it wasn't for baseball, I don't know what I would have done," he said.

John Greene, 1st Platoon's leader, finished his active-duty commitment at the end of 1970. He had considered staying in to be a career military officer, but the Army made that decision for him with its end-of-war drawdown. Although he had a four-year reserve commitment, Greene was called up for only a two-week activation at Fort Drum, New York, so he was able to continue school. He earned a master's degree from the University of Houston and completed law school at South Texas University.

Technically, most soldiers returning from their Vietnam combat tours still owed Uncle Sam six months on their two-year commitment, but many of them got early discharges after being wounded or by extending their combat tour by a few weeks. In a few other cases, stateside officers would extend soldiers an early release. Jerry Nash wasn't one of those. The Army held onto him as long as it could. After he returned to the United States in late 1970, he was assigned to Fort Benning, Georgia, where his services were rarely necessary. One day a week, Nash would take an ambulance out to the base's firing range in case a trainee shot himself, which didn't happen. Aside from that, his time was largely his own.

After the Mother's Day Ambush, which took the life of 22-year-old Sabo and caused 24-year-old Koziol – who would carry the nickname "The Old Man" for the rest of his life – to be moved into a non-combat role, Clanton, then 22, became one of the oldest men in Bravo Company's 2nd Platoon. He served as a squad leader, effectively being a sergeant without the stripes, as the men injured and killed on May 10 were replaced with troops fresh from the States.

Koziol, who grew up in Omaha, Nebraska, had a similar experience to Nash. He finished up his combat tour in the supply depot and headed back to the United States on October 1, 1970, completing his military commitment in Fort Riley, Washington. Although he said his troubles weren't as profound as Clanton's, the transition was still difficult.

"It's very hard to get over that when you get back," Koziol said.

Ben Currin and Mike DiLeo delayed that transition by staying in the Army, and both forged a link between the modern 101st Airborne Division, which had become an air assault unit by the Vietnam era, and its founding roots as a paratroop unit. Currin and DiLeo were both selected for the Army's elite parachute team, the Golden Knights. DiLeo, who would retire in 1992 at the rank of command sergeant major, was on the Golden Knights team in 1973.[1] That year, the team made what DiLeo called a memorable jump over Busch Stadium in St Louis before a Cardinals football game.

DiLeo jumped with the exhibition team, including group skydiving performances which he said required great precision, with the team members maneuvering within inches of each other without actually touching. "It was a lot of fun, traveling around the country jumping out of planes," he said.

The Golden Knights were founded in 1959 during the Cold War's height in response to the Soviet Union's sweep that year of the parachute jumping world championships. The full squad includes the Black and Gold Demonstration teams and the competition teams – DiLeo and Currin both jumped with the Gold Demonstration team.[2]

Currin left an even bigger mark on the Golden Knights. He was on the demonstration team from 1986 to 1991. From 1988 to 1990, he was a team leader and helped run tryouts for the 1988–89 season. He called the Golden Knights time, which ended his Army career, "a humbling experience." Tryouts are grueling, not just for candidates, but also for the evaluators. Each year's camp, held in September and October, narrows the field to a handful of soldiers selected after putting the hopefuls through at least 100 jumps.

"Skydiving was not necessarily the top priority," Currin said about the year he ran tryouts. "It was being a model soldier, your appearance, your ability to be a team player."

One of his most memorable jumps came in January 1988, when he led a demonstration team on a jump to deliver the US, POW/MIA, and American Football Conference flags into Denver's Mile High Stadium before the Broncos' AFC championship game against the Cleveland Browns. As expected, making a parachute jump into the Rocky Mountains in the dead of winter was a tricky proposition, with high winds that threatened to force cancellation of a jump scheduled to take place in front of a national television audience prior to a game that would determine one of the teams that would take part in that season's Super Bowl. As the Army's top parachutists, Golden Knights team leaders are given decision-making power over whether a jump can be made safely. Instead of aborting the jump, Currin did some on-the-fly – literally – calculations and moved the jump zone by nearly a mile to allow wind currents to carry his team safely into the stadium. In Currin's estimation, the combat experience earned at the beginning of his Army career served him well as an elite parachute jumper at the end of it.

"You're dealing with life-and-death situations and that changes the complexion of everything in the military," he said. "You have to look ahead. You have to be ready for any kind of eventuality."

Rich Lane also stayed in the military – "27 years going where Uncle Sam told me to go" – and retired in 1993 as a colonel. After his combat tour with Bravo Company, he served as an officer in the 82nd Airborne Division, Special Forces and was a battalion commander in the 10th Mountain Division. His postwar career also included a stint as ROTC instructor at the University of California at Berkeley, one of the hotbeds of anti-war dissent during the Vietnam era. Lane was less angry than mystified over the protests.

"Altruistically, the great thing about our country is that you can protest your government," he said of the demonstrations. "I was always amazed at students, who were smart, that were led around by instigators."

He finished up with the Hawaii-based Joint Special Operations Command in 1993, leading from a desk while other soldiers were in the Middle East during Operation *Desert Storm* in the First Persian Gulf War.

"I felt terrible being in Hawaii while that was going on," Lane said.

Immediately after retiring from the Army, Lane worked for the department of commerce in South Carolina, but returned west because his wife wanted to be closer to her native state of California. The move worked out well for them – he worked 16 years for the PGA Bob Hope Classic, which brought Lane's life full circle. Few, if any, entertainers did more than Hope to support troops during the Vietnam War. For years, Hope chose to be away from his own home during the Christmas season so he could entertain those who were ordered to be away from theirs. Ironically, Lane himself saw Hope live for the very first time after he began working for the renowned comedian. During his 1968 combat tour, Lane had missed Hope's big Vietnam Christmas show after being wounded.

Some of the Bravo Company soldiers, including Brown and Sabo, planned to start or finish college when they returned from Vietnam. Rios had considered going to law school when he was drafted. Sabo never made it home, and Brown and Rios lost any interest in setting foot on a college campus after they returned. Vietnam had the polar opposite effect on Freeling. His year experiencing death and destruction turned him into a focused college student. A month to the day after he returned home, Valentine's Day 1970, Freeling married the college sweetheart he left behind when the Army called. Even before the wedding, he had returned to college. And in spite of getting a late start to the semester, Freeling, who had flunked in his first try at higher education, passed all of his classes. And he kept passing his classes until he graduated, and until he eventually taught at the University of Nebraska-Omaha.

"It took a guy who didn't even want to go to college the first time, which was apparent by the fact that I only lasted a year, and it made me into quite a studious person," he said.[3]

Other Bravo Company veterans – at least those who were afforded the opportunity to grow old – had grown up during their time overseas. Bill Sorg, who had been in the company supply depot for the final four months of his combat tour, took a little time for himself before heading out into the working world. He went on to work in various jobs – at a glass factory, construction, and in a stone quarry. While Sorg took up with his life pretty much where he had left off, at least from an occupational standpoint, he found that most of his old friends were up to activities that he had once enjoyed, but couldn't any more. One weekend, some of his pals invited him along on a camping trip. For Sorg – who had slept outdoors too many nights, and spent too many sleepless nights outdoors in the Army – camping held absolutely no appeal.

"I had matured so much that the stuff my friends were doing was stupid," Sorg said. "How do I tell them I don't want to do that?"

His reprieve came in the form of a rainstorm that forced them into a hotel. Even though he had slept outside in the rain on an almost daily basis in Vietnam, Sorg was glad to spend that night in a hotel bed.

After a year aching to return home and continue with his life, Jerry Nash, the company medic, found the adjustment more difficult than he expected. The Jerry Nash who left for Vietnam in 1969 had been a gregarious, outgoing man. The one who returned in 1971 had changed – "I didn't want to talk to anyone," he said.

Angry and dealing with undiagnosed post-traumatic stress disorder, Nash went back home to Tennessee and began working with his brother at a Goodyear dealership, which was difficult because it forced him to deal intimately with the public. It didn't last long. Nash punched his boss in a fit of anger and was fired. But that, and another incident in which he almost came to blows while on a recreational boating trip, was the warning that set his life on a better path. Right about the time Nash lost his job at Goodyear, he was out with family on a boat when the storm began turning foul. Another boater cut him off as he rushed to dock before the storm hit and Nash, by his own admission, overreacted.

"It was almost like my fuse was very short," Nash said. "It didn't take much to set me off."

So Nash decided, without the benefit of any treatment, that he had to change. His wife, Elaine, was already working as a teacher – they had met while Nash was attending school at Tennessee Tech – and he followed her into that profession. After 12 years as an elementary school principal, he retired as a regional school administrator where he oversaw federal programs. Working in education forced Nash to overcome the anger he brought home from Vietnam – or at least suppress it – and reclaim the personality he had before going to war.

"I had to do my job," he said. "In education, you can't be seen in a beer joint. You had to keep your nose clean."

Men like Clanton, Koziol, and Rios – who served during that 1969–70 tour of duty with Sabo – were in country during a time when public support for the war evaporated. As early as 1966, opposition to the Vietnam War was evident on college campuses. But it wasn't until after the Tet Offensive that the general public began to see the war as a folly thanks to the strategic failure of the Tet Offensive. By 1970, college protests like the one that turned fatal at Kent State – a few days before the Mother's Day Ambush – turned into a vanguard of popular sentiment against the war.[4] That opinion affected the Vietnam combat soldiers, according to a military-commissioned study that determined the combination of an unsupportive civilian attitude toward the troops, assigning soldiers as individuals rather than as units, and the nature of combat itself were all contributing factors to high rates of post-traumatic stress disorder, to the point that the US military realized it needed to provide more support services to address psychological difficulties as a result of difficulties experienced by Vietnam veterans. About three in every ten Vietnam veterans have sustained post-traumatic stress disorder over the course of their lives, according to a review by Air Force psychologists.[5]

Those studies described the full experience of Koziol, Rios, and Clanton. And even for many of those who didn't immediately display outward signs of post-traumatic stress, picking up with their lives at the place where they left off was too great a challenge. Leslie Sabo and Clanton were among the few soldiers in 2nd Platoon who were married. But after Clanton's return from war, his wife began complaining that the man who came back resembled the husband who left only in appearance and name, effectively scuttling the marriage.

Looking back in 2008 from a perspective of more than 30 years, Clanton didn't argue with his ex-wife's assessment. After spending a year in the most serious circumstances, he wasn't exactly ready to get on with his adult responsibilities. The result was an inconsistent temperament.

"She kept talking about how I changed. War has that effect on people," Clanton said. "When I got back at first, I wanted to relax. I didn't want to be on guard all of the time."

Clanton's marriage wasn't the only one to fall apart after his return. Rick Brown had wed his high school sweetheart just before shipping to Vietnam and he celebrated his first anniversary on November 1, 1970, by ending his combat tour and departing for home. That union ended in divorce, although the deterioration took a lot longer for Brown than it had for Clanton – they divorced in 1980. Brown blamed himself, or more accurately, the pain he brought home from Vietnam, for the separation.

"I wasn't easy on my wife and I wasn't easy on my children," said Brown.

Ruben Rueda's marriage didn't even make it back home. Only weeks after starting in Bravo's combat grind in mid-1969, he received a "Dear John" breakup letter, which sent him into a near suicidal funk. As a result, he seized every opportunity to perform hazardous duty, including venturing into the caves and tunnels on Hill 474. On

May 10, 1970, Rueda was walking point when the North Vietnamese sprung the Mother's Day Ambush. The war cost him not only a marriage, but his Catholic faith. When he returned home, Rueda said he was angry with both God and man, which boiled over when someone told him to pray for forgiveness, because Rueda was firmly convinced that he was entitled to offer forgiveness, rather than be a supplicant asking for it.

"After what I did, I've gotta ask the Pope for forgiveness?" he said. "I lost my religion over it."

The war turned Rueda into a man of peace. Before he was drafted, Rueda had been an avid hunter who credited his time in the woods for saving his life in the Vietnam jungles. But he had lost his taste for hunting after getting back home from war. Bill Sorg, a 2nd Platoon soldier wounded on April 8, also came home with no taste for handling guns.

"I didn't want to have anything to do with killing," Rueda said. "I lost the spirit for destroying life."

While Vietnam destroyed some of Bravo Company's marriages, wives turned out to be a saving grace for Bravo vets Mark Rogers and Doug Lange, who credited the support they got from their wives as a key factor in easing their transition to civilian life, even as they suffered themselves.

"Those ladies had to put up with so much crap, and when we came home, they had to put up with us," Lange said.

By Norm Friend's admission, few wives had to put up with more than his own spouse, Ardie. She gave birth to their son, Scott, the same day as her husband was spirited away by the Army. By the time Norm returned home, Scott was two years old, and hadn't seen his father for more than a few days his entire life. After a harrowing combat tour, and a hostile reception upon returning home, Norm Friend faced the heartbreaking prospect of having a son who didn't even know who he was.

And Ardie didn't know him all that well, either. The man she fell in love with two years earlier was gone. The man who returned from combat was withdrawn and sometimes hurtful.

"I was so excited to have the person who left come back," she said. "But that person never came back."

In some ways, Ardie said things were worse for Norm than they were for vets who sustained severe war wounds because her husband's wounds – unlike the scars left behind by bullets and grenade shrapnel – weren't visible. Norm Friend, like Clanton, sustained no visible damage but returned home to a society that not only held their combat service in contempt, but also saw their emotional wounds as a sign of weakness. Friend said he drank heavily and buried himself in his work as a long-haul truck driver, which kept him out of the house for stretches as long as 36 days. Ardie admitted that she sometimes looked forward to those absences.

"I'm thankful every day that he came home," Ardie said. "But I prayed to God that he would go. I would be able to regenerate myself while he was gone."

While both Norm and Ardie Friend admitted that he was emotionally abusive in the years after returning from Vietnam, it never crossed over into the physical.

"She's never been hit in her life," Norm said.

"Because he knew he'd have to sleep," Ardie responded.

But as rough as some of the marriages were after the men returned, a couple of Bravo Company's wives would gladly have traded places.

CHAPTER 20

It was a slow day at the big supermarket in Grand Haven, Michigan, and clerk Candace Sullins Moore thumbed through a copy of the Parade Sunday newspaper magazine supplement when she found an article describing the process for notifying family members that their loved ones were killed or missing in Vietnam. The article was of special interest to Candace because her husband of less than a year was in the middle of his combat tour. She had just read the part that described how the detail usually consisted of two soldiers, one white and one black, when she looked into the parking lot and saw two soldiers, in dress uniforms, walking toward her store.

One was white and the other was black.

"I knew they were coming for me," she said.

Ernest Moore, Candace Sullins' husband, was among eight soldiers who died on May 10 in the Mother's Day Ambush. The next morning, Moore's body was found, still at his 60mm machine gun. Although they wouldn't meet for another 30 years, the lives of Candace Sullins and Rose Sabo Brown were connected from that day forward.

Almost to a man, Leslie Sabo's comrades in Bravo Company remember him for three things – courage under fire, a great sense of humor in difficult situations, and his devotion to the newlywed wife he left behind in Ellwood City.

"He adored his bride," said Mark Rogers, who served alongside Sabo in 2nd Platoon.

For Rose, the years following her first husband's death were difficult. By her own admission, some of those problems stemmed from her own decisions. If Leslie Sabo's family – his wife, parents, brother, sister-in-law, and nephews – were bound by tragedy, a decision made by Rose Sabo Brown, one she would come to regret, drove a wedge into it. Before 1970 was out, Rose had a new husband following her second marriage in less than a year. She said her former in-laws didn't forgive her for that.

To Rose, the new man hadn't been entirely new. She had known him for a few years, when he dated a neighbor of hers, and he was a friend of her cousin. She became reacquainted with the man during her husband's tour of duty in Vietnam, after Rose took a new job, going from her job at Airways Luggage in West Pittsburg, a small hamlet tucked between Ellwood City and New Castle, to working as a clerk at a newsstand in Ellwood City. They got together regularly on her breaks, but Rose maintains that it wasn't a romantic relationship on her end. However, she claimed to have discovered later that Brown's designs on her went well beyond talks about her husband. She said the man had made a bet with Rose's cousin that he would eventually strike up a romantic relationship with the war widow. But Rose said she was never unfaithful to her husband. Just the opposite, in fact.

"All we ever did was talk. I'd talk about Leslie the whole time," she said. "I never dated him."

In 1970, Ellwood City's population was nearly 25 percent larger than it would be 30 years later, after the big steel mills had been closed down or relocated. But even then, the town was small enough to sustain a rumor. Enough people knew that Rose was married to a soldier – hundreds of people had attended her wedding – so they knew that she was hanging around with a man other than her husband.

And they talked.

"People started talking, spreading nasty rumors about me," she said. "When people talk about you, it's like, 'Why did you say something like that?'"

Rose said the rumors became worse after Leslie was killed. One of those stories, which she denies, had her going into Brown's apartment for a rendezvous. That story got back to Leslie's brother, George. Rose said that and similar stories alienated her from the Sabo family. Rose said the woman leaving the apartment was another person who looked like her. She blamed the rumors – and her fragile state of mind after her first husband's death – for her decision to remarry while many people believed she still should have been in mourning.

"People wouldn't leave us alone. He said 'Let's get married' and I said 'OK.' It was horrible. People were so cruel," she said. "People had no idea what I was going through."

But to anyone disinclined to believe Rose's account, the timing was suspicious. She gave birth to a daughter less than a year after the second marriage. The couple also would later have a son.

"I tried to get pregnant with Leslie," she said, referring to the one month they had together in October of 1969. "With the asshole, I got pregnant on my wedding night."

Rose said her second husband was emotionally abusive. They divorced some years later and she never pursued a relationship again. Rose regretted her second marriage, which she said came during a time when she was still reeling from the combat death of her first husband. After 2002, when some of Leslie Sabo's comrades got in contact with her for the first time, Rose discovered that she wasn't the only Vietnam War widow who went through an ill-advised second marriage. She recalled the sad tales of other women who remarried after their husbands died in combat with outcomes similar to Rose's.

"We all got married after our husbands got killed and we all regretted it," she said.

Candace Sullins stopped short of calling her second marriage a regret, even though it, too, ended in divorce.

In one incident, Candace said she was seen with a male relative, which triggered rumors that she was stepping out with a new man.

In fact, Candace did remarry more than a year after Ernest Moore's death and moved to Chicago, a few hours' drive to the southwest, in part to escape the small-town rumor mill. She said Moore's family might have been disappointed in her decision to remarry, but they still maintained a friendly relationship. She attends Bravo Company reunions with A. J. Moore, Ernest's younger brother.

"They still call me their daughter-in-law," Candace said. "His mother always considered my son her grandson."

But like Rose Sabo Brown, Candace was troubled by dark thoughts about her first husband.

"I always dreamed that Ernest came back and he was disappointed in me."

A. J. Moore was still in high school when the soldiers came for him. He said Ernest had planned on working for a year before going to college, but his Selective Service number came up before he could enroll and obtain a college-student draft deferment. After Ernest died in the Mother's Day Ambush, A. J. delivered the bad news to his younger sisters, one of whom was in elementary school, but the soldiers couldn't immediately locate their parents. A. J. went out to find them because he didn't want them to find out through the small-town grapevine. Eventually, Ernest Moore's parents were located in the nearby town of Muskegon. Like Candace and Rose, A. J. Moore, a talented metalworker who has plied his craft manufacturing tributes to Ernest and his Bravo Company comrades, would one day be adopted into the Bravo Company fraternity.

Grand Haven is located on the western coast of Michigan, not far from Grand Rapids and Chicago. In 1970, the year Leslie Sabo and Ernest Moore were fighting and dying in Southeast Asia, Grand Haven had a population of about 11,000, slightly larger than Ellwood City. Today, the permanent population of Ernest Moore's hometown is still only slightly larger than that of Leslie Sabo's, although Grand Haven's summer population swells with tourists who come to see the nearby sand dunes – the Grand Haven area along Lake Michigan boasts some of the world's finest sand.

After her husband's death, Candace said she felt as if the whole town was watching her and judging whether her behavior was appropriate for the town's Vietnam War widow, a sentiment that Rose Sabo Brown certainly understood.

George Sabo, Leslie's brother, was never convinced of Rose's proclamations of devotion to Leslie. He said she remarried within months of Leslie Sabo's death because she had got pregnant and at least one of Sabo's relatives said she had sent Leslie a "Dear John" breakup letter shortly before he was killed. Rose denied those claims. But if Leslie's death was difficult for Rose, it wasn't any easier for Leslie Sabo's parents or his brother's family. Even before Ellwood City began building monuments to his brother and all the other soldiers killed in Vietnam – as of December of 2008, there were three monuments to six soldiers, including Leslie, from the town itself and four more from the surrounding area – George was packing to leave town for good.

George was finishing his studies at Youngstown State University, his father's alma mater, when Leslie was training for his combat tour. By his seventh year of part-time study in the engineering curriculum, George decided he didn't want to be an engineer. So he and a friend, Jerry Mitchell, picked two majors – industrial marketing and industrial relations – and flipped a coin to decide which one they would take. The coin dictated that George would study industrial marketing.

"We were looking at the quickest way to get out of school," George said. "I never did a day's work in industrial marketing and he never did a day's work in industrial relations."

His first job after college would be as an engineering manager for Rockwell International in New Castle. In 1971, less than two years after his brother's combat death, George's job with Rockwell took him to Ohio. He would be joined by thousands of Ellwood City and western Pennsylvania residents forced by economic reality to choose between staying in their hometown and keeping gainful employment. Within ten years of the tube mill's closure in 1974, both of the town's movie theaters were gone and the downtown business district was a shadow of its heyday during George and Leslie's teenage years.

George would go on to work for the automobile manufacturing division of Johnson Controls as a manager and landed in the Detroit suburb of Dearborn, Michigan. He would retire as an executive vice president for the company in 2006 at the age of 63, just about the same age that Leslie Sabo Sr. was when he buried his younger son. George's three sons – the boys that Leslie ironically promised to raise if anything happened to his brother – grew into manhood. At the time of their uncle's death, Anthony, the eldest, was only eight. Michael, the youngest, was not yet five. The three boys grew to manhood in eastern Michigan. Anthony went to work in construction, Steve became a school teacher, and Michael pursued a career as a detective for the Dearborn, Michigan, police department.

Leslie Sabo Sr. had shepherded his family through the turbulence of Hungarian politics during World War II, then spirited it out of Eastern Europe just ahead of that nation's takeover by the Soviet Union and into what he must have thought was safety in the United States, only to see his son die at the hands of an entirely different band of communists. When he learned of Leslie Jr.'s death, he cursed Richard Nixon for sending his son into Cambodia. The father outlived his son by only a few years. The heart problems that had been stalking Leslie Sr. since middle age claimed his life in 1977 at the age of 70.

Elisabeth Sabo remained in the family home, on Pershing Street in Ellwood City's Ewing Park neighborhood, for another 15 years before she was no longer able to live by herself. She moved to a nursing home in Dearborn, near her son, grandchildren, and great-grandchildren. She died on April 27, 2008, at the age of 96. Her obituary was published in the *Ellwood City Ledger*, almost exactly one year after the newspaper initially reported that Leslie Sabo was being considered for the nation's highest military honor. Elisabeth, who began life as a Presbyterian in a Catholic nation, was buried alongside her husband and son in the same plot at Holy Redeemer Catholic Cemetery on the outskirts of Ellwood City.

George Sabo, his parents, and his family got on with their lives, but that doesn't mean they did it painlessly. Forty years later, George found that even talking about his brother brought back the anguish he felt immediately after Leslie's death and the Army's decision not to provide his family with the full story of the Mother's Day Ambush, and then to institutionally forget what that story was, delaying their efforts to find meaning in his death. Ultimately, it fell to the men who served with Leslie and were with him in his final hours to comfort his family.

But first, they had to heal themselves.

CHAPTER 21

When George Koziol returned home to Nebraska in the late spring of 1971 after completing his military hitch, he was confronted with the moral quandary of how to honor a debt that is beyond the capacity of any mortal to repay, to a man who is beyond the reach of any mortal currency. Koziol watched from the cargo door of a helicopter as the closest friend he would ever have died while saving his life.

After the Vietnam War, the American soldiers who had participated, many of whom were teenagers when they were sent off by their government to kill and die for their country, turned out to have been the experimental psychological subjects whose lessons have benefited future generations of servicemen and women. Navy Lieutenant Commander Shannon Johnson, a psychologist who worked with combat soldiers from the Second Persian Gulf War, said those whose lives are saved by the sacrifice of their comrades are given a tremendous gift, and left with a tremendous emotional weight.

"The guilt that those left behind have is sometimes compounded by a sense of unworthiness," she says. "They cannot accept that their lives were worth more than the life of their loved comrade. They are left with the heavy burden of trying to measure up to the great sacrifice so that they could live on. For some, the burden is too much."[1]

Ruben Rueda, who had lost his marriage while in Vietnam, and gave up his faith and passion for hunting when he returned home, would sever ties completely with his memories and the men he shared them with. It would be more than 40 years before he saw any of them again.

"I felt a lot of guilt," he said.

Dick Freeling – who hit his DEROS date in early January and was gone before the January 28 firefight that took the lives of Steven Dile, Frank Madrid, Pete Guzman, and John Shaffer – felt the same guilt when he made it home and realized that some of the guys he knew were still fighting and dying. Freeling even considered re-enlisting until his wife pointed out that, by the time he went through training again, all the guys he served with would have been discharged. That dose of logic was enough to convince Freeling to remain a civilian and eased some of his guilt.

"I had a real problem that I wasn't there again," he said. "It's like I left something undone."[2]

For George Koziol, adjusting to civilian life was exacerbated by survivor's guilt over the fact that he made it through the Mother's Day Ambush, and he admitted that he felt the pressure of living his life not just for himself, but for a friend who took his place in death. But even without that, he said the battle-honed edge he brought home didn't dissipate easily, which made even the most routine acts difficult.

"I'll tell you why you can't sleep after you get back home," he said. "When you were over there, you had that other guy covering your back."[3]

Koziol admitted that he came home in no mood to dwell on the Vietnam War, which – along with the guilt – goes a long way toward explaining why he and the other men who knew about Leslie Sabo's heroism remained silent while his Medal of Honor recommendation languished with the rest of his file in the National Archives.

"It was difficult to talk about it for a long time," he said. "You try to forget what happened in Vietnam."[4]

One of the ways Bravo Company's veterans tried to forget what happened was by not talking about it. "Kid Rick" Brown was angry when he got home. The military didn't offer him any help, and the public reaction of hostility toward Vietnam veterans simply exacerbated the problem. But Brown did receive some compassion, and from an unlikely source – his boss at Somers Rubber Company, where he went to work. Many veterans, aware of public opinion and wary of being regarded as pariahs, didn't share their service records with their employers or co-workers. Brown's boss knew that he had been in Vietnam and allowed him some latitude.

"He said, 'If you get angry, take a walk around the block,'" Rick Brown said.

Brown admits to having to take a few walks around the block, literary and figuratively, as he bottled up the emotional fallout from his combat tour.

"My own family didn't know anything," he said. "I told them, 'I'm not talking about it.'"

If Sabo's Medal of Honor recommendation was, as Alton Mabb would surmise three decades later, just something that "fell through the cracks," it's also worth noting that circumstances made those cracks considerably larger than normal. And the United States, from the college kids who protested the war to the politicians who supported it, and even the men who fought in it, developed a case of collective amnesia about the Vietnam War. That mental outlook generated a fog which obscured the tale surrounding Sabo's death.

That attitude made it even more difficult for those returning home from Vietnam, even if they hadn't been the beneficiaries of a fellow serviceman's sacrifice. Those who survived the Mother's Day Ambush faced the same, if not greater, emotional challenges than the combat soldiers who would follow them. But the Vietnam vets' problems went undiagnosed and untreated, for decades in some cases, while those who suffered were left to heal themselves.

Within two years of his return from military service, Richard Clanton divorced and remarried. For years since his tour in Vietnam, Clanton was plagued by self-reproach that was, in its way, even worse than the guilt Koziol felt. Clanton suffered emotionally from the knowledge that he wasn't with Bravo Company on May 10, 1970. While his 2nd Platoon mates fought for their lives – almost 33 percent fatalities and virtually 100 percent wounded – Clanton felt he had betrayed them by not being there.

"In my mind, I had deserted them," he said. "My recollection was that someone [else] was carrying my radio. So maybe they took something that was meant for me."

Koziol said he understood the demons Clanton wrestled with for nearly 30 years, because he had overcome them himself. For Koziol, the guilt was a little more acute because of his belief that Leslie Sabo took his own place in death. Koziol probably spent more downtime with Sabo, and forged a closer relationship with him than with any other soldier in Bravo Company, which heightened his sense of guilt and loss.

"I don't think George had it that great for a few years after Vietnam," Clanton said. "It was a difficult thing for George to face."

Clanton and Koziol weren't alone among Bravo Company's veterans in dealing with those memories. For years, though, they were all dealing with those memories alone. And those demons claimed at least one victim. A veteran, who had been a team leader in combat during the war, wound up homeless and died prematurely.

"He was KIA but died years and years later," said Bravo veteran Lee Paterson.

By the time the veterans of Bravo Company began gathering for reunions in 2003, Koziol had quieted his own guilt and pain enough to offer Clanton absolution for the feeling that he had abandoned his comrades in the Mother's Day Ambush. At that first reunion, Koziol told Clanton something that lifted his guilt over not being with his comrades on May 10, 1970, and the feeling that someone else was injured or killed in his place.

"He told me, 'Rick, you were at places I wasn't. You were in firefights I wasn't,'" Clanton said. "'We all have our time and you just weren't meant to be there.'"

Over the previous 30 years since returning from Vietnam, Clanton said he had heard similar sentiments from others, but it took Koziol's words to serve as a salve that could not have been provided by a psychologist, counselor, or even from a family member, but only from someone who had the same experience.

"It didn't mean as much from them as it did for someone who was there."

Many of the men in Bravo Company grew up as the sons of men who won World War II, came home and never talked about what they experienced in Europe, North Africa, and the Pacific islands, because that was what "real men" did. After their own combat experience, Clanton said he had absolutely no desire to talk about the war and he thought his comrades felt the same way.

"We just wanted to close that memory of our lives."

For 30 years, that was exactly what happened. But when the soldiers of Bravo Company closed that memory door, it hid the story of Leslie Sabo's heroism in a dusty, seldom-seen shelf in the National Archives.

CHAPTER 22

The first thing Alton Mabb Jr. noticed about Sergeant Leslie Halasz Sabo Jr.'s Army service record was its thickness.

"There must have been 100 pages in that file," Mabb said of the day he stumbled upon the folder that contained the official story of Sabo's final year in this world.

When it comes to Army files, size matters. The typical service register includes only a few pages, listing the soldier's service in a no-nonsense manner. Embellishments, except in the cases of courts martial or battlefield distinction, are largely a waste of paper. To Mabb, a columnist for *Screaming Eagle* magazine, the folder attracted his interest as more than just fodder for his next article. In his day job, Mabb is a customer service representative for the Internal Revenue Service. But his passion is for making sure that his fellow Vietnam veterans receive the recognition they deserve through his work with *Screaming Eagle*, the publication of the 101st Airborne Division Association.

He earned that column-writing job the hard way. Mabb was with the reconnaissance unit in the 2nd Battalion of the 502nd Infantry Regiment, 101st Airborne Division, as part of a mortar crew in

Vietnam. *Screaming Eagle* isn't just the method Mabb uses to express his journalistic leanings. It's part of his identity, being part of that storied tradition that began with the June 6, 1944 drop into Normandy.

"The same thing goes with the World War II guys," he said. "It's a part of America because of that shoulder patch, because of that eagle."

On that day in the spring of 1999, Mabb was doing research in the National Archives, on the campus of the University of Maryland, when a librarian handed him a box of files. One of those files – which attracted Mabb's attention on account of its thickness – was Leslie Sabo's military record. Inside Sabo's folder, Mabb discovered a story of heroism unknown to all but a handful of people, a list which, at the time, did not include Sabo's mother, brother, adult nephews, widow, or his childhood friends in Ellwood City.

Among all the millions of people who have served in the US military since the beginning of the Civil War, fewer than 3,500, as of 2014, have received the Medal of Honor. In 1862, when the Department of War, now called the Defense Department, created an award for valor in wartime, General George McClellan, then the Army chief of staff, opposed it because he worried that it might be awarded not on merit, but on the basis of social class and political influence, which was then the custom in Europe. Nearly half of all the Medals of Honor given out were given for acts of distinction during the Civil War, because that was, at the time, the US military's only decoration for battlefield valor.[1]

In 1941, with another war looming, the US military adopted its current medal hierarchy, which established the following decorations, in ascending order, for combat distinction: Bronze Star, Silver Star, Distinguished Service Cross (Distinguished Flying Cross in what was then the Army Air Corps and is the Air Force today; Navy Cross in the Navy and Marine Corps), and the Medal of Honor. Under those rules, the Distinguished Service Cross is awarded for combat heroism not worthy of the Medal of Honor, and so on for the Silver Star and Bronze Star. A Medal of Honor must be approved by the entire military command structure – including the secretary of the military branch in question, the Secretary of Defense, and eventually the

President of the United States. Along the way, any one of those officials can deny the recommendation and stop the process.[2] Since the current standard was set, only slightly more than 800 people have received the award. If all of those servicemen were placed in a single military unit, it would barely amount to a fully-manned battalion. McClellan would be pleased to know that the Medal of Honor is now given only for the most extreme acts of conspicuous intrepidity, to use the phrasing common to award citations.

Ironically in war, an enterprise more readily associated with killing, Medals of Honor are given more often for saving lives than for taking them.[3] Sabo, who was killed on May 10, 1970, during the Army's incursion into Cambodia, was the ninth of ten Ellwood City-area men to die during the Vietnam War. Based on an eyewitness account at the time, Sabo's commanders recommended him for the Medal of Honor. And it bothered Mabb that no medal was ever awarded.

"The guy got lost in the shuffle and I didn't care for that," said Mabb, who served with the 101st in 1970–71, toward the end of the division's activity in Vietnam.[4]

So Mabb, of Jacksonville, Florida, put pressure on the government – military and civilian – to recognize the sacrifice of a man who, with the exception of service with the 101st Airborne in Vietnam, had very little in common with him.

But that was enough.

"Part of it is being a proud member of the 101st Airborne Division," Mabb said. "It's also for us as Vietnam veterans. Maybe there's a little Don Quixote."

Totally by accident, Mabb discovered Sabo's military file. After that file turned up, Mabb immediately began ringing all the bells he could on Sabo's behalf. He devoted his column in *Screaming Eagle* to cracking the unresolved mystery of Sabo's Medal of Honor recommendation. Mabb also contacted his congresswoman, US Representative Corrine Brown, who represents the Jacksonville area.

"Based on my experience, I would claim that as worthy of a Medal of Honor," Mabb said of the documents in Sabo's file. "It started out as a quest. I sort of took it on because someone has to speak for the dead."[5]

But Mabb also knew that he couldn't speak for the dead without using the voices of those men who survived the Mother's Day Ambush because of Sabo's sacrifice. After finding the file, Mabb's next *Screaming Eagle* column included a request for contact information on a list of men who had served in Bravo Company's 2nd Platoon, including George Koziol and Richard Rios. In response to that column, Richard Clanton, whose name was not included on the *Screaming Eagle* list because he wasn't with the unit the day Sabo was killed, contacted Mabb and got him in touch with Koziol and Rios.

By the time Mabb started his own investigation of Sabo's death, veterans like Koziol and Clanton were reaching a place where they were finally emotionally prepared to talk about the Mother's Day Ambush and the rest of their experiences in Vietnam. Because Sabo received no military decoration for his actions on May 10, 1970, it was obvious to Mabb, a military historian by avocation, that the Medal of Honor investigation was never completed. Each of the other seven men killed in the ambush received medals for combat valor ranging from Bronze Stars to a Silver Star. Many of the survivors – including Koziol, who got a Bronze Star and Waybright, the company commander, who received the Silver Star – were honored for their actions. But unlike Sabo, none of them were recommended for the US military's highest honor.

Because Sabo had received no decoration aside from an interim Army Commendation Medal, Mabb quickly surmised that the Medal of Honor recommendation hadn't been rejected, but that the Army's evaluation of the request had never been completed. And that annoyed him to no end. A letter, dated March 17, 2002, from Mabb to US Representative Corrine Brown laid out the situation with Sabo's stalled request and included the demand "What Happened?", a question that, even in its written form, fairly dripped with frustration and anger. Mabb advocated for Sabo with a fervor that surprised even those who had served alongside the Pennsylvania soldier.

"Tony didn't know Les. Tony didn't know us and he took it on anyway," Rick Clanton said.

To Mabb, it didn't matter that he didn't know Leslie Sabo or any of the other men in Bravo Company because he still took the fate of Sabo's memory personally. To Mabb, it was important because he saw Sabo not as a stranger, but a brother he never met.

"I'm proud of being a Vietnam veteran. Part of it is justice, part of it is being a proud member of the 101st Airborne Division," Mabb said.

But while Sabo's comrades honored the Soldiers' Creed with his body, the Army apparently did not do the same for his memory, a fact that frustrated Mabb.

"That company got the shit kicked out of it for a while," he said. "There seemed to be something from my experience that seemed not to be right."[6]

The file Mabb discovered went a long way in solving the mystery of how Sabo's Medal of Honor recommendation went missing. In the letter to Representative Brown, he reported that the documentary trail ended on July 1970, when the 3rd Battalion, 506th Regiment was returned to 101st Airborne Division command – it had been attached to the 4th Infantry Division for Operation *Binh Tay*. A complete Medal of Honor investigation usually requires multiple interviews with witnesses, and Mabb said those interviews probably never took place because the lines of communication between command of the 4th and 101st divisions were broken after *Binh Tay* was completed. Waybright said he forwarded the Medal of Honor recommendation out of deference to his men who supported the action. As a matter of procedure, Medal of Honor requests have to move to the very top military echelons. In Sabo's case, Waybright would have sent Koziol's document to battalion, then regimental command, and to the 101st Airborne Division.

Koziol and Alton Mabb both think that might have had something to do with why the Medal of Honor recommendation got sidetracked. An additional complicating factor was that, on May 15, 1971, almost one year to the day after Sabo was killed, the 506th Regiment was deactivated and sent home. The 4th Infantry had already been rotated home and, with all the clerical duties involved in the move, it's not difficult to imagine the Medal of Honor recommendation being misplaced and forgotten.

"Things can get lost in the shuffle," Koziol said. "When we came out of Cambodia, we went one way and the 4th Infantry Division went another."[7]

Koziol and Mabb both thought Sabo's Medal of Honor recommendation might have got to brigade or divisional command in either one or both divisions, and staff in the 4th Infantry said that, since Sabo was a Screaming Eagle, the 101st Airborne would review the award testimony. Meanwhile, command in the 101st likely thought that since the 4th Infantry Division had run the operation in Cambodia, it would address the issue.

Ultimately, the leaders of both units left behind the memory of a fallen soldier.

CHAPTER 23

In his work as a manager at a company that installs touchscreen cash registers, Carmen "Butch" Buccelli is known for two things – an ever-present dish of pistachios and a near-photographic memory. Buccelli became a pistachio junkie during his days accompanying Leslie Sabo, the man who would, for less than a year, be his brother-in-law. It turned out that Sabo plays a significant role in Buccelli's memories as well. Four decades after Sabo shipped off to Vietnam, and said farewell to his family for the last time, Buccelli could easily recall the good times they had while Sabo courted his sister.

And Buccelli remembers the not-so-good days after Sabo's death just as easily.

"Up until the day my father died, that was the saddest day of my life," Buccelli said about hearing of his brother-in-law's death.

Most of the people who knew Leslie Sabo can be placed neatly into one of two categories. There were the family and friends who knew him during the first 20 years of his life, and the comrades who fought alongside Sabo as he slogged through the jungles of Vietnam, who faced the enemy with him and ultimately battled alongside him in his final hours. Carmen Buccelli Jr., who nurtured a friendship with Sabo in peacetime and followed him to war, had a foot in both of those worlds.

When Buccelli got the news of Sabo's death, he took leave from Army training at Fort Hood, Texas, to attend the funeral. Buccelli is the last person left alive to have seen inside the bag, marked "Remains Unfit For Viewing," that the military sent home from Cambodia. P. O. Contrucci, the funeral director who conducted Sabo's arrangements, was a friend of the family and he took Carmen Sr. and Jr. to his prep room. The experience – and the memory of it – would haunt Buccelli for years. Contrucci sprayed an air freshener and ordered the Buccellis to stand back before cutting the bag open, which gave both men their final look at Sabo's body. They would later tell Rose and other relatives that Leslie Sabo was identified by his wedding ring.

That was a lie out of respect for the sensitivities of Sabo's loved ones by hiding the actual horrific condition of his remains. In fact, Sabo was wearing no ring and Buccelli remembered there was no way to identify the body as Sabo's.

"You barely could tell it was a human body," Buccelli said. "There were jagged bones where his legs would have been, where his head would have been."

As an active-duty soldier, Buccelli was permitted to participate in his brother-in-law's funeral ceremony by presenting his sister with the flag that had draped Sabo's coffin.

Less than two years after Sabo was laid to rest, Buccelli arrived in Vietnam himself, as an artillery reconnaissance platoon sergeant in the 196th Infantry Division, based in Da Nang at the time. Rose Sabo Brown, Leslie's widow and Buccelli's sister, said she was going through some of her brother's documents a few years ago, when she came across a journal her brother wrote while he was in country. She said the document included a report of her brother's first enemy kill, when he continued firing his weapon and repeatedly shouted, "This is for Leslie!" even after the enemy soldier was dead.

Carmen Buccelli admitted that he was angry that the North Vietnamese had not only killed the man who was like a brother – and a hero, even before he faced combat – to him, and might have desecrated his body, but would admit only that he had been "aggressive" in engaging the enemy during his tour. And his duty – as a forward observer seeking out enemy mortar and artillery emplacements – gave him plenty of opportunity to carry out the vengeance he craved.

"That was on my mind the day I knew I was going over there," he said.

Buccelli said that quest to even the score for Leslie was a contributing factor in a decision by his unit's leaders to cut his tour short. In 1972, a portion of the 196th Division was ordered to rotate home as part of a scheduled troop drawdown. Buccelli said he was picked to return to the United States because his fervor might have put him and other soldiers at risk. Like other veterans returning home from Vietnam, Buccelli said he was told not to wear his uniform when he arrived in San Francisco, where war protesters would be waiting with a hostile reception.

"They were literally up on the bridges in the airport, spitting and throwing things," he said. "It even happened in little Ellwood City."

Buccelli said he has noticed a change in the overall attitude people have toward Vietnam veterans since those days when he trod carefully through the airport in San Francisco. By the mid-2000s, nearly 35 years after returning from his time in combat, Buccelli said he has begun to feel that the nation has finally welcomed him home. But even when people have tried to express their support for his service, it sometimes comes off as patronizing, like the people who have told him that they understand that he was only following orders.

"I'd want to say, 'What do you think I did?'" Buccelli said. "I may have been aggressive, but I did nothing immoral."

Not long after being discharged, Buccelli left his hometown for good. He settled in the Denver area, where he met his wife, Debra. They now have three kids and nine grandchildren, including a grandson who was born on May 11, 2005, one day after the 35th anniversary of Leslie Sabo's death. The baby's grandfather was grateful that the birth didn't come 24 hours earlier.

"I did not want him born on that day," he said.

While Buccelli said he never completely recovered emotionally from the death of his brother-in-law, his family and his career have given him a level of comfort. So, he said, has learning the true story of Sabo's service and death. Even so, official recognition of his ex-brother-in-law's heroism doesn't tell Buccelli anything he didn't already know.

In the past dozen or so years, Buccelli said he has been able, at long last, to take pride in his service. When he bought a Harley-Davidson motorcycle a few years ago, Debra got him a jacket with a Vietnam veterans' patch affixed to the back and he often attaches a Vietnam veterans' or POW/MIA flag on the back of his cycle when riding. On the road, Buccelli said he often crosses paths with other vets – riding Harleys is a popular hobby among those who served in Vietnam. Those encounters, according to Buccelli, are a little like family reunions.

"There are a lot of people who just say, 'Man, welcome home,'" he said.

Another attraction between Vietnam veterans and motorcycles has a connection to one of the most common addictions they brought home from the war. While plenty of those veterans – including a few from Bravo Company – consumed drugs and alcohol, they also sought the adrenaline surge that had once been fed by combat. Richard Rios wound up working in a government job, but admitted that he engaged in dangerous behavior. While it didn't include motorcycling, he admitted feeling isolated from those who hadn't shared his experience.

"I was a loner. If I did talk to someone, they had to be a Vietnam veteran," he said. "I masked my emotions for a couple of decades."

Ben Currin went from combat with Bravo Company to jumping with the Golden Knights elite parachute team to motorcycling after retiring from the Army. Even in his 60s, a Harley-Davidson is Currin's main form of transportation in season. And in Oxford, North Carolina, it's a long season. A few years ago, he joined his regional Patriot Guard Riders outfit. The Patriot Guard Riders were formed in 2005 to counter the virulent anti-gay-rights group from Westboro Baptist Church in Topeka, Kansas. The church – which, in reality, consisted chiefly of patriarch Fred Phelps and his extended family – espoused the opinion that God was punishing America for its public acceptance of homosexuality by killing its soldiers. When soldiers killed in Iraq and Afghanistan during the Global War on Terror returned home, Westboro members turned up at funerals bearing signs inscribed with sayings like "Thank God For Dead Soldiers." In response, Patriot Guard Riders, whose motto is, "Standing for Those Who Stood for Us," formed groups of motorcyclists across the nation and counterprotested, in many cases by forming human shields between the Westboro contingent and mourners. Many of those riders, like Currin, are Vietnam veterans who want to make sure that fallen soldiers and their families won't be confronted with the animosity that awaited them a generation earlier.

Buccelli said he has felt the same rejection and admitted that his Vietnam jacket patch sometimes still draws hostile reactions. In 2006, Buccelli was on a motorcycle trek when a car, loaded with people who, by his estimation, had been born long after the Vietnam War ended, pulled up alongside him at a stoplight. Just before pulling away, one of the kids stuck a head out the window and shouted, "Baby killer!"

"How would they even know what that meant," Buccelli said as he remembered the encounter.

Before he had come to terms with his own war experience and the death of the brother-in-law he loved like a brother, Buccelli's reaction would have been far different. Afterward, he let the insult roll off that patch on his jacket.

"Me, 20 years ago, I would have chased them down," Buccelli said. "When it happened, I let it go."

Those taunts of "baby killer" like that directed at Carmen Buccelli on his motorcycle in 2006, have their origin in the March 16, 1968, massacre in My Lai, in which more than 300 Vietnamese civilians were killed – virtually all of whom, by most accounts, were women and children. The massacre, and reports of other incidents, were used to smear all Vietnam veterans, even those like Buccelli and Bravo Company's soldiers who never fired their weapons at anyone other than known enemy soldiers.

But if March 16, 1968, marked the nadir of America's involvement in Vietnam – perhaps the darkest day in US military history – it also offered a moment of redemption. Planning for the operation in My Lai called for several helicopters to provide cover for the ground troops. Chief Warrant Officer Hugh Thompson was at the controls of one of those choppers. In a 1998 *60 Minutes* interview, Thompson said he saw that his fellow soldiers were killing unarmed civilians, none of whom were fighting-age males. He likened it to Nazi mass murders during World War II. By his estimate, the victims included 179 children younger than two years old.

Thompson put his helicopter on the ground between the soldiers and a group of civilians hiding in a bomb shelter, confronted the US troops, and even threatened to turn the guns of his aircraft on his fellow Americans if the killing continued. His actions ended the attack. Thompson then went into the shelter, talked the Vietnamese out, and supervised their evacuation. Once he was airborne, he saw some people moving among hundreds of dead bodies in a ditch and landed again to rescue an injured child. During a 2003 speech at the US Naval Academy, Thompson said the enormity of what he was doing impacted on him after he finally coaxed the Vietnamese out of their bunker.

"When they started coming out, reality hit me," he said. "What are you going to do now, big boy?"

For his actions, Thompson got little but trouble. Because he threatened to shoot Lieutenant William Calley if the rampage wasn't stopped, Thompson expected that he was headed for the federal prison at Leavenworth, Kansas, where insubordinate soldiers and other military lawbreakers are jailed. At the time, he sweated over statements like the one made by a congressman who said, as quoted by Thompson, "If anybody goes to jail in the My Lai stuff, it will be the helicopter pilot Hugh Thompson."

"After it broke in the United States, I was not a good guy," Thompson said.

The Army itself undertook an investigation, led by General William R. Peers, which Thompson himself regarded as "very thorough." The fact that there had been an investigation itself was all-but-unique in military history – the Japanese or German military, just to name two, never investigated any World War II atrocities committed by their troops and if they hadn't lost the war, they never would have been called to account for their acts. Peers recommended more than two dozen people for courts martial, although only six people were ever tried and only one, Calley, was ever convicted. The lieutenant was sentenced to life in prison. In the immediate aftermath, though, it was Calley who received the public sympathy that should have gone to Thompson.

After three days of imprisonment, President Richard Nixon ordered Calley moved to house arrest at a relatively comfortable apartment in Fort Benning, Georgia. There was a hit song recorded in his honor and the military, under severe public pressure, reduced his sentence to 20 years and again to ten years. He was paroled after a term of three years house arrest.

Thompson avoided jail, but a generation would pass before he was recognized for his own valor. In 1998, more than 30 years after My Lai, Thompson and his crew, Glenn Andreotta and Larry Colburn, were each awarded the Soldier's Medal. Andreotta's award was posthumous; he was killed in action less than a month after the My Lai massacre.

In the mystery of how Leslie Sabo's heroism disappeared down a memory hole for nearly three decades, another answer can be found in the war's two competing narratives, as exhibited in the My Lai massacre. On one side, there was the anti-war version, which painted all the soldiers as "baby killers." On the other was the pro-war account, which held that the US lost Vietnam because its soldiers didn't kill enough Vietnamese. The war's actual foot soldiers found themselves whipsawed between those two perceptions.

In 1971, when the soldiers from Bravo Company who faced the Mother's Day Ambush began returning home, the United States was into a third year of scaling back its involvement in the Vietnam War, in accordance with public opinion. Before the year ended, both the 101st Airborne Division and 4th Infantry Division had been rotated stateside, and the US military ceased major combat action by the end of 1973. When Saigon, soon to be renamed Ho Chi Minh City – in honor of the man who, depending upon the historical perspective, was either a butcher who gave the Communists a foothold in Southeast Asia or liberated it from its colonial-era shackles – fell in the spring of 1975, it capped what is generally recognized as the United States military's first battleground defeat. In the United States, people on both sides of the narrative divide wanted to forget about a conflict that consumed more than 58,000 lives, billions of dollars in capital, and dominated United States foreign policy for more than a decade. And the Army, which had misplaced Leslie Sabo's Medal of Honor recommendation, was institutionally disinclined to pick the bones of the only war the United States had ever lost.

CHAPTER 24

It might be difficult to believe today because it seems so deeply appropriate, but the National Vietnam Veterans Memorial, as initially conceived, was controversial. The physical design – a gargantuan gash in the ground near the Mall in Washington, DC for a partially embedded wall that would contain the names of more than 58,000 men and women killed during the war – was deemed to be unsightly. The designer, Maya Lin, was Chinese-American, which was seen in some circles as an affront to Vietnam veterans, some of whom still commonly used the word "gook" in conversation.[1]

But the monument's execution justified Lin's vision. That gash became hauntingly symbolic of a war that left a national psychological wound which, at the time of construction, was still gaping. The monument's list of names serves as a drawing point for the comrades of those who perished on the battlefield. Since it was dedicated on Veterans Day 1984, the wall has become one of the national capital's most popular sightseeing spots. And the memorial has served as a site for one of the world's most unusual rituals. By the thousands, Vietnam veterans visit the wall, leaving behind personal items such as used combat boots or dog tags as offerings in memory of those who never made it home.[2] The wall has also been a source of healing for veterans like "Kid Rick" Brown.

"The visit to the wall turned my life around in a way I didn't know."

One way to measure the Vietnam Memorial Wall's success is by the proliferation of its officially sanctioned imitators. The national wall quickly spawned two one-half-scale replicas that still tour the nation to this day and, as more households purchased personal computers and connected to the Internet, The Virtual Wall. The memorial's online version would eventually serve as the digital town square that would connect all of the most important people in Leslie Sabo's life – the soldiers he fought alongside, and his family and friends from Ellwood City who, 30 years after he perished in a Cambodian jungle clearing, still didn't know the circumstances of his death.

In 2002, Olga Sabo, Leslie's sister-in-law, posted his photograph on The Virtual Wall online site, and Rose Sabo Brown posted a message on the webpage. Through the website, the Bravo Company veterans, starting with Richard Clanton, reached out to Sabo's family. The Virtual Wall enabled Sabo's long-ago comrades to confront their own personal demons by opening up about their Vietnam experiences and gave them the opportunity to share their memories at a point in their lives when they were ready to relive them. Clanton said for years he put off meeting with his fellow Bravo Company veterans until he was approached by Mabb about Sabo's Medal of Honor recommendation. But that gathering finally took place at the national memorial in Washington, DC, on May 10, 2003, the 33rd anniversary of the Mother's Day Ambush. His reticence proved unfounded.

"The minute I got out of the car at the hotel, it was like we had been apart for only three months," Clanton said.

Among those attending the 2003 reunion was Rose Sabo Brown, who had only just learned the true story of her first husband's death. In what would become a recurring theme for those who knew Leslie Sabo in peacetime, Rose said she was surprised that his citation went missing for so long, but not that he sacrificed his life for his comrades. She found the experience of meeting those who served alongside her husband intense yet gratifying in part because seeing the end result of Leslie's sacrifice lent a purpose not only to his death, but her own personal difficulties – her unhappy subsequent marriage and the questions she had after his death – she said she experienced in the ensuing years.

"It was the most emotional experience I've ever had in my life," she said. "Their wives said, 'We feel so bad, we're standing here with our husbands because of your husband.' I was so glad to have met them."

Rose turned 60 in 2008. Unlike her brother and Sabo's mother and brother, she remained in the Ellwood City area. After she divorced her second husband, Rose moved to a rural community just outside New Castle, Lawrence County's seat, and took a job nearby for a company that sorts prescription drugs for pharmacies. If talking about Leslie Sabo with his wife helped his wartime comrades recover from the war's ill effects, the healing went both ways.

"It's easier to handle now that I know everybody," Rose said. "I still cry, but it's not as emotional.

"I told them, 'After meeting you and being with you, I can see why he gave his life for you.'"

After that first meeting, Rose said she kept in touch with Clanton, Koziol, and the rest of Leslie Sabo's comrades, thanks in no small part to another form of information superhighway technology – online chat rooms. For the veterans, those conversations proved cathartic. Men like Koziol and Clanton, who had been unable to even talk about their combat experience, used the Internet and their own personal connections to one another to have lighthearted banter about the worst day of their lives. For Clanton, the healing process carried him from one extreme to the other. After avoiding his past for nearly three decades, Clanton helped establish Bravo Company's website and chats extensively online almost daily with his fellow veterans.

In one chat room exchange, Koziol misidentified Clanton by the name of another Bravo Company veteran. Clanton responded by writing, jokingly, "I realize you are getting old and can't see well."

Koziol, who was in his mid-20s during his combat tour, replied: "Its [sic] not getting old, its [sic] getting older. I was old in Nam, that's why they called me the 'Old Man' then. And also my eyes must have got screwed up from all the red and green tracer bullets going back and forth in Nam. Maybe the VA [Department of Veterans Affairs] has a 'Pill' for me to take. You go to the doctor and every time you come home, they give you another 'Pill' to take."[3]

That conversation took place during 2005, two years after the Bravo Company veterans first met the widow of the man who saved many of their lives.

The difference might have been that, 30 years after Leslie Sabo's death, they were at last telling his story. And without meeting the only remaining guardians of that chronicle, the soldiers who lived because of his sacrifice, it would remain elusive for the loved ones Sabo left behind when he departed for Vietnam. For George Sabo, learning about the details of his brother's death didn't make the pain go away, but it helped him, too. After Olga posted Leslie's picture on The Virtual Wall website, Clanton contacted her with an email, in which he told George that his brother did not die, as the Army told them, when an ammunition dump exploded, but while saving the lives of his comrades.

"When we heard that, we were just stunned," Olga said. "Because that's not what we heard."

Even though most, if not all, of the men who served with Leslie Sabo knew the details surrounding his death, Olga spoke up in their defense.

"They always knew how Leslie died, but they didn't know how to get ahold of us," she said.

Part of the time lapse might have happened through the desire of some veterans to put the war behind them once they came home and rejoined "the world." Or, as Clanton put it, "Life gets in the way."

Like Rose Sabo Brown, George Sabo was more surprised that the military had misplaced the record of his brother's heroism. Clanton's assertion that Leslie Sabo had given his life to save perhaps dozens of his comrades was much easier for him to believe.

"He was always thinking about other people," George Sabo said. "It was not surprising that he gave his life for other people."[4]

In 2007, nearly four years after Clanton first contacted him, George attended a Bravo Company reunion. He said it was striking to see how the men who served alongside his brother in combat had aged. George admitted that, because his brother was frozen in death at the age of 22, he had a problem seeing the men with whom Leslie had forged bonds that reached beyond mortality, as 60-year-old men.

"I remember Leslie as a young man," George recalled. "To see these guys as 50- and 60-year-old men… It was hard to picture them as the young boys they were. It was like, 'I remember my brother being that age.'"

But Olga said that she and her husband struck up an "instant friendship" with the Bravo Company men. Just as important, she realized that her brother-in-law lives on in the men whose lives he saved. While George and Olga said those men were appreciative of the gift they got from Leslie, they also gave something back to his brother.

"They have really opened up a wealth of information to us," she said. "It made me want to cry, it was very sentimental, but it at the same time, it was like [being] home with Leslie."

As young children, George and Leslie Sabo accompanied one another across Europe and the Atlantic Ocean, into the United States. For a time during their formative years, they became closer than friends, even than brothers. And for George, Leslie's loss opened a wound that defied healing, even after nearly 40 years. When he was interviewed in September of 2008, George patiently answered questions for about two hours in an Ellwood City restaurant before he abruptly stood up and said "We're done," not out of rudeness, but because he had reached the emotional limit of how long he could talk about his brother.

Even so, Olga Sabo admitted that meeting Leslie's fellow Bravo Company veterans has helped her husband deal with the tragedy.

"It was so wonderful to see that Leslie was not forgotten," she said.

George and Olga continued to keep in touch with the men Leslie served with, as much to stay connected with his legacy as to learn more about the Medal of Honor application as it wound silently – and slowly – through the military command structure.

In fairness to the men of Bravo Company, preserving Leslie Sabo's memory hadn't been their job. Even while suffering from physical and emotional injuries sustained in the Mother's Day Ambush, men in the company, particularly George Koziol, sat down, collected the eyewitness documentation of Sabo's heroic acts, and committed them to paper and the Army's command structure. Ultimately, if Sabo's memory was poorly tended, if anyone is to blame for concealing his story for 30 years from the people who knew him best in peacetime, the Army should have to accept responsibility.

It was 2006 before Sabo's Medal of Honor recommendation cleared the Army hierarchy. Although it is military policy not to comment on ongoing Medal of Honor evaluations, US Representative Corrine Brown, D-3, Florida, obtained a copy of a letter written in 2006 from then-Army Secretary Francis Harvey to then-Defense Secretary Donald Rumsfeld. Brown forwarded the letter to Alton Mabb, her constituent, who sent copies to Sabo's fellow veterans and family members. In the letter Harvey stated that, in his view, Sabo's actions were worthy of a Medal of Honor award.

That was an important threshold, because the US Code dictates that the Secretary of the Army can authorize the award of the Distinguished Service Cross to a soldier who has not been honored if the military took no action on the recommendation, "because the statement was lost or through inadvertence" within two years.[5] Even though both Harvey and Rumsfeld would resign less than a year after that letter was written for reasons that had nothing to do with Sabo, it was added to the fallen soldier's growing file. Even though Mabb agreed with Harvey that Sabo deserved the Medal of Honor, he said the Distinguished Service Cross would have been more than a consolation prize. It would be a statement from the government that even after 40 years, Sabo's heroism wasn't forgotten.

"That guy was bumped off on Mother's Day and that really fucks me up," Mabb said.[6]

The men who served with Sabo never forgot, even when it hurt too much to remember. By taking up Sabo's cause, Mabb spurred those men, particularly George Koziol, to campaign on the fallen soldier's behalf. Richard Clanton noted the fervor with which Koziol devoted himself to seeing Sabo receive the recognition he deserved.

"He wanted people to know what [Sabo] did," Clanton said.

Koziol was hardly alone, though. Clanton, Rick Brown, Richard Rios, James Waybright, and others took an interest in the effort. Mabb said that was hardly a surprise. After facing combat overseas and indifference or even hostility at home, he said the Vietnam veterans had forged bonds that might have been greater than the bonds expressed by those who had served in other wars. And by the time Mabb unearthed evidence of Sabo's valor, those men were ready not just to face their demons but to conquer them together just as they faced the North Vietnamese decades earlier.

The fact that Sabo gave his life, not for the Democratic Way, not for the Domino Theory – a justification for the war which held that, if Vietnam fell to communism, it would be followed by strategically vital nations such as Thailand and India – but for his buddies, never escaped Mabb's notice. And he said that, just as Sabo saved the lives of his Bravo Company comrades, recognition of his memory hinged on them returning the gesture. Without their efforts – especially the work of Koziol, who had the best view of his actions – Mabb said restarting the long-dormant probe of Sabo's Medal of Honor recommendation would have been a non-starter.

"It's all about witnesses," Mabb said. "You can be the most heroic dude, but if nobody can see it, it doesn't matter."

Koziol saw it and, by the time Mabb unearthed Sabo's file in the National Archives, he was ready to testify to his comrade's heroism emphatically.

"I don't know what else a guy could do to help other soldiers," he said. "Giving him the medal would say that no one is forgetting what Leslie did for others and it's time the military stepped up and did something."

But Koziol didn't live to see his friend receive the recognition he had earned so long ago. After a long battle with cancer, "The Old Man" died on January 27, 2008, at the age of 62. For Koziol's fellow Bravo Company veterans, his death was a harbinger of mortality for the keepers of Sabo's memory. By the time of Koziol's death, Sabo had been dead almost twice as long as he had lived. George Sabo turned 65 in September of 2008. Although he reached that milestone in excellent health, George didn't have another four decades to wait for his brother's public recognition.

For Elisabeth Sabo, time ran out on April 27, 2008, when she died at the age of 96. After living in Michigan, George transported his mother's body back home to Ellwood City, where she was buried at Holy Redeemer Catholic Cemetery alongside her husband and younger son. George said he hadn't spent much time discussing Leslie's valor with his mother because, even after more than 35 years, his death still left an emotional void that couldn't be filled.

The deaths of Koziol and Elisabeth Sabo provide a poignant reminder that those who actually knew Leslie Sabo were facing their own mortality. His fellow Bravo Company veterans were nearing retirement age. Richard Clanton, just to list one example, was a grandparent. Even George's sons, who weren't much beyond toddler age when Leslie shipped off to Vietnam, were in their mid-to-late 40s with children of their own.

By that time, the push to see Leslie Sabo's sacrifice recognized at long last seemed to have been making progress.

But just as the goal appeared near, another obstacle appeared. After misplacing the evidence of Leslie Sabo's courage for more than three decades, the US military was forced by statute to delay even further. US Code dictates that the Medal of Honor must be awarded no more than three years after the date of the act being honored, a statutory limitation that had long since expired. That rule required special legislation to waive the time limit for Sabo's Medal of Honor award.[7]

After being concealed in the National Archives for 30 years, Sabo's memory was buried more than 500 pages into the 2008 US Military Authorization Act. An obscure passage in the 800-section proposal, which served as approval for all of the military's actions for the following year, waived the three-year statute of limitations for Korean War veteran Woodrow Keeble, three participants in the Andrews Raiders operation during the Civil War, and Sabo.

Keeble's story was a near-direct parallel to Sabo's. On October 20, 1951, Master Sergeant Keeble was acting leader of the support platoon for Company G, 19th Infantry Division, a post typically held by a lieutenant. The company was ordered to attack a heavily defended enemy position atop Hill 765 near Sangsan-ni, Korea. When the attacking element became pinned down by heavy fire, Keeble crawled beneath the enemy's machine-gun fire and moved in close to the North Korean position. Once within range, Keeble eliminated three machine-gun positions with hand grenades, in spite of heavy fire and grenade assaults against him. His action enabled the company to dislodge the North Koreans from Hill 765.[8]

Keeble – who had earned two of his four Purple Hearts and a Bronze Star for his actions fighting on Guadalcanal in the Pacific Theater, one of the most brutal campaigns of World War II – was immediately recommended for the Medal of Honor, but the paperwork was misplaced. Keeble's commanders, undaunted, sent up a second recommendation, which again was lost. Given that Keeble was an American Indian of the Sisseton-Wahpeton tribe, it's possible that his Medal of Honor documentation wasn't lost so much as deliberately misplaced by racists in the military hierarchy. When Keeble's commanders tried to submit his recommendation for a third time, the Army informed them that the medal's time limit had expired and no request would be accepted, even though it was the fault of the Army itself for losing, or intentionally destroying, Keeble's records until the statutory time expired.[9]

Keeble died on January 28, 1982, at the age of 64, without being recognized for his Korean War heroism.

The Civil War awards should have been little more than a rubber stamp approval – although they weren't approved in 2008 – because the Medal of Honor was the only combat valor award in the Civil War, which meant an act that would today be worthy of a Bronze

Star earned a Medal of Honor. Further, all of the other 19 Andrews Raiders had already been awarded the Medal of Honor.[10]

Usually, the authorization bill is a routine operation. But after being delayed for decades by bureaucratic snafus and neglect, politics would play a role in the process to recognize Sabo for his sacrifice. The 2008 authorization bill was brought before Congress in early 2007, a few months after Democrats took control of both the US House of Representatives and the Senate in an election that was seen as a referendum on the US-led war in Iraq, which began in March of 2003 and was going badly at the time. With their newfound control of the legislative branch, the House of Representatives leadership inserted a provision that would have established a timetable for a withdrawal of combat troops from Iraq, which President George W. Bush regarded as a deal-breaker. So when the authorization bill reached his desk in December of 2007, Bush – who went his entire first term as President without vetoing a single bill – rejected it, a move that prompted Mabb to say he "was crushed."

But the setback was only temporary. Another version, without the withdrawal timetable, hit Bush's desk the following February, and was signed. Once the authorization bill passed, it cleared the way for the Pentagon and White House to consider Medal of Honor awards for Keeble, Sabo, and the three Andrews Raiders. Keeble, who had been dead for more than a quarter-century, received his Medal of Honor on March 2, 2008, after a long campaign on his behalf.

Sabo's effort was supported on Capitol Hill by US Representatives Corrine Brown, who represents Alton Mabb in Congress, Melissa Hart, who represented Ellwood City from 2001 to 2007, and Jason Altmire, who defeated Hart in her 2006 bid for re-election. US Representative James Gerlach – who represented the Philadelphia suburbs in Congress and grew up in Ellwood City during the Vietnam War – also backed the effort to see Sabo receive the nation's highest military honor.

But when Bush left office on January 20, 2009, the order that would have granted Leslie Sabo his long-overdue recognition remained unsigned. US Senator Arlen Specter began making inquiries on Sabo's behalf in the summer of 2009. His timing, though, could not possibly have been better. By the time he started advocating for the fallen Pennsylvanian, Specter had established himself as one of the US Senate's pivotal votes. Specter, a Republican for more than 40 years, switched parties in April of 2009 and became instrumental to President Barack Obama's legislative agenda, including the 2009 economic stimulus program and the 2010 Affordable Care Act health care law.

To say, or even hint, that a US Senator could influence the military hierarchy to grant a serviceman a Medal of Honor he didn't deserve would both cheapen the award and defame the men who have received it. But it's possible that the lobbying efforts of four senators on Keeble's behalf might have resulted in the same decision, only quicker. Specter's initial probe elicited a "don't call us, we'll call you" response from the Army. In an August 20, 2009 letter to Specter's legislative office, Lieutenant Colonel Stewart L. Stephenson, chief of the Army's military awards branch, said the Department of the Army was reviewing Sabo's award, even though Francis Harvey, a former Secretary of the Army, had already recommended Sabo for the Medal of Honor nearly three years earlier. Stephenson also cited Army policy, which prohibits commenting on the status of open Medal of Honor investigations.

"The review is being conducted in compliance with the legislative requirements and in accordance with all applicable policies and procedures," Stephenson wrote.[11]

Bravo Company veteran Richard Rios, who was in that Cambodian clearing on May 10, 1970, during the Mother's Day Ambush, said it was imperative and overdue for the nation to honor Sabo.

"I think Leslie Sabo rose to the occasion and traded fire with the enemy and saved the lives of the soldiers around him, and sacrificed his life for the soldiers around him," Rios said.

The other surviving Bravo Company veterans were no less adamant about that.

CHAPTER 25

One of the first sights that greeted visitors to Marietta, Ohio, during the last weekend of July 2009 was the message, "Welcome Bravo Company, 3/506th Infantry Regiment" on the marquee of a Pizza Hut located just off Interstate 77. A handful of similar sentiments festooned the strip malls and fast-food restaurants in Marietta, a city of about 15,000 people located where the Muskingum River meets the Ohio River southeast of Cincinnati. Marietta happens to be the residence of Jim Waybright, commander of Bravo Company during Leslie Sabo's tour of duty in Vietnam. In addition to the big overhead marquees, many of the stores in Marietta's downtown business district welcomed Bravo Company to town with color-copied signs bearing the 101st Airborne Division's Screaming Eagle shoulder patch logo.

Bravo Company's 2009 reunion started on Tuesday July 21, and ran through the following Sunday morning. All three of the Marietta-area newspapers, two dailies and one weekly, ran front-page stories about the gathering, which culminated on Saturday July 25, in an hour-long ceremony commemorating the 18 Bravo Company men killed in action during the first five months of 1970. Those men are memorialized with bricks at Marietta's Walk of Fame. Sabo's brick includes the letters "MOH," to denote the Medal of Honor. Waybright ordered the brick immediately after passage of the 2008 Defense Authorization Bill, which included a waiver of the Medal of Honor time limit for Sabo. Bravo Company's former commander said he "jumped the gun a little bit," because he had been certain Sabo's award would be approved quickly after passage of the time limit waiver.

Bravo Company veterans Rick Brown and Richard Rios said Waybright saved lives with his leadership during the Mother's Day Ambush and his decision to hold 1st Platoon in reserve on the morning of May 10, 1970, which meant there was a cavalry to come to the rescue that evening. For his part, Waybright credited Lieutenant Teb Stocks for stabilizing the rear element of Bravo Company's column and Lieutenant John Greene for leading 1st Platoon on the rescue mission in the fading light that evening.

Stocks, who was attending his first reunion, broke down as he spoke, which prompted Waybright to mention that, "he never cried over there." After the Mother's Day Ambush, he was transferred to a battalion staff post in the 82nd Airborne Division and was eventually mustered out of the Army in the postwar troop drawdown. After his discharge, Stocks experienced guilt over having lost men under his command and repeatedly asked himself if he could have done anything to prevent those losses. In the late 1970s, a few years after leaving the Army, Stocks finally hit his knees in search of an answer to that question.

"I asked the Lord to forgive me," Stocks said. "And He said, 'You've done nothing to be forgiven for.' He said, 'You need to forgive yourself.'"

While Stocks sought solace in faith, other Bravo Company veterans muddled through and now look to Department of Veterans Affairs counselors and meeting with one another at the reunions. The company has been meeting roughly once a year since not long after Alton Mabb began making inquiries among Bravo Company veterans about Leslie Sabo's Medal of Honor documentation.

In a way, Sabo played a role in bringing the men of Bravo Company back together. Mabb's requests for information from Clanton, Rios, and Koziol in 1999 also played a role in the decision to organize the company's first reunion the following year. For Brown, reconnecting with his fellow Vietnam veterans gave him the motivation to confront his own personal demons in a deeper way. He decided to contact the families of the men killed during his tour in Vietnam. While looking at The Virtual Wall Vietnam memorial website, Brown found a page dedicated to Leslie Sabo established by his widow.

Brown had decided that the families of those who didn't come home needed to know about their sons and husbands, especially in the case of Leslie Sabo, a hero whose sacrifice had gone unrecognized for decades. But he didn't know if he could do it.

"For three days, I didn't know what I wanted to do," he said. "It finally hit me on the third day. She needs to know."

Brown then emailed Rose Sabo Brown, who learned for the first time about the circumstances surrounding her husband's death. Since then, Brown has been locating the families of his fallen battlefield comrades to tell them about how their loved ones spent their final weeks and days. For Brown, it has been part of the healing process. After loading Sabo and five of the other fatalities from the Mother's Day Ambush onto a helicopter on May 11, 1970, Brown experienced a period of near-amnesia for several days. Even decades later, Brown said he experiences nightmares, in which he relives the ambush, several times a week.

"It seemed like that was one way to put the past behind us," he said of his efforts to reach out for the families of his fallen comrades.

Rick Brown suffered just as much for those who didn't make it home as he did over the indifference and hostility from the countrymen he had defended in Vietnam. He was particularly struck by the existential ramifications from seeing his fellow Currahees fall.

"What really bothered me was that I knew they were dead and their families didn't," he said. "Watching that chopper go off, I thought, 'My God, they don't know.' I wanted them to know that we cared. We cared about each and every one of these guys."

Driven by that desire, Brown would take it upon himself to visit the families of the men who went with him into battle, but never returned. The gesture has been appreciated by those family members like George Sabo.

"Because of these reunions, I've been able to put faces to the names of the men my brother served with," he said.

The visits weren't always easy. Brown's trip to Illinois for a meeting with Frederick Harms' parents was particularly harrowing. Harms, who was killed in the Mother's Day Ambush, was known to his colleagues as a good-natured, highly-valued radio telephone operator in 3rd Platoon. But Harms' death devastated his family and the emotional wound was still raw, even 30 years later.

"The tears were just running down his face," Brown said of his meeting with Harms' father. "You could just feel that it was hard to take."

But if reaching out to the families of his fallen comrades was sometimes difficult for Brown, it also gave him a gift that even he hadn't anticipated. During the 2009 reunion, Brown, who had been twice divorced, began dating Candace Sullins, whose husband, Ernest Moore, was among those killed on May 10, 1970, in the Mother's Day Ambush. Brown and Sullins married in April 2014.

While some of the soldiers, like Clanton, Rios, and Koziol confronted their demons – again, to use Clanton's characterization – from the day they returned home, others didn't face their own difficulties until later. After the war, Ben Currin stayed in the Army, rose to the rank of sergeant, served as a drill instructor and jumped out of airplanes with the elite Golden Knights demonstration parachuting team. Contrary to his comrades who had problems reintegrating themselves into a civilian society that saw them as "baby killers" or failures, Currin was admired by the raw Army recruits he trained. Those newly minted soldiers saw the Screaming Eagle patch on Currin's shoulder and Combat Infantryman Badge on his chest – symbols of experiences that gave him instant credibility during basic training. Currin remained in the Army for more than 20 years, into the 1990s. It wasn't until after leaving the military that he began having issues with post-traumatic stress disorder (PTSD).

"When it hit me, it hit me hard," Currin said.

Rios, who had been a PTSD counselor at a Department of Veterans Affairs (VA) hospital at least once a week in his hometown at Austin, Texas, said he hears that's become common among Vietnam veterans who came home and suppressed their combat memories in favor of getting jobs, raising families, and just moving on with their lives. Now in retirement – the oldest Bravo Company veterans are in their late 60s and "Kid Rick" Brown turned 60 in 2011 – they have time to contemplate their past and are experiencing the sleepless nights that have plagued Brown over much of the last 40 years. Rios said that he and his fellow soldiers would still probably need to see their VA counselors, but Bravo Company's reunions play a large role in the veterans' healing process.

"How can you talk about this to somebody out on the street?" Rios asked. "The brotherhood is so strong among Vietnam combat veterans."

It took more than 30 years for the men of Bravo Company to gather for the first time after their year in Vietnam. But once they did, they forged bonds even stronger than those that linked the World War II Currahees because they shared not only the experience of combat, but also the feelings of alienation and loneliness upon returning home that they alone could understand.

Rios said he often thinks about how his own life might have been different if Vietnam service hadn't come calling. Before being drafted, he had graduated from the University of Texas and had designs on attending law school. After a year of combat in Vietnam, that plan changed.

"When I came back, I had my own personal issues for about 20 years," he said.

Rios engaged in what he called destructive behavior for much of that time before seeing a counselor for the first time in 2000. And unlike too many of his fellow Vietnam veterans, Rios came out on the other side of PTSD. For him, the sessions continued until 2011.

"I thought, 'I can't be doing this,'" he said. "But it really helped."

For Brown, it took the reunions, and George Koziol, to get him into counseling. When "Kid Rick" and "The Old Man" reconnected, Brown began talking about his nightmares. Koziol diagnosed Rick's sleeping visions and urged him to seek counseling. Brown began his VA sessions in 2003.

"It's helped me a lot," he said. "And a lot of other guys said it helped them."

"Doc" Nash, the medic whose face was one of the last 13 of Bravo Company's 18 men killed saw in this world, entered PTSD treatment in 2009, after decades of suppressing the issues stemming from his time in Vietnam. The VA peer counseling sessions and Bravo Company's reunions have value for the same reason – both enabled men to talk about their experience with the only people who could truly understand them.

"I can open up more around them than I can with my wife or children," said Bill Sorg.

After the Saturday night ceremony to honor the fallen soldiers of Bravo Company, Waybright and Stocks went with a few other veterans to dinner at a restaurant at the downtown Marietta Hotel Lafayette, which played host to the reunion. While leaving, an employee presented them with a cocktail napkin, which had been left anonymously at the hotel bar and was inscribed with the following handwritten message:

"B Company 101st: Thank you for what you did in 'The Nam' for those of us who didn't go."

It was signed "A Patriot."

And that's a long way from "baby killer."

Just before midnight on Sunday July 26, as the last full day of Bravo Company's reunion in Marietta rolled to an end, veterans Dick Bowling, Lee Paterson, and Ben Currin led the group in a performance of a song, written by Koziol and sung to the tune of the Beatles' "Yellow Submarine," which would have been familiar to a group of men who went through their teenage years in the mid-1960s. Koziol's lyrics tell the tale of a carefree upbringing in America during the 1950s and '60s followed by horrific combat, a difficult return, to a measure of healing in the embrace of his fellow soldiers that the Bravo Company veterans didn't just sing, but empathized with.

When they got together in July of 2009 in Marietta, the Bravo Company veterans had been healing themselves for the better part of a decade. Those pardons that could come only from a comrade might have been the most significant accomplishment of Bravo Company's reunions. Rios, a 2nd Platoon survivor of the Mother's Day Ambush, said the get-togethers bring together the only people who can share the laughter and the tears from their year away from "the world." Some of the stories that provide the former are a little off-color and begin with the consumption of alcohol in copious quantities. During the 2009 reunion, one Bravo Company veteran told a story about one night when he got drunk and passed out in an unlit bunker and awoke to find a woman, presumably a prostitute, who by his estimation was about "110 years old." The soldier maintained that nothing happened, but the woman made the soldier's fellows think something did, much to their amusement. Tony "Yogi" Krizinski, a Bravo Company veteran at the 2009 reunion, said the stories from Vietnam held a meaning that only another combat veteran could understand.

"There were so many things over there that were really funny and so many things that were really sad."

And because of gatherings like the one in Marietta, the men of Bravo Company have been able, at long last, to remember their lost youth and innocence, and to laugh about Vietnam, to cry about it and even to sing about it.

As gratifying as those annual gatherings were, they were only a prelude to what might have been the greatest reunion any Army unit has ever had.

CHAPTER 26

Yesterday I received your letter and was very happy to hear from you. I received Tony and Stevie's letters a while ago. Tell them it was good to hear from them. I am happy that you liked my pictures. I've sent more since then. Also I am very proud of Tony for making the team. I'd love to see him play. Tell George I think his grades are really good, I can't imagine how he can take so many hours and still get good grades. You mentioned my being in a new mountain. Our battalion is now stationed at An Khe. We've had four days at the rear. Here at An Khe we have a large PX [postal exchange] and a service club. It almost seemed like we were back at some fort in the US. I was very surprised to see your picture in the Ledger which I did about two weeks ago, so I cut it out and put it in my photo album and have been carrying it since. By the way, I saw George was the head of a committee. How does he have time for this. I'm going to finish this letter so I can give it to somebody to mail before they pick us up. Say hi to everyone for me. I'm taking R&R in mid-July, it won't be much longer now and I'll be home.

Leslie Sabo letter to George and Olga
Dated April 25, 1970
(This was Leslie's final letter to his brother)

The applause lasted for nearly a full minute, with President Barack Obama leading the tribute.

Somewhat arbitrarily, the Obama administration set 1963 as the Vietnam War's beginning, which meant the 50-year anniversary observances began with that year's Memorial Day celebration. In fact, the Vietnam War commemoration began on May 16, 2012, the day Obama awarded the Medal of Honor to Leslie Halasz Sabo Jr. Obama, in his speech during the ceremony, wasn't even subtle about it. More than two dozen of Leslie Sabo's long-ago comrades were invited to the White House, where the President, in an unusual recognition for a ceremony to honor an individual soldier, asked Waybright, Stocks, Greene, Brown, Rios, and more than two dozen additional men who accompanied Sabo into Vietnam and Cambodia to stand and be recognized for their valor.

The applause started off solemn and polite. Then, General James Amos, Commandant of the Marine Corps, stood. After that, the whole house rose, as if it were at a concert or a baseball game, and gave Leslie Sabo's comrades the long-overdue admiration they earned 42 years earlier.

"Instead of being celebrated, our Vietnam veterans were often shunned," Obama said in his speech during the ceremony. "They were called many things when there was only one thing they deserved to be called and that was American patriots."

Exactly one month before the ceremony, on April 16, the White House, through the office of US Representative Jason Altmire, who represented Ellwood City in the House of Representatives – acting with White House approval – contacted the *Ellwood City Ledger*, Sabo's hometown newspaper, to officially announce that the Austrian-born Hungarian-American, who had been dead for 41 years and 11 months, would become the 247th Vietnam veteran to receive this nation's most prestigious military award. The President released the information a day later to the full media.

Around the nation, members of Leslie Sabo's family – related by blood shared and blood shed – made plans to descend upon Washington, DC for the White House ceremony on May 16 and the Hall of Heroes induction on May 17 at the Pentagon. Bravo Company rescheduled its annual reunion, which was to have been held later in the year, to coincide with the celebration of a hero's life. Rose Sabo Brown would be accompanied by the children she had with her second husband, and their children. George Sabo would bring Olga, their three sons and wives, and their seven grandchildren – including a granddaughter, the first girl born in the Sabo family since the 17th century. White House officials said Sabo Brown could invite 100 people. There were more than 130 on her list. Altmire, who had been keeping tabs on Sabo's Medal of Honor citation as it wound through the military bureaucracy since 2006, would attend, along with several surviving Vietnam War Medal of Honor recipients.

Ruben Rueda, Bravo Company's mongoose who was walking point on the day Leslie Sabo died, attended his first reunion. So did Lawrence Neff, Sabo's platoon leader who was wounded and airlifted out of Cambodia a few days before the Mother's Day Ambush. Carmen Buccelli – whose father earned the Silver Star in Europe during World War II, and who forged a brother's bond with Leslie Sabo on pre-dawn pistachio runs and afternoons in the pool hall off Lawrence Avenue in Ellwood City, saw the mangled remains of Leslie Sabo, presented the flag that had been draped over his brother-in-law's coffin to his own sister, and fought and killed in Vietnam – would be there too.

Typically, uniformed military personnel, ranked sergeant or higher and chosen from the military branch being honored, serve as ushers during Medal of Honor celebrations. Their duties include directing the guests in the proper direction, flanking the President during the White House ceremony, and just generally looking impressive. One colonel who participated in Sabo's ceremonies said there is no shortage of volunteers to serve that particular duty –

which is, after all, an extension of the Soldiers' Creed's admonition to "never leave a fallen comrade." Before the official ceremony, Rose Sabo Brown, and George and Olga Sabo sat down with Barack Obama and First Lady Michelle Obama. During the meeting, they shared Leslie's story with the President and his wife, and told of the searing pain left behind, even 42 years later, by his death. Rose said Michelle Obama shed tears with the family.

"One of the soldiers [in the Army's honor guard] said she never does that," Rose said.

The President's speech was pitch-perfect. Obama touched on all the relevant narratives of Leslie Sabo's life and service almost from the very first words of an address whose audience wasn't limited merely to the less than 150 people in the White House's East Room, but to every American who has served in combat and their families.

"Today is a solemn reminder that when an American does not come home from war, it is our military families and veterans who bear those sacrifices for a lifetime," the President said. "The spouses like Rose, who still displays in her home her husband's medals and decorations. The siblings like Leslie's big brother, George, who still carries the childhood memories of his little brother tagging along at his side. These are our veterans, like the men of Bravo Company, who still speak of their brother with reverence and with love."

If the veterans of Bravo Company – and by extension, all of Vietnam's combat veterans – suffered from the pain of losing their comrades, that agony was aggravated by a country that misinterpreted the meaning of their sacrifice and blamed the soldiers for the politicians' mistakes. An injustice that President Obama acknowledged: "To our shame, our veterans did not always receive the recognition and thanks they deserved, a mistake that must never be repeated," the President said.

"Throughout history, those who have known the horror of war and the love behind all great sacrifice have tried to put those emotions into words," the President said. "After the First World War, one soldier wrote this, 'They are more to me than life, these voices. They are more to me than motherliness and more than fear. They are the strongest, most comforting thing there is anywhere. They are the voices of my comrades.' Those were the voices that Leslie Sabo heard that day, the voices of his comrades pinned down at the risk of being overrun. He saved his comrades, who meant more to him than his own life."

Back at the Sheraton National's hospitality suite that night, the Bravo Company veterans corrected the President's omission by remembering, one by one, each of the 18 Bravo Company Currahees who died in combat between January 25 and May 10, 1970, reprising a traditional ceremony that had begun nearly a decade earlier, when Bravo Company held its first reunion. The roster of Bravo Company's fallen included soldiers, like Larry DeBoer and Ernest Moore, who had been with Bravo Company for only a few weeks before they were killed in the Mother's Day Ambush, not that it mattered to them.

"Whether they were with us for two or three weeks or two or three months, they are all Currahees," said Rick Brown, who himself finished his Vietnam combat tour with the 4th Infantry Division after being transferred out of Bravo Company through infusion.

As with the 2009 gathering, it was a night for laughter and for tears, for remembering and even for White House-caliber hijinks.

"The President sure serves some damn good whiskey," one Currahee said as he held aloft a tumbler of Maker's Mark purloined from the White House.

The following day – after many of the veterans had been reinforcing bonds originally forged in the rain, and sun, and tragedy of Vietnam until well into the morning – the men of Bravo Company awakened for another day of remembering and pride with Leslie Sabo's induction onto the Pentagon's Wall of Heroes. The military presence for this ceremony was far more palpable than it had been the previous day, with Secretary of Defense Leon Panetta, Army Secretary John McHugh, and Army Chief of Staff General Ray Odierno as the main speakers. Sergeant Antonio Giuliano, an opera-trained performer, sang the national anthem. Major General Donald Rutherford, the Army's head chaplain, said opening and closing prayers, just as he had in the White House a day earlier.

During his remarks, Panetta cited his own heritage and said, "The Sabo brothers had good taste in women. They both married Italian girls." Left unmentioned by the defense secretary was that a single man in Ellwood City who refuses to date Italian women necessarily spends a lot of Saturday nights at home.[1]

All three of the speakers, starting with Odierno, recounted the story of Sabo and his sacrifice while mentioning that, while his sacrifice had been forgotten for more than four decades, it would be remembered from that day forward.

"With this Medal of Honor, a warrior is held up to the American people as an example to all fellow men and women as the embodiment of the highest ideal," Odierno said. "Specialist Sabo is the epitome of a hero and he will never be forgotten."

Panetta mentioned Sabo's birth in Austria during the chaotic days after World War II to point out that the hero's life spanned two wars and three continents to begin in Europe and end in Asia. In between, Sabo lived in Ellwood City, which shaped the kind of man he would become, as McHugh said while referring to the town's motto, "What Ellwood City builds, builds Ellwood City."

"Well, Ellwood City built a hero," McHugh said.

During his remarks, Panetta apologized on behalf of the Army, Department of Defense, and the US government to the Sabo family, and said the prospect that a war hero's sacrifice could go unrecognized on his watch was, "the kind of thing that scares the hell out of me every day." George Sabo, speaking for his family, accepted Panetta's apology and said it wasn't necessary. The former engineer upstaged his better-known fellow speakers, in offering heartfelt thanks to everyone involved – including Tony Mabb, whose contributions had already been noted the previous day by President Obama – with helping his brother receive the Medal of Honor.

And even though the Army's forgetfulness meant Leslie Sabo Sr. died without knowing that his youngest son was a hero, and his mother had succumbed to old age without seeing Leslie receive the recognition of a grateful nation, George said there was a positive sign to the long delay in awarding his brother the Medal of Honor.

"If it wouldn't have taken that long, I wouldn't have had seven grandchildren here," George said. "When you think about the honor and the ability to pass this honor on to four generations of Sabos and having my grandchildren say, 'I was here,' that's wonderful."

George, displaying the grace that he inherited from his father, took a moment to thank Leslie Sabo's comrades, who worked to restore the legacy of a man who saved many of their lives and shared the words that his younger brother would have said if he had been there to say them.

"The Sabo family considers them all heroes, and this medal is for them," he said.

On what would be his final hours in the United States, Sabo bought bouquets of flowers for his mother and mother-in-law for Mother's Day, and another for his wife on her birthday. The Mother's Day flowers were delivered on the day he died and the birthday bouquet was delivered the day after his burial, a coincidence that featured prominently in Obama's speech.

With the President's help, Sabo's widow returned the gesture. Less than two weeks after the Medal of Honor ceremony, Obama marked the war's 50th anniversary with a Memorial Day speech at the National Vietnam War Memorial. When the President finished, he and Michelle Obama escorted special guest Rose Sabo Brown – who, 42 years earlier, had received flowers from beyond the grave – as she placed a flowered wreath at the wall's base, only a few yards from the inscription bearing her first husband's name.

CHAPTER 27

Initial Proposed Medal of Honor citation for Specialist Leslie Halasz Sabo

(Killed in action, May 10, 1970)

For conspicuous gallantry and intrepidity at the risk of his own life above and beyond the call of duty in the Republic of Vietnam on 10 May 1970, Spc. 4 Leslie H. Sabo Jr. distinguished himself while serving as a rifleman against hostile forces in the Se San area during the Cambodian Operation west of Pleiku. Specialist Sabo was in the rear element of a reconnaissance patrol when it was ambushed by a large enemy force. He immediately turned his fire in the direction of the attacking enemy and with automatic weapons fire and grenades, he was able to halt the insurgents from moving forward even though he was wounded while doing so. Then, from his defensive position, Spc. 4 Sabo saw a wounded comrade about 10 meters to his right and, disregarding his own wound, rushed to help the fallen soldier. A grenade was thrown into the friendly area from a nearby enemy ditch and Spc. 4 Sabo threw himself on top of the wounded soldier to protect him from the blast. He was again wounded in the back from the grenade. He then took one of his own grenades and assaulted the ditch, threw his grenade into the ditch and killed two enemy soldiers. Now seriously wounded Spc. 4 Sabo retrieved three bandoliers of ammunition and was able to make it back to his original defensive position. As he threw extra ammunition to another comrade, he was again shot in the leg and fell behind a small tree. As two wounded soldiers were trying to get to a tree line to be evacuated out of the combat area, enemy fire was pointed in their direction, preventing them from getting to the helicopter. Spc. 4 Sabo, with multiple wounds, stood up from behind his only cover, a small tree, and opened fire on the enemy that were preventing the evacuation. While their fire was now diverted toward Spc. 4 Sabo, the two wounded soldiers were able to get to the helicopter safely. Spc. 4 Sabo was hit by automatic weapons fire multiple times and died from his wounds. Through his indomitable courage, complete disregard for his own safety and profound concern for his fellow soldiers, he averted loss of life and injury to the members of his platoon. Spc. 4 Sabo's extraordinary heroism at the cost of his own life are in the keeping with the highest traditions of the military service and reflect great credit upon himself, his unit and the United States Army.

Medal of Honor citation
Awarded May 16, 2012 by President Barack Obama

Specialist Four Leslie H. Sabo Jr. distinguished himself by conspicuous acts of gallantry and intrepidity above and beyond the call of duty at the cost of his own life in Company B, 3d Battalion, 506th Infantry, 101st Airborne Division in Se San, Cambodia, on May 10, 1970. On that day, Specialist Four Sabo and his platoon were conducting a reconnaissance patrol when they were ambushed from all sides by a large enemy force. Without hesitation, Specialist Four Sabo charged an enemy position, killing several enemy soldiers. Immediately after, he assaulted an enemy flanking force, successfully drawing their fire from friendly soldiers and ultimately forcing the enemy to retreat. In order to resupply ammunition, he sprinted across an open field to a wounded comrade. As he began to reload, an enemy grenade landed nearby. Specialist Four Sabo picked it up, threw it and shielded his comrade with his own body, thus absorbing the brunt of the blast and saving his comrade's life. Seriously wounded by the blast, Specialist Four Sabo nonetheless retained the initiative and then single-handedly charged an enemy bunker that had inflicted severe damage on the platoon, receiving several serious wounds from automatic weapons fire in the process. Now mortally wounded, he crawled toward the enemy emplacement and, when in position, threw a grenade into the bunker. The resulting explosion silenced the enemy fire, but also ended Specialist Four Sabo's life. His indomitable courage and complete disregard for his own safety saved the lives of many of his platoon members. Specialist Four Sabo's extraordinary heroism and selflessness, above and beyond the call of duty, at the cost of his life, are in keeping with the highest traditions of military service and reflect great credit upon himself, Company B, 3d Battalion, 506th Infantry, 101st Airborne Division and the United States Army.

The Medal of Honor ceremonies for Leslie Sabo featured recorded readings of Sabo's Medal of Honor citation, which differed significantly from the original citation penned by a temporarily deaf George Koziol in a hospital bed as he recovered from wounds sustained in the Mother's Day Ambush. The approved citation was based upon an investigation by an awards committee from the Department of Defense, which would have interviewed some of the ambush survivors, although Koziol – who died of cancer in January of 2008 before the award process was reopened – was unavailable by the time the new investigation began.

Considering that Sabo's friends and family in Ellwood City had circulated conflicting accounts of exactly how Sabo died for years after he was killed, it was ironic that the biggest difference between the two accounts dealt with Sabo's final act. Koziol said he saw Sabo suppressing a North Vietnamese bunker with fire from his

M-1 rifle to enable the initial medical helicopter, with Koziol on board, to get safely away. Other witnesses confirmed that Sabo, working alone, fired on the bunker, which gave 1st Platoon an opportunity to secure a landing zone for medical evacuation helicopters. In the official citation, Sabo fell when he attacked the bunker with a hand grenade at close quarters, so close that the grenade blast killed both him and the enemy.

Several veterans from Bravo Company interviewed after the Medal of Honor ceremony confirmed Koziol's account of Sabo's acts during the Mother's Day Ambush.

Not that anyone was complaining about it. Sabo's comrades were too satisfied with the long-overdue recognition, not only for his sacrifice, but for their service, to quibble over the citation's wording. And in any event, they had gained a sense of perspective with their experience from Vietnam, where there were too many reports written by REMFs that bore little or no resemblance to what the combat soldiers saw out in the field.

"Sometimes, the official account isn't what really happened," said one Bravo Company veteran.

"Everyone knows he was protecting the guys from the Medevac," another asserted.[1]

For its part, the Army stands by the wording of the official approved Medal of Honor citation signed by President Obama. Troy Rolan Sr., a spokesman for the Army's Public Affairs office, said the document is based upon statements submitted with the nomination file. Those statements were taken "close to the time of the incident," according to an email statement by Rolan.

That is not to say these events did not occur, simply that the individuals interviewed did not note these actions when they made their official statement on the battle. Each individual on the battlefield has a different perspective and memory of events and their order ... the citation attempts to capture the key events that are corroborated by more than one individual and should not be seen as an all-encompassing timeline of this hero's actions that day.[2]

The apparent conflicts in those statements raise the question of which account actually took place. And the answer just might be "both."

As night fell on May 10, 1970, and the Hueys lifted the most badly wounded soldiers off the battlefield, the Americans were still taking fire from an enemy bunker along the tree line. From behind a small tree, First Lieutenant John Greene heard the sporadic enemy attacks but wasn't able to get a good look at them.

"I had some cover, but I couldn't move without going into a hail of bullets," he said.

Suddenly, a loud explosion rent the night.

"After that, there was no more enemy fire."

Greene speculated that the explosion might have been the suicide grenade attack referenced in Sabo's official Medal of Honor citation, which would not only reconcile the two accounts, but also solve one important mystery stemming from Sabo's death. Even though Sabo appeared – as far as Koziol could tell – to have been killed earlier in the machine-gun crossfire while helping 1st Platoon clear the landing zone, it is not only possible but, in light of the apparently conflicting accounts, likely that he was only severely – perhaps mortally – wounded. Throughout most of the afternoon and evening, Sabo had performed one heroic act after another to hold off the North Vietnamese advances. The explosion might have been Sabo's final blow against the enemy.

If a wounded Sabo, unable to throw a grenade any significant distance, were able to drag himself toward the enemy position, he would have pulled the pin and let the device "cook off" – to use Rolan's description – before dropping it into the bunker. The resulting explosion would not only have killed the enemy, but also Sabo.

As well as killing Sabo, the blast would have damaged his remains, which would have explained why his body returned home in a bag marked "Remains Unfit For Viewing."

Regardless of which account – or both – is correct, there's no dispute that Sabo made a soldier's sacrifice. He chose to die on the floor of a dusty, muggy, sweltering jungle clearing so that his comrades could make it home.

For the veterans of Bravo Company, Leslie Sabo's Medal of Honor ceremonies were the culmination of more than a decade's worth of effort, 40 years of pain and healing, and a validation of the one thing that brought them all back together so many years after their combat tours ended. After an experience that profound, a letdown was to have been expected.

"Everyone experienced some kind of mental or physical setback when they got back from DC," Ben Currin said.

But that didn't last long. When Currin talked about the physical illness after returning from the ceremony and reunion, it was in the warmth of a western Pennsylvania summer evening, immersed in the afterglow of honoring Sabo's memory while exercising his post-service career passion, motorcycling. He had ridden from North Carolina by way of Ohio – where he visited Jim Waybright, Rick Brown, and Norm Friend – to New Castle, Pennsylvania for a motorcycle run to raise money for a monument to Sabo in Ellwood City. Rose Sabo Brown, Sabo's widow, rode in Currin's sidecar that day.

Lee Dile, the brother of Sergeant Steven "Hungry" Dile, took part in the motorcycle run, too. Steven Dile was among the first of Sabo's Bravo Company comrades killed, on January 25, 1970, when he was hit by enemy fire while he and Jack Brickey were trying to silence two North Vietnamese machine guns. Lee Dile said the efforts to remember Sabo also honor his brother.

"It keeps his memory alive and it makes his sacrifice mean something," he said.

In the wake of Sabo's Medal of Honor award, those memory-preserving events were numerous. In Ellwood City alone, there were no fewer than five observances for the most decorated war hero in the history of Lawrence County. Ellwood City, one of those small towns that contribute more than their share of young men to the cause when old men in big cities start a war, didn't restrain itself in the slightest to honor Sabo. On Memorial Day, less than two weeks after the White House ceremony and while Rose Sabo Brown was a guest of the President and First Lady, George Sabo served as grand marshal at Ellwood City's annual parade and gave a speech afterward. Five weeks later, organizers of the Ellwood City Arts, Crafts, and Food Festival had a ceremony in Leslie Sabo's honor.

On a brilliant early fall afternoon on September 30, 2012, the monument, paid for partly with proceeds from the motorcycle run, was unveiled in Ellwood City's Legion Park, not far from memorials to the borough's war dead from World War I, World War II, Korea, and Vietnam. The ceremony was held more than 35 years after his name was etched into the Vietnam monument, just across Spring Avenue from Christ Presbyterian Church, where Sabo attended services as a child. Many of Sabo's wartime comrades – including Jim Waybright, Jerry "Doc" Nash, "Kid Rick" Brown, Currin, and Friend – made their first trip to Sabo's hometown.[3]

"If everyone in Ellwood City is made from the same stuff as Leslie Sabo, you've got a heck of a town," Waybright said during his keynote address.

US Representative Jason Altmire, who helped shepherd the waiver of Sabo's Medal of Honor time requirements through Congress, also attended the ceremony and remarked that holding the event outside a church Sabo once attended in the community where he grew up was particularly fitting.

"Thank God for places like Ellwood City," the congressman said. "The reason that Leslie Sabo became the man he was, a hero to the entire country, happened in Ellwood City."[4]

One day after the Legion Park ceremony, Sabo's family traveled to the state capitol in Harrisburg for the unveiling of his stone on Pennsylvania's Soldiers' and Sailors' Grove and passage of joint state House and Senate resolutions honoring him. Lawrence County recognized Veterans Day on November 11 with an event to rename the Ewing Park Bridge in Sabo's honor. The bridge, originally built immediately following World War I and rebuilt in 2005, is Lawrence County's largest bridge. George Sabo, whose eloquent memorials to his brother upstaged some of the US government's highest-ranking officials, again gave a heartfelt speech. Evoking their childhood living in Ewing Park and numerous crossings of the bridge's previous incarnation to get downtown, George Sabo said renaming it as Sergeant Leslie H. Sabo Jr. Bridge was particularly symbolic.

"It's a structural memorial that will be a reminder to us that a hero lived here. And it connects Leslie's life history from his time in Ellwood City to his service with 2nd Platoon, Bravo Company, 506th Regiment, 101st Airborne Division."[5]

During the long effort to see him receive the Medal of Honor, Sabo himself served as a bridge of sorts. Sabo's memory served to reconnect his former wartime comrades and helped lend meaning to his and other families whose sons went off to Vietnam with Bravo Company and never made it back home.

"The loss of my brother, who was my hero, defines my family. My blood family consists of me, my family, and my son. Ever since these guys sought me out, they became my family," said Rick Scarboro, whose brother, Lieutenant Thomas Scarboro, died April 8, 1970, in the Crow's Foot.

Sabo's formal monument, in Ellwood City's Legion Park, will outlive his brother, his widow, and his long-ago comrades, to remind the community where he grew up of his sacrifice, and the gift he left behind to his fellow soldiers and his nation.

A few weeks after the monument's dedication, on an October Saturday morning as the leaves on Legion Park's trees were turning orange, yellow and brown, a lone figure entered the park and walked up a ramp between two walls etched with the names of Ellwood City's World War I dead. With an air of solemnity, he approached the front of Sabo's monument, emblazoned with the text of his Medal of Honor citation.

The man read the words, snapped off a salute, and walked away.

EPILOGUE

As the men of Bravo Company first assembled in late 1969, they were still young men barely out of high school – or in some cases, college – with most of their lives still ahead of them. By the time they gathered in May of 2012 for Sabo's Medal of Honor ceremonies, most of them were retired and many of them were doting over grandchildren. The time they spent as combat soldiers was long in their past and, as measured in time, amounted to only a year out of six decades. But that time had been the most significant period of their lives, in triumph and tragedy.

Through his sacrifice, Leslie Sabo saved many of them. The efforts to honor him amounted to a final victory for the men who came home and built lives after war had irrevocably changed them.

Tommy Baker became a manufacturing executive, and settled in Mount Morris, Pennsylvania. His adult life came full circle when his company invested in a facility in Vietnam.

Mike "Tex" Bowman, settled down in Bonham, Texas, and is retired after a career in the Veterans Affairs system.

Jack Brickey, from a family of railroad workers, retired from the Norfolk Southern Railway and returned to Allen Park, Michigan. His older brother, Miles, was the first to get a railroad job, and "the rest of us just followed." Before going to Vietnam, Brickey had been a football standout at Allen Park High School. As an adult, he was an assistant coach while his son was on the varsity team. He is married to Gail and has three adult children, two sons and a daughter.

Rick Brown returned home to Columbia Station, Ohio, and retired after 38 years as a salesman in the hydraulic and industrial equipment field. By reaching out to the family of his fallen comrades, he got more than closure. On April 26, 2014, a few weeks before his 63rd birthday, he married Candace Sullins, Ernest Moore's widow.

Rick Clanton, whose first wife said she no longer knew him after his tour in Vietnam, celebrated the 40th anniversary of his second marriage in 2013. By that time, he had three daughters and six grandchildren. He eventually retired as publication manager for Swix Filtration Products, based in Gastonia, North Carolina. Clanton initiated online efforts to bring his former comrades back together and he's still comfortable with the Internet. He can regularly be found on Facebook, where his "Rickfucius" persona shares witticisms with followers.

Ray D'Angelo, aka Dangelo, was discharged after being wounded on May 7 and the subsequent horrific hospital treatment, moved to Arizona, and retired from an ironic career repairing medical diagnostic equipment.

Bruce Dancesia, of Binghamton, New York, retired as a buyer for IBM. He and his wife, Christine, have a son and daughter.

Michael DiLeo, who spent May 10, 1970, "directing traffic" at Fire Support Base Currahee, remained in the Army and did a hitch with the Golden Knights parachute team, retired in 1992 with the rank of command sergeant major. He settled in Kennesaw, Georgia, and meets Teb Stocks regularly for lunch.

Dick Freeling, who served in Bravo Company with Sabo for only a few weeks, married Nancy, his college sweetheart one month to the day after his return from Vietnam. He rededicated himself to college studies and eventually worked as a college professor.

Norm Friend, who lived not far from Brown, in Cuyahoga Falls, Ohio, retired as a driver with Consolidated Freightways trucking company.

John Greene, 1st Platoon's leader who led a quick march across an open field to break the North Vietnamese siege on May 10, 1970, worked as a public solicitor for Harris County before he retired from the legal profession in 2012. He lives in Conroe, Texas, just north of Houston.

Joe Hanks became Bravo Company's reunion photographer. He wound up in Detroit, not far from George Sabo's family in Dearborn, Michigan. A professional photographer, he found himself struggling for work as the digital age shook up that occupation. He supplemented his income with work at Home Depot. But his photos of Bravo Company gatherings have become part of the unit's official unofficial archives. He was accompanied to the Medal of Honor ceremonies by his wife, Diane.

Joseph Jaggers retired from the Army at the rank of major general. Through his combat service and his work consulting with the military on helicopter development, he was inducted into the US Army Aviation Hall of Fame.

Rich Lane, who took over command of Bravo Company from Waybright, retired from the Army as a colonel and went on to work in the corporate sales department for the PGA Bob Hope Chrysler

Classic. After his second retirement, he moved to Surprise, Arizona. "My golf game hasn't improved but my temperament has," he said. He has three children, two daughters who live in Washington State and a son in New York City.

Jerry Nash, the medic who earned a Bronze Star in the Mother's Day Ambush, returned to Tennessee, and had a long career in education. He and his wife, Elaine, live in Sparta. They have an adopted daughter and two grandsons.

Larry Neff, Leslie Sabo's platoon leader, moved to Hudson, Ohio. He retired as an official with Chrysler.

Lee Paterson met Bravo Company when it returned from Cambodia – "They joined me, rather than me joining them," he joked – and retired as superintendent of Roseburg Public Schools in Roseburg, Oregon. He and his wife, Robin, have a son and daughter.

Richard Rios abandoned his pre-combat-tour plan to enter law school and moved to the Houston suburb of Spring, Texas. He and his wife, Blanca, married in 1976, and he is retired from government work.

Ruben Rueda, the company's "mongoose" who rejected his father's offer of $5,000 to dodge the draft and run for Canada, returned to California and worked in construction. He lives in Hawthorne, California.

Dave Soden, the final casualty of the Mother's Day Ambush, became a dairy farmer in Starrucca, Pennsylvania, near Joe Honan's hometown of Scranton, and the man left temporarily blind by the blast of a rocket propelled grenade on May 10, 1970, sometimes works as a high school basketball official. Soden has the clear eyes and strong chin that you'd expect to see in a farmer, veteran, and basketball referee.

Bill Sorg designs and manufactures the commemorative T-shirts for Bravo Company's reunions. He lives in Elmore, Ohio, and is retired from a limestone processing company. He and his wife, Diane, have a son and daughter.

Teb Stocks, the deeply respected leader of 3rd Platoon with the heavy Southern accent who helped solidify Bravo Company's defenses in those crucial early moments of the Mother's Day Ambush, was promoted to captain and had hoped to make a career of the Army. However, he was forced out during the post-Vietnam War drawdown, he believes, because he was an officer without a college degree. Stocks worked in demolition for a construction company until his retirement. He and his wife, Delain, have two sons.

Ron "Shaky" Stone lives in Rockford, Illinois, and worked as a plant manager for Rock Valley Oil, the company that welcomed him home after his combat tour.

Jim Waybright returned to Marietta, Ohio, and retired as a factory manager. In retirement, Waybright, still known as Captain Jim to the men under his command so long ago, works occasionally as a substitute school teacher.

APPENDIX

Roster for Bravo Company, 3rd Battalion, 506th Infantry Regiment, 101st Airborne (Air Assault) Division, July 1, 1970

The roster was compiled almost two months after the Mother's Day Ambush, when eight 2nd Platoon troopers were killed and 29 soldiers from 2nd and 3rd Platoons were wounded, and just after Richard Lane assumed command of the company from Captain Jim Waybright.

Headquarters Platoon

Company commander: Captain Richard Lane.
First Sergeant Willie Nickleberry, Sergeant First Class Clarence Curtis, Staff Sergeant Joseph Brown, Staff Sergeant Arthur Sherwood, Specialist Michael Anderson, Specialist Joseph Hanks, Specialist George Koziol, Specialist Michael McDonough, Specialist David Rojas, Specialist Robert Sherwood, Specialist Crandall Simpson,

Specialist William Sorg, Specialist Philip Stebbins, Specialist Ronald Stone, Specialist James Tischer, Private First Class Lofton Conner, Private First Class James Hurst, Private First Class Joseph Kretschmer, Burke (medic), Tinh (interpreter).

1st Platoon

Platoon leader: First Lieutenant John Greene.
Platoon sergeant: Staff Sergeant Onorio Romo.
Squad leaders: Staff Sergeant Richard Rogers, Sergeant Vernon Bruner, Sergeant Roy White.
Team leaders: Sergeant James Bass, Sergeant Donald Callahan, Sergeant Lewis Dick, Sergeant Richard Godsy, Sergeant Ronald Leslie, Sergeant Lawrence Stefan, Specialist Ben Currin.
Platoon: Specialist James Beatty, Specialist Michael Bowman, Specialist James Elrod, Specialist Norman Friend, Specialist Albert Hughes Jr., Specialist Anthony Krizinski, Specialist Ronald Lynn, Specialist Daniel Maxey, Specialist Herschel McSperitt, Specialist Tommy Payton, Specialist Lyle Roberts, Specialist Randall Stice, Specialist William Watling, Specialist Melvin Robben, Private First Class Richard Carlisle, Private First Class Steven Elliano, Private First Class Timothy Galliher, Private First Class Gene Gause, Private First Class Walter Hawkins, Private First Class Albert Manier, Private First Class Benjamin Miller, Private First Class Mark Parisi, Private First Class Roscoe Peterson, Private First Class Randall Skorheim, Schmidt (medic), Private Harold Pierce.

2nd Platoon

Platoon leader: First Lieutenant Lawrence Neff.
Platoon sergeant: Staff Sergeant Charles Buckner.
Squad leader: Sergeant James Bell.
Team leaders: Sergeant Dale Blaubach, Sergeant Dennis Cholger, Sergeant James Cokebank, Sergeant Albert Marcotte, Sergeant James Morrow, Sergeant Richard Tombaugh, Sergeant William Wafford.

Platoon: Specialist Lyle Buss, Specialist Richard Clanton, Specialist Johnny Ivey, Specialist Eddie Jennings, Specialist Darrell Johnson, Specialist Josue Lopez, Specialist Melvin McBride, Specialist Paul McLeod, Specialist James Nesbit, Specialist Mark Nishino, Specialist Jack Phillips, Specialist Carlos Pidilla, Specialist Mark Rogers, Specialist Randy Schlachter, Specialist Chalmer Strunk, Private First Class Richard Dehoyos, Private First Class Lawrence Dugas, Private First Class James Hall, Private First Class Orlando Harris, Private First Class Richard Jeckstadt, Private First Class Mark Lovay, Private First Class Kenneth McCauley, Private First Class Donald Martella, Private First Class James Nemeth, Private First Class David Ross, Private First Class Tommy Powell, Howington (medic), Wen (Kit Carson scout).

3rd Platoon

Platoon leader: First Lieutenant Teb Stocks.
Platoon sergeant: Michael DiLeo.
Squad leaders: Sergeant Robert Bellamy, Sergeant John Emhoff, Sergeant John Roethlisberger.
Team leaders: Sergeant Gerald Britain, Sergeant Joseph Empson, Specialist Roger Cope.
Platoon: Specialist Jerry Cowan, Specialist William Grzonka, Specialist Phillip Hostetter, Specialist Willie Johnson, Specialist William Kennedy, Specialist Ruben Rueda, Specialist Jacob Spencer, Specialist Howard Watson, Specialist James Weinberg, Specialist Reid Schmotzer, Private First Class Paul Beider, Private First Class Paul Bosling, Private First Class Hiram Carrasquillo, Private First Class Doyle Causey, Private First Class Glenn Guillory, Private First Class Allen McCulty, Private First Class William McEachin, Private First Class Richard Mickelson, Private First Class Ronnie Moreland, Private First Class Richard Morland, Private First Class Lee Paterson, Private First Class Larry Rayner, Private First Class Rick Sasama, Private First Class Bobby Sees, Private First Class William Threets, Private First Class Gregory Walker, Private First Class Ronald McHenery, Micklus (medic).

Unassigned

Sergeant Mario Venteicher, Sergeant Stanley Wilson Jr., Specialist John Abboud, Specialist Donald Mayblum, Specialist Richard Rios, Private First Class Grady Smith Jr.

All three platoons had a Kit Carson scout, usually a captured Viet Cong or North Vietnamese soldier repatriated and assigned to provide information on enemy forces and terrain.

NOTES

Prologue

1. Ambrose, S., *Band of Brothers* (New York: Simon and Schuster, 1992).
2. Poole, E., "Vietnam veteran proud to serve his country," *Ellwood City Ledger*, Memorial Day supplement (May 22, 2009). The 101st Airborne intelligence officer, Charles Garbett, returned home to become a prominent attorney in Lawrence County, Pennsylvania.

Chapter 1

Additional information in this chapter comes from interviews in 2008 with George and Olga Sabo, Norm and Ardie Friend; in 2012 with Rick Brown, Ray D'Angelo, Michael DiLeo, Ardie Friend, Norm Friend, and Ruben Rueda; in 2013 with Norm Friend, Bill Sorg, and Bruce Dancesia; and in 2014 with Jack Brickey.

1. Tony, Stevie, and Michael are George's children, and Roe is Rose, Leslie's wife.
2. "Little John" Roethlisberger is not believed to be a relative of Pittsburgh Steelers' quarterback Ben Roethlisberger. Longtime Steelers beat reporter Jim Wexell put that question to Roethlisberger – the football

player – who said he was not aware of any relatives who served with the 101st Airborne Division during the Vietnam War (Facebook chat in 2012 between the author and Wexell).

3.   Barnes, "Family never forgets Vietnam vet and son," Chambersburg *Public Opinion*, (October 12, 2011).

4.   Berry, J., *My Gift to You* (New York, NY: RJ Communications, 2006), pp.295–296.

5.   Ibid. p.344.

6.   Appy, C., "Working Class War," in Andrew Rotter (ed.), *Light at the End of the Tunnel: A Vietnam War Anthology* (Lanham, Md.: Rowman and Littlefield, 2010), p.394.

7.   Freeling, Richard, interview by Kayla Gehle, Library of Congress Veterans History Project, August 27, 2005, Library of Congress, Washington, DC.

8.   Ibid.

9.   Berry, *My Gift to You*, pp.318–319.

10.   Ibid. pp.355–356.

11.   Ibid. pp.305–306.

12.   When the terrorist-controlled United Airlines Flight 93 broke from its intended Newark-to-San Francisco course and turned back toward Washington, DC on September 11, 2001, its precise position was over Columbia Station, according to an article that appeared in the *New York Times* on April 13, 2006. The passengers on board that plane attempted to retake control from the terrorists, who opted to crash the passenger jet into the ground in Pennsylvania near Shanksville, Somerset County, about 35 miles from the author's hometown of Ruffs Dale, Westmoreland County.

13.   Berry, *My Gift to You*, pp.333–334.

14.   Freeling interview, Library of Congress.

15.   Poole, E., "Act of Courage," *Ellwood City Ledger* (April 9, 2007), p.1.

Chapter 2

1.   News of the My Lai massacre, which took place on March 16, 1968, broke in a report on November 12, 1969, in an Associated Press story by Seymour Hersh. Eight days after the Hersh story, major US news magazines and CBS News reported the incident.

2.   Davidson, Lieutenant General P., *Vietnam at War: The History 1946-1975*, 1st ed. (Novato, Calif.: Presidio Press, 1988), p.35.

3.   Ibid. pp.40–42.

4.   Ibid. pp.262–264.

5.   Ibid. p.288.

6.   McMaster, H.R., *Dereliction of Duty: Lyndon Johnson, Robert McNamara, The Joint Chiefs of Staff and the Lies That Led to Vietnam* (New York: HarperCollins, 1997), p.40.

7.   Davidson, *Vietnam at War*, p.291.

8.   Ibid. p.292.

9.   McMaster, *Dereliction of Duty*, p.191.

10.   Davidson, *Vietnam at War*, p.405.

11.   Turse, N., *Kill Anything That Moves: The Real American War in Vietnam* (New York: Metropolitan Books, 2013) pp.42–44. Turse, armed with newly-unclassified documents and court-martial records, reveals that My Lai was not an isolated incident.

12.   Davidson, *Vietnam at War*, pp.443–445.

13.   In a 1995 interview, North Vietnamese General Bui Tin said the Americans could have won the war by cutting the Ho Chi Minh Trail in Laos (Kolb, Richard, "Hitting the Ho Chi Minh Trail," *VFW* (February 2011), p.32). While no one in a leadership position ever said why Giap laid siege to Khe Sanh during the Tet Offensive, the most plausible explanation, given Tin's statement, is that North Vietnamese military leaders feared the US Marines would destroy the trail in Laos and, with it, any chance for the North to win the war.

14.   Davidson, *Vietnam at War*, pp.445–446.

15.   *Infantry* magazine staff, *A Distant Challenge* (New York: Jove, 1983).

16.   Davidson, *Vietnam at War*, p.446.

17.   Boylan, K., "The Red Queen's Race: Operation Washington Green and Pacification in Binh Dinh Province, 1969–70," *Journal of Military History*, 73 (October 2009), pp.1,195–1,199.

18.   Freeling interview, Library of Congress.

19.   Davidson, *Vietnam at War*, p.548.

20.   On page 1,199 of the October 2009 issue of the *Journal of Military History*, history professor Kevin Boylan said the Hamlet Evaluation System designated villages controlled by the Republic of Vietnam and United States with A, B, and C grades, contested hamlets as D and E grades, and Viet Cong controlled as "V." Boylan called it "suspect" and said, "It would undoubtedly have been more accurate to classify A-B

hamlets as 'government controlled,' C hamlets as 'Contested,' and
D-E-V hamlets as 'Vietcong controlled.'"

21. Boylan, "The Red Queen's Race," pp.1,207–1,217.

22. Ibid. pp.1,212–1,213.

23. Gooch, Ron, "February 2 – 1970," *Vietnam Journal*, December 21,
1969 to April 8, 1970: 3-506 Infantry, 101st Airborne, Company B,
2nd Platoon (April 8, 1970).

24. The full quote, from page 760 of Sheehan's book, *A Bright Shining Lie:
John Paul Vann and America in Vietnam* (New York: Random House,
1988) is "The Yellow Star Division was the real phoenix of Binh Dinh,
destroyed and risen more times than the intelligence officers on the
Saigon and US side would have wanted to know." Sheehan's quote refers
specifically to the PAVN 3rd Division's participation in the 1972 Easter
Offensive.

25. Boylan, "The Red Queen's Race," pp.1,218–1,219.

26. Freeling interview, Library of Congress.

Chapter 3

Additional information in this chapter comes from interviews in 2008 with
George and Olga Sabo; in 2009 with Norm Friend and Richard Rios; and
with Jack Brickey in 2014.

1. Poole, "Act of Courage."

2. Much of the information on airlifting soldiers into a hot zone comes
from Pennsylvania Republican state Senator Robert Robbins, a
company commander in the 101st Airborne Division in 1967. After his
first tour of duty, Captain Robbins served as an advisor to a Republic of
Vietnam army unit and earned the Soldier's Medal, the US military's
highest award for valor not involving contact with the enemy, for
rescuing South Vietnamese soldiers from a burning personnel carrier. In
dismissing his act of heroism, Robbins said he was merely going back
for his own rucksack, which was full of candy. After graduating from the
US Military Academy at West Point, Robbins joked affectionately that
he opted for infantry command because he had, "a low IQ" and referred
to himself and other infantrymen as "tree eaters," because of their
aggressiveness in battle.

3. Moore, Lieutenant General H. and Galloway, J., *We Were Soldiers Once
… And Young* (New York: Random House, 1992), pp.112–113, 136.

4.   Joseph Galloway, Facebook chat with Eric Poole, October 2012.

5.   "Biography of Maj. Gen. Joseph N. Jaggers," *Army Aviation Association of America Hall of Fame*, Army Aviation Association of America, retrieved November 15, 2012, http://www.quad-a.org/index.php?option=com_content&view=article&id=123&Itemid=76.

6.   Prine, C., "Through the Looking Glass," *Military.com*, July 24, 2011, n. page. Print. http://www.lineofdeparture.com/2011/07/24/through-the-looking-glass/.

7.   O'Brien, First Lieutenant J., "Binh Dinh's Season of Change," Staff of *Infantry* magazine, *A Distant Challenge* (New York: Jove, 1980), p.255.

8.   Dawidowicz, L., *The War Against the Jews* (New York: Bantam Books, 1975).

9.   Montgomery, J. F., *Hungary: The Unwilling Satellite* (New York: Devin-Adair Co., 1947), p.84.

10. Ibid. pp.132–150.

11. Nagy-Talavera, N., "Simon Wiesenthal Center Multimedia Learning Center," *The Anatomy of a Massacre: Sarmas 1944*, Simon Wiesenthal Center, n.d. Web. October 22, 2008, www.wiesenthal.com. After the war, Adolf Eichmann escaped to Argentina, where he was captured by Israeli agents. Ron Rosenbaum, a columnist for the Slate online magazine and author of *Explaining Hitler*, said Eichmann was such a Nazi zealot that he continued working toward the "Final Solution" even in late 1944 and into 1945, when the cause was clearly lost and other German leaders were less interested in ethnic cleansing than in purging their own records of evidence that they participated in genocide.

12. Gabriel's name was listed in Elisabeth Sabo's obituary, which was published May 3, 2008, in the *Ellwood City Ledger.*

13. Montgomery, *Hungary*, p.200.

14. Ibid.

Chapter 4

Additional information in this chapter comes from interviews in 2012 with Richard Rios and Rick Brown, and in 2014 with Jerry Nash and Jack Brickey.

1.   Davidson, *Vietnam at War*, pp.303–304.

2.   Berry, *My Gift to You*, pp.278–290.

3.   O'Brien, "Binh Dinh's Season of Change," pp.255–260.

4.   Boylan, "The Red Queen's Race," p.1,219.

5. Ibid.

6. Berry, *My Gift to You*, pp.278–290.

7. Nemeth, J., "Unclassified Official Account of the 3rd BN, 1970," *506th Infantry Regiment*, 506th Infantry Regiment Association. Web. August 9, 2012, http://www.506infantry.org.

8. Berry, *My Gift to You*, pp.297–299.

9. United States, National Weather Service, *Palm Sunday Tornado Outbreak*, Washington, DC: National Weather Service, 2005, http://www.crh.noaa.gov/dtx/palmsunday/. An F5 tornado reportedly has wind speeds in excess of 300mph in its vortex.

10. Nemeth, "Unclassified Account."

11. Berry, *My Gift to You*, p.300.

Chapter 5

Additional information in this chapter comes from interviews in 2007 with Richard Rios, and in 2008 with George and Olga Sabo.

1. Montgomery, *Hungary*, pp.201–223.

Chapter 6

Additional information in this chapter comes from interviews in 2008 with George and Olga Sabo; in 2009 with Rick Brown and Richard Clanton; in 2012 with Bruce Dancesia, Richard Rios, Dave Soden, and Ruben Rueda; in 2013 with Norm Friend; and in 2014 with John Greene and Jack Brickey.

1. The *Taylor*, which had been commissioned in 1943, was known as a "magic carpet" ship by World War II troops who were carried home by it and other transport ships. By the time it brought the Sabos across the Atlantic Ocean, the *Taylor* had been acquired by the US Army Transport Service, which used it to bring the Sabos and thousands of other immigrants to the United States. After the unsuccessful Hungarian revolution in 1956, refugees escaping reprisals from the Soviet Union followed the Sabos' path on the *Taylor* to the United States. In 1963, the ship passed to command of the US Air Force and was renamed the *Gen. Hoyt S. Vandenberg*. The *Vandenberg* remained in service in the Air Force, and later the Navy, until 1993. Three years later, it stood in for a Russian science vessel for filming of the movie *Virus*, which was released in 1999 and starred Jamie Lee Curtis, William Baldwin, Donald Sutherland, and Joanna Pacula. The *Vandenberg* was sunk – with the

Cyrillic lettering affixed to its hull for *Virus* still visible – in 2009 off the coast of Florida with the intent that it would become an artificial reef.

2. "Rooster," a 1992 song by the band Alice in Chains, references the avian mix-up with the lyrics, "Walking tall Chickenman/They spit on me in my homeland," Jerry Cantrell Jr., the band's lead guitarist, wrote "Rooster" in homage to his father, Jerry Cantrell Sr., who served two tours in Vietnam with the 101st Airborne Division.

3. Gooch, Journal.

4. Nemeth, "Unclassified Account."

5. Berry, *My Gift to You*, p.304.

6. Ibid. p.305.

7. Gooch, Journal.

8. Berry, *My Gift to You*, pp.310–312.

9. Ibid. p.313.

10. Turse, *Kill Anything That Moves*, pp.164–165.

11. Poole, "Act of Courage."

12. Vietnam Gear website, http://www.vietnamgear.com/kit.aspx?kit=156. Retrieved July 21, 2012.

Chapter 7

Additional information in this chapter comes from interviews in 2009 with George and Olga Sabo, and in 2012 with Ruben Rueda.

1. *Ellwood City Ledger* staff, "100 Years of Ellwood City" special publication to celebrate Ellwood City's 100th anniversary (Citizens Publishing, Ellwood City, 1992).

2. US Census Bureau, 1950 Census.

3. Binder, M., "In 1955 downtown was source of almost everything," *100 Years of Memories* (Citizens Publishing, Ellwood City, 1992). p.59.

4. Poole, E., "Monastery celebrates 30th anniversary," *Ellwood City Ledger*, June 2006.

5. Poole, "Act of Courage." This quote from Pam Powell is interesting in that, when she said it, she had no idea of the details about Leslie Sabo's death. Like most Ellwood City residents – including Sabo's own family for many years – Powell had been told conflicting stories alleging that Sabo had perished in a relatively mundane way, when he had, in fact, sacrificed his life to save dozens of his comrades.

Chapter 8

Additional information in this chapter comes from interviews in 2009 with George and Olga Sabo; in 2012 with Rick Brown, Lee Paterson, Richard Rios, and Teb Stocks; in 2013 with Jim Waybright and Norm Friend; and in 2014 with John Greene.

1. Berry, *My Gift to You*, pp.353–354.

2. Perhaps the most prominent popular reference to "fragging the louie" comes in *Animal House*, John Landis' 1978 movie set in the 1960s. At the movie's conclusion, screen captions are used to tell the final fates of the film's characters. For the villainous "ROTC Nazi" Doug Neidermeyer, the screen card reads "Killed by his own troops in Vietnam." A few years later, in *Twilight Zone: The Movie*, Landis directed a segment set during the Vietnam War, in which a soldier says, in a thick Hispanic accent, "I knew we chouldn't have chot Lieutenant Neidermeyer."

3. Milliken, J. W., *Enter and Die* (Xlibris, Indianapolis, 2009), p.27.

4. Ambrose, *Band of Brothers*, pp.233–235.

5. Berry, *My Gift to You*, p.314.

6. Gooch, Journal.

7. Nemeth, "Unclassified Account."

8. Moore, Captain J. W., "Impressions on a Third Tour," *A Distant Challenge*.

9. Freeling interview, Library of Congress.

10. Moffett, H., "Troops Attack VC Area," *Vassar Miscellany News* (Vol. LI, 16), February 15, 1967. Retrieved from http://newspaperarchives.vassar.edu/cgi-bin/vassar?a=d&d=miscellany19670215-01.2.25#.

11. O'Brien, "Binh Dinh's Season of Change."

12. Gooch, Journal.

13. Berry, *My Gift to You*, pp.318–319.

14. Ibid. pp.317–318.

15. *Ellwood City Ledger* staff writer and photographer Marino Parascenzo took the "Seven Cents Profit" photograph. Parascenzo went on to become the Pittsburgh Post-Gazette's lead golf writer for many years. In 2008, he received the Professional Golf Association's award for lifetime achievement in journalism, joining a category that also includes Pulitzer Prize winners Dave Anderson and Jim Murray, and Dan Jenkins, author of the best-selling novels *Semi-Tough* and *Dead Solid Perfect*.

Chapter 9

Additional information in this chapter comes from interviews in 2012 with Ruben Rueda and John Greene, and in 2013 with Norm Friend.

1. Poole, "Act of Courage."

2. Freeling interview, Library of Congress.

3. Poole, "Act of Courage."

4. Nemeth, "Unclassified Account."

5. Associated Press, "Mlive.com: Everything Michigan" website; http://www. mlive.com/factbox/20070808_edmund_fitzgerald.ssf. Retrieved January 11, 2009. At the time Leslie Sabo was working on the Great Lakes, the *SS Edmund Fitzgerald* was the largest craft sailing on the Great Lakes routes. The *Fitzgerald* would become the most famous of all the Great Lakes freighters when it went down on November 10, 1975, with all 29 men on board lost. As of 2009, its sinking, which was immortalized by the song "The Wreck of the *Edmund Fitzgerald*," by Canadian singer-songwriter Gordon Lightfoot, was the most recent major shipwreck on the Great Lakes.

6. Woods Hole Oceanographic Institution Human Resources Office website, http://www.whoi.edu/services/HR/jobdescp/marine/ordinary_ sea.html, retrieved November 23, 2008.

7. Cooper, C. L., *The Lost Crusade* (Cornwall, N.Y.: Cornwall Press, 1970), p.521.

8. At the time, Ellwood City Lincoln High School, which drew from a population swelled by the children of steelworkers and owners of businesses that supported the steel industry, consistently had graduating classes numbering more than 300 students. So it was possible that, even in the relatively small town, Leslie Sabo and Rose Buccelli could attend classes for six years in grades seven through twelve and never cross paths.

9. Poole, "Act of Courage."

Chapter 10

Additional information in this chapter comes from interviews in 2007 with Rose Sabo Brown; in 2008 with Carmen Buccelli and Richard Rios; and in 2014 with John Greene.

1. Poole, "Act of Courage."

2. Chad Stuart and Jeremy Clyde official website; http://www. chadandjeremy.net/.

Chapter 11

Additional information in this chapter comes from interviews in 2008 with Lawrence Phillips and Rose Sabo Brown, and in 2009 with Rick Brown, Richard Clanton, and Ben Currin.

1.   Berry, *My Gift to You,* pp.339–347.

Chapter 12

Some parts of the Mother's Day Ambush narrative include information from the book *Twelve Days in May,* by Jerald Berry, public information officer for 3rd Battalion, 506th Infantry Regiment in 1967–68. Entirely by coincidence, Berry appeared to have interviewed an entirely different set of Bravo Company veterans than I did. Berry interviewed Allen McCulty, Bobby Garnto, Joe Hanks, and Dave Soden. My interviewees on the Cambodian operation were Jim Waybright, Ray D'Angelo, Mike "Tex" Bowman, and Teb Stocks. Both Berry and I interviewed Rick Brown, John Greene, and Richard Rios. However, this book does not use quotes or accounts from any of Berry's interviews with Brown, Greene, and Rios.

1.   Frank and Louise are Olga Sabo's sister and brother-in-law, Frank and Louise Carrozza. Tony Carrozza, one of Frank and Louise's children, worked for a time as head printer with the author at the *Ellwood City Ledger.*

2.   Davidson, *Vietnam at War,* p.59.

3.   Berry, J., *Twelve Days in May* (Libby, Mont.: Xlibris, 2010), introduction.

4.   McMaster, *Dereliction of Duty,* p.86.

5.   "Moscow International Film Festival." MIFF, Moscow International Film Festival, n.d. February 21, 2014, http://www.moscowfilmfestival.ru/miff34/eng/archives/?year=1967.

6.   Gordon, B. K., "A Survey of Asia in 1968: Part I," *Asian Survey,* Vol. 9, No. 1, (Berkeley: University of California Press, January 1969), pp.58–68. According to Gordon, *Shadow over Angkor,* which Sihanouk wrote, produced, and starred in, was likely a fictionalized account of a coup attempt in 1959. Article Stable URL: http://www.jstor.org/stable/2642095.

7.   Ibid. p.624.

8.   Berry, *Twelve Days in May,* p.65.

9.   Ibid. pp.40–41.
10.   Ibid. pp.51–52, 280–281.
11.   Fold 3 (February 6, 2012), "Kit Carson Scouts," retrieved from http://spotlightsfold3.com/2012/02/06/kit-carson-scouts/.
12.   Berry, *Twelve Days in May*, p.87.
13.   Ibid. p.79.

Chapter 13

Additional information in this chapter comes from interviews in 2008 with George and Olga Sabo and Rose Sabo Brown; in 2012 with Ray D'Angelo and Rick Brown; and in 2014 with John Greene.

1.   Wallechinsky, D., *The Twentieth Century: History With the Boring Parts Left Out*, p.219.
2.   Lieutenant Colonel J. Jaggers (Major General, retired), Confidential after-action report, May, 1970. (Acquired courtesy of Alton Mabb.)
3.   Berry, *Twelve Days in May*, p.81.
4.   Army News Service (May 17, 2012), "Medal of Honor recipient remembered," www.army.mil/article/80098.
5.   Nemeth, "Unclassified Account."
6.   Berry, *Twelve Days in May*, pp.89–91.
7.   Ibid. pp.91–92.
8.   Ibid. p.298.
9.   Ibid. pp.255–256.
10.   Ibid. p.248.
11.   Ibid. pp.189–190.

Chapter 14

Additional information in this chapter comes from interviews in 2009 with Teb Stocks, Mike "Tex" Bowman, and Alton Mabb; in 2012 with Rick Brown and Ruben Rueda; with Jim Waybright in 2008, 2009, and 2012; and in 2014 with John Greene.

1.   Poole, "Act of Courage."
2.   Army News Service, "Remembering a Hero" (May 17, 2012), www.army.mil/article/80098.
3.   Jaggers, after-action report.

4.   Berry, *Twelve Days in May*, pp.192–93.
5.   Poole, "Act of Courage."
6.   MyFamily.com, Bravo Company website.
7.   Ibid.
8.   Poole, "Act of Courage."
9.   Ibid.
10. Nolan, K. W., *Into Cambodia* (Novato, Calif: Presidio Press, 1990), pp.193–194.
11. Berry, *My Gift to You*, p.340.

Chapter 15

Additional information in this chapter comes from interviews in 2009 with Mike "Tex" Bowman, Rick Brown, John Greene, and Teb Stocks; in 2012 with Ruben Rueda; and in 2014 with Jerry Nash.

1.   "Douglas AC-47D 'Spooky,'" Douglas AC-47D 'Spooky' The Aviation Zone website, retrieved August 31, 2014.
2.   Jaggers, after-action report.
3.   Ibid.
4.   Berry, *Twelve Days in May*, p.189.
5.   Poole, "Act of Courage."
6.   Because the identity of the wounded soldier that Sabo shielded from the grenade blast has never been ascertained by any of the soldiers who are known to have survived the Mother's Day Ambush, it's probably reasonable to assume that he was either one of the other seven Americans killed in the battle, or that he died in the years immediately following his Vietnam combat tour with Bravo Company.
7.   MyFamily.com, Bravo Company website.
8.   Poole, "Act of Courage."
9.   Ibid.
10. Ibid.
11. Berry, *Twelve Days in May*, p.205.
12. Ibid. p.203.
13. Poole, "Act of Courage."
14. Ibid.

Chapter 16

Additional information in this chapter comes from interviews in 2009 with Teb Stocks and John Greene; in 2009 and 2012 with Rick Brown; in 2012 with Michael DiLeo; and in 2014 with John Greene.

1. Berry, *Twelve Days in May*, pp.210–211.
2. Ibid. p.213.
3. Nemeth, Bravo Company after-action report.
4. Berry, *Twelve Days in May*, pp.213–214.
5. Ibid. p.253.
6. Ibid.
7. "Senate demands withdrawal from Cambodia," Associated Press, May 12, 1970 (retrieved from *Ellwood City Ledger* archives).
8. Jaggers, after-action report.
9. Ibid.
10. Nemeth, Bravo Company after-action report.

Chapter 17

Additional information in this chapter comes from interviews in 2007 and 2008 with Rose Sabo Brown, and in 2008 with George and Olga Sabo.

1. Poole, "Act of Courage."
2. "Spc. 4 Sabo missing in action," *Ellwood City Ledger*, May 16, 1970.
3. "Spc. 4 Sabo killed in Cambodia," *Ellwood City Ledger*, May 18, 1970.
4. Sabo was the last resident of Ellwood City borough to die during the Vietnam War, but Robert "Punky" Kuner Jr. was killed June 15, 1970, 36 days after Sabo. Kuner was a resident of North Sewickley Township, not far from Ellwood City and the location of Holy Redeemer Catholic Cemetery, where Sabo is buried.
5. "Spc. 4 Sabo to be laid to rest," *Ellwood City Ledger*, May 24, 1970.
6. When Contrucci retired, he sold the funeral home to Joseph Tomon, who later cut a lucrative deal with a drug store chain for the former Contrucci property and moved his funeral home just outside Ellwood City. Tomon, a longtime fan of the Pittsburgh Penguins, branched out his business – he is one of the world's top hockey memorabilia dealers. His collection includes game-worn sweaters dating to the 1930s, the sweater worn by Penguins' star Sidney Crosby in the first Winter Classic outdoor hockey game in Buffalo, and a cancelled paycheck issued to Jaromir Jagr. For

years, Tomon has had exclusive rights to the Penguins' game-worn sweaters, which means that anyone who owns an authentic sweater game-worn by Mario Lemieux, Crosby, or Evgeni Malkin has an artifact that almost certainly passed through Tomon's funeral home.

7. Poole, "Act of Courage."
8. Ibid.

Chapter 18

1. Jaggers' biography, retrieved from http://www.quad-a.org/index.php?option=com_content&view=article&id=123&Itemid=76.
2. Poole, "Act of Courage."
3. Berry, *My Gift to You*, pp.360–379. Sergeant James Vincent Ballay, of Alpha Company, was killed by friendly fire on May 12 during the Cambodian Incursion. He was less than a month, including a two-week rest-and-relaxation leave, from completing his tour of duty. According to Berry's book (p.358), soldiers from Alpha Company approached an outpost held by the battalion's Delta Company, when a member of the latter unit misidentified a Hawaiian Alpha Company soldier as Vietnamese and opened fire. In the ensuing fog of combat, Ballay was killed and several other Americans were injured.
4. "Facts about Ripcord," FSB Ripcord Association, 2013, http://www.ripcordassociation.com/c.aspx?n=Facts-about-Ripcord.
5. Nemeth, after-action report.

Chapter 19

Additional information in this chapter comes from interviews in 2009 with Rick Clanton; in 2012 with Ben Currin, Michael DiLeo, Norm Friend, Doug Lange, and Ruben Rueda; in 2013 with Ron Gooch and Bill Sorg; in 2014 with Jack Brickey, John Greene, and Jerry Nash.

1. Golden Knights official website, retrieved from www.goldenknightsaa.com.
2. Ibid.
3. Freeling interview, Library of Congress.
4. Philip Caputo, *The Kent State Shootings*, from the National Public Radio website, http://www.npr.org/templates/story/story.php?storyId=4630596, retrieved January 24, 2009.

5. Campise, R., Geller, S. K., and Campise, M. E., "Combat Stress," *Military Psychology* (Guildford Press: New York City, 2006), p.217.

Chapter 20

Information in this chapter comes from interviews in 2008 with George and Olga Sabo and Rose Sabo Brown, and in 2009 with A. J. Moore, Mark Rogers, and Candace Sullins.

Chapter 21

Additional information in this chapter comes from interviews in 2007 with Rick Clanton and in 2009 with Rick Brown.

1. Zoroya, Gregg, "In Iraq, coping after a hero saves you," *USA Today*, September 27, 2007.
2. Freeling interview, Library of Congress.
3. Poole, "Act of Courage."
4. Ibid.

Chapter 22

Additional information in this chapter comes from an interview in 2008 with Alton "Tony" Mabb.

1. Center for Military History website, www.history.army.mil, retrieved November 9, 2008.
2. US Code, Section 3744.
3. In an error-filled 2010 radio broadcast, religious conservative radio talk-show host Bryan Fischer of the American Family Association used the occasion of a Medal of Honor award to Afghanistan War hero Army Staff Sergeant Salvatore Giunta, to decry what he called the "feminization of the Medal of Honor." In a blog posting to mirror his radio address, Fischer said the Medal of Honor was no longer being used to recognize soldiers who "killed the enemy," such as in the Normandy Invasion assault on the cliffs of Pointe du Hoc, which Fischer – or, more likely, one of his staffers – misspelled as "Pointe do Hoc." Additionally, the Army awarded no Medals of Honor for the Army Rangers' attack on Pointe du Hoc, and the operation's purpose was to destroy German artillery guns believed to have been placed in a bunker (the guns had not yet been installed). Neutralizing the guns was

necessary to prevent the Germans from using them against invading US troops landing at Utah and Omaha beaches – in other words, to save the lives of other soldiers.

4. Poole, "Act of Courage."

5. Ibid.

6. Ibid.

7. Ibid.

Chapter 23

No notes.

Chapter 24

Additional information in this chapter comes from interviews in 2007 with Alton "Tony" Mabb; in 2008 with George and Olga Sabo, Richard Rios, and Rose Sabo Brown; and in 2009 with Rick Clanton.

1. "Between Art and Architecture: The Memory Works of Maya Lin," American Association of Museums website, www.aam.us.org/pubs/mn/ mayalin.cfm, retrieved March 11, 2009.

2. "Vietnam Veterans Memorial Fund FAQs," Vietnam Veterans Memorial Fund website, www.wmf.org, retrieved March 11, 2009.

3. MyFamily.com website, Bravo Company 3/506th Infantry page.

4. Poole, "Act of Courage."

5. US Code, Section 3744 (d), paragraph (2), retrieved from the uscode. house.gov website on March 4, 2008.

6. Poole, "Act of Courage" (the quote does not appear in "Act of Courage," but was obtained in an interview for that story).

7. US Code, Section 3744, section (b), paragraph (1).

8. Medal of Honor citation for Woodrow Wilson Keeble, http://www. army.mil/medalofhonor/keeble/citation/index.html, retrieved March 20, 2009.

9. Donna Miles, "Korean War Hero Receives Posthumous Medal of Honor," March 3, 2009, American Forces Press Service, http://www. defenselink.mil/news/newsarticle.aspx?id=49159, retrieved March 20, 2009.

10. The Andrews Raiders operation, also known as the Great Locomotive Chase, was led by Union civilian spy James Andrews, along with 22

volunteers from an Ohio military regiment. It was a daring effort to steal a Confederate train and run it all the way back to Union lines. Andrews and his men successfully took the train on April 12, 1862, and raced against the Southern military and sympathizers. That race was lost when the locomotive ran out of fuel, and Andrews and seven of his cohorts were executed as spies. Eight others escaped from captivity and made it back to Union lines and six more were exchanged for Confederate prisoners of war. Of the 23 men involved in the operation, 19 – including at least two men who did not actually participate in the operation because they either overslept or were captured and forced to enlist in the Confederate Army – have received the Medal of Honor. Andrews, as a civilian, was not eligible, and the other three were named in the 2008 Defense Authorization Act. One of the Andrews Raiders, Private Jacob Parrott, was the first man to receive the Medal of Honor. Parrott was among those who escaped from the Confederates and was later promoted to lieutenant.

11. Lieutenant Colonel Stewart L. Stephenson, August 20, 2009, letter to US Senator Arlen Specter. (Letter provided by Rose Sabo Brown.)

Chapter 25

Additional information in this chapter comes from interviews in 2008 with George and Olga Sabo, and in 2009 with Rick Brown, Ben Currin, Tony "Yogi" Krizinski, Jerry Nash, Richard Rios, Bill Sorg, Teb Stocks, and Jim Waybright.

Chapter 26

1. According to the 2010 US Census, nearly 25 percent of Ellwood City borough residents are ethnic Italians.

Chapter 27

Additional information in this chapter comes from an interview in 2012 with Richard Scarboro.

1. The narrative in Chapter 12 of this book was based on multiple accounts provided by the soldiers of Bravo Company who witnessed it. After the Medal of Honor ceremony, several of those veterans confirmed that account, which differs from the official account on Sabo's Medal of Honor citation. However, the author, in an editorial decision, chose not

to single out any single veteran as disputing the White House-approved account and therefore used anonymous direct and indirect quotes as the only unattributed statements in this book.

2. Rolan, T. Jr, "Re: photo request for book by Eric Poole - 1 of 3 (UNCLASSIFIED)," Message to Eric Poole, January 8, 2014 by email.

3. The fund-raising campaign was led by Sam Teolis, a World War II veteran who was mayor of Ellwood City at the time Sabo was serving in Vietnam.

4. Eric Poole, "Community honors hometown war hero," *Ellwood City Ledger* (October 1, 2012).

5. Eric Poole, "Bridge dedicated to Sabo," *Ellwood City Ledger* (November 12, 2012).

SELECT BIBLIOGRAPHY

Interviews

Bowman, Mike, July 2009
Brickey, Forrest "Jack," January 2014
Brown, Richard, July 2009, June 2012
Buccelli, Carmen, December 2008
Clanton, Richard, March 2008
Currin, Ben, July 2009, May 2012
Friend, Norm, July 2009, May 2012, November 2013
Greene, John, July 2009, January 2014
Krizinski, Tony, July 2009
Lane, Richard, January 2014
Mabb, Alton, April 2008
Moore, A. J., July 2009
Nash, Jerry, January 2014
Phillips, Lawrence, April 2009
Rios, Richard, April 2008, July 2009, June 2012
Robbins, Robert, March 2008
Rogers, Mark, July 2009
Rueda, Ruben, June 2012

Sabo, George, September 2008, June 2012
Sabo, Olga, September 2008
Sabo Brown, Rose, December 2008
Scarboro, Rick, May 2012
Stevenson, Robert, September 2008
Stocks, Teb, July 2009
Sullins, Candace, July 2009
Waybright, James, December 2008, July 2009, June 2012

Previously unpublished elements of additional interviews with George Koziol, Alton Mabb, George Sabo, and Rose Sabo Brown in March 2007 for a newspaper story are included and cited in footnotes as being part of the story "Act of Courage," which appeared in the April 9, 2007, issue of the *Ellwood City Ledger.*

Books

"100 Years of Ellwood City," by the staff of the *Ellwood City Ledger*, special supplement to commemorate the borough's centennial (Ellwood City: Citizens Publishing, 1992).

Ambrose, Stephen, *Band of Brothers* (New York: Simon and Schuster, 1992).

Berry, Jerald, *My Gift to You* (New York: RJ Communications LLC, 2006).

Berry, Jerald, *Twelve Days In May* (Libby, Mont.: XLibris, 2010).

Cheney, Elisabeth, *Evolution of Presidential War Powers* (Boulder, Colo: Colorado University, 1988), citing Nixon, Richard, *No More Vietnams.*

Cooper, Chester L., *The Lost Crusade* (Cornwall, New York: Cornwall Press, 1970).

Dawidowicz, Lucy, *The War Against the Jews* (New York: Bantam Books, 1975).

Infantry magazine staff, *A Distant Challenge* (Nashville, Tenn: The Battery Press, 1983).

Kennedy, Carrie H. and Zillmer, Eric A., eds., *Military Psychology* (New York: The Guilford Press, 2006).

Loewen, James W., *Lies My Teacher Told Me* (New York: Simon and Schuster, 1995).

McMaster, H.R., *Dereliction of Duty* (New York: Harper Perennial, 1997).

Montgomery, John Flournoy, *Hungary: The Unwilling Satellite* (New York: Devin-Adair Co., 1947).

Nolan, Keith William, *Into Cambodia* (Novato, Calif: Presidio Press, 1990).

Websites

Associated Press, "Mlive.com: Everything Michigan" website, www.mlive.com/factbox/20070808_edmund_fitzgerald.ssf.

"Between Art and Architecture: The Memory Works of Maya Lin," American Association of Museums website, www.aam.us.org/pubs/mn/mayalin.cfm.

Caputo, Philip, *The Kent State Shootings*, from the National Public Radio website, http://www.npr.org/templates/story/story.php?storyId=4630596.

Center for Military History website, www.history.army.mil.

Chad Stuart and Jeremy Clyde official website, http://www.chadandjeremy.net/.

"Douglas AC-47D 'Spooky,'" Douglas AC-47D 'Spooky' The Aviation Zone, website (August 31, 2014).

History of the 101st Airborne Division website, http://screamingeagles__10.tripod.com/101st_played_an_important_part_i.htm.

Kunich, John and Lester, Richard, "The Wallenberg Effect," published by The Journal of Leadership Studies website, www.au.af.mil/au/awc/awcgate/readings/wallenberg.htm.

McLeroy, Carrie, "First Sioux to Receive Medal of Honor," Army News Service, www.army.mil.news/2008/02/22/7566-first-sioux-to-receive-medal-of-honor (February 22, 2008).

Miles, Donna, "Korean War Hero Receives Posthumous Medal of Honor," American Forces Press Service, http://www.defenselink.mil/news/newsarticle.aspx?id=49159 (March 3, 2009).

MyFamily.com – Bravo Co. 3/506th Inf. (Airmobile) 101st ABN DIV CURRAHEE!…" website (March 19, 2007).

Nagy-Talavera, Nicholas M., *The Anatomy of a Massacre: Sarmas 1944*, Simon Wiesenthal Center's Multimedia Learning Center website, www.wiesenthal.com.

Official Army Medal of Honor Website, http://www.army.mil/medalofhonor.

"Sink the Vandenberg," Artificial Reefs of the Keys website, http://www.bigshipwrecks.com/history/timeline.htm.

Swomley, John M., "Neo-fascism and the religious right," *Humanist*, www.findarticles.com/p/articles/mi_m1374/is_n1_v55/ai16399959 (January–February 1995).

"Vietnam Veterans Memorial Fund FAQs," Vietnam Veterans Memorial Fund website, www.wmf.org.

The Vietnam Veterans Memorial Wall website, www.thewall-usa.com.

Woods Hole Oceanographic Institution Human Resources Office website, http://www.whoi.edu/services/HR/jobdescp/marine/ordinary_sea.html.

Yingling, Lieutenant Colonel Paul, "A failure in generalship," *Armed Forces Journal*, www.armedforcesjournal.com (May 2007).

Zacharia, Janine, *Jerusalem Post online*, "Lantos' List," www.jpost.com.

Newspaper articles

"Senate demands withdrawal from Cambodia," Associated Press, May 12, 1970. (Retrieved from *Ellwood City Ledger* archives.)

"Spc. 4 Sabo missing in action," *Ellwood City Ledger* (May 16, 1970).

"Spc. 4 Sabo killed in Cambodia," *Ellwood City Ledger* (May 18, 1970).

"Spc. 4 Sabo to be laid to rest," *Ellwood City Ledger* (May 24, 1970).

Poole, Eric, "Act of Courage," *Ellwood City Ledger* (April 9, 2007).

Zoroya, Gregg, "In Iraq, coping after a hero saves you," *USA Today* (September 27, 2007).

Poole, Eric, "Commissioner ends long career," *Ellwood City Ledger* (December 27, 2007).

Poole, Eric, "Writer honored by PGA," *Ellwood City Ledger* (January 18, 2008).

Poole, Eric, "The voice for a hero goes silent," *Ellwood City Ledger* (February 2, 2008).

Obituary, Elisabeth Sabo, *Ellwood City Ledger* (May 3, 2008).

Hohmann, James, "Soldier who threw himself on grenade to save others is recognized," *Los Angeles Times* (June 3, 2008).

Poole, Eric, "Soldiers worthy of credit," *Ellwood City Ledger* (October 22, 2008).

Poole, Eric, "The Last Battle," *Ellwood City Ledger* (October 26, 2008).

Other sources

Galanski, John, email to Raylene Boots (February 17, 2009).

Jaggers, Lieutenant Colonel Joseph, confidential after-action report (May, 1970).

Mabb, Alton E. Jr., letter to US Representative Corrine Brown, dated March 17, 2002.

Moral Courage in Combat: The My Lai Story, forum at the United States Naval Academy led by Dr Albert C. Pierce, director of the Center for the Study of Professional Military Ethics (2003).

Stephenson, Lieutenant Colonel Stewart L., letter to US Senator Arlen Specter (August 20, 2009).

US Census Bureau (1950).

US Code, Section 3744.

INDEX